classic
recipes

classic recipes

igloo

Published by Igloo Books Limited
Henson Way
Kettering
Northants
NN16 8PX
info@igloo-books.com

This edition printed in 2005

ISBN 1-84193-308-2

Printed in China

Author: Victoria Chow
With thanks to Yew Yuan Chow and James Mitchell

Project management by Metro Media Limited

Contents

Introduction

Classic dishes have usually become so because of their popularity. Many of the meals we order when we go to a restaurant are the classic recipes, and many of these will be found in these pages. Whether you like to treat yourself by going out and having Chinese or Italian, Mexican or typically English food, likely as not it's not something you do every day. So if you'd love to indulge yourself more often but can't afford to, this book will be a boon offering dozens of classic recipes to make and enjoy at home. Whether you are planning a dinner party or a romantic meal for two, there are recipes here to suit all tastes and time-frames.

In the classic starters chapter you will find mouth-watering oriental fare such as Hot & sour soup and Sesame seed prawn toasts alongside delicacies from India, such as Naan bread and Mixed bhajis. As well as soups and breads, there are fruits and mousses to try out.

There is also a wealth of main course recipes to choose from such as Irish stew, Coq au vin and Bouillabaisse. Macaroni cheese, Waldorf salad and Tagliatelle with lemon sauce are among the treats in the vegetarian chapter.

No meal would be complete without ta dessert. The examples here range from the rich Dark chocolate cake to the comforting warmth of Pear & blackberry crumble. As well as classic cakes and tempting tarts, the hot desserts section has seasonal classics such as Mince pies and Christmas pudding. But if the weather is warm then turn to the cold desserts section for a refreshing range of sorbets and ice-cream recipes to cool you down. This chapter also sees the innocent delights of Fruit salad and Angel cake set next to the devilish temptations of Mississippi mud pie and Crème caramel.

With meat and poultry, pasta and pizza, salad and seafood, and delicious dessert recipes to choose from there is scope for you to indulge in a different national delicacy each day of the week. Enjoy!

Starters

To create the right impression from the outset – whether at a family gathering or a more formal sit-down meal – try something from this chapter. From finger food like Cheesy potato skins and Breaded mushrooms, to more sophisticated fare, such as Chicken liver pâté and Salmon mousse, these recipes will get your meal off to a great start.

Gazpacho

SERVES 4–6

INGREDIENTS:

2 slices white bread (crusts removed, torn into pieces)
900ml/1½pt tomato juice
6 ripe plum tomatoes
1 red onion
1 red pepper
1 small cucumber
3 garlic cloves

1 teaspoon Tabasco sauce
1 tablespoon sherry vinegar
Salt and pepper

For the croûtons:
3 tablespoons olive oil
2 slices soft white bread (crusts removed, cut into 1cm/½in cubes)

- Put the bread in a large bowl and cover with the tomato juice.
- Plunge the tomatoes in just-boiled water for 30 seconds and skin. Cut them in quarters, strip out and discard the seeds, then cut the flesh into 1cm/½in cubes.
- Cut the red onion into 8mm/¼in slices.
- Grill the red pepper then place in a plastic bag for 5 minutes, then remove the skin and dice the flesh.
- Peel the skin from the cucumber. Cut cucumber lengthways into 1cm/½in slices, then cut these into strips and finally cut these strips into cubes.
- Peel and chop the garlic cloves as finely as you can.
- Stir all these together with the tomatoes into the contents of the bowl. Add the Tabasco sauce and sherry vinegar. Season generously with salt and pepper. Put clingfilm over the top and refrigerate for 6 hours or overnight.
- To make the croûtons, season the olive oil and toss the cubes of bread in it, then fry them gently in a non-stick pan until they are nicely crisp and golden brown.
- Ladle the chilled gazpacho into 4 to 6 soup bowls and scatter the croûtons on top.

Hummus

SERVES 8

INGREDIENTS:

225g/8oz dried chickpeas (soaked overnight) or 500g/1lb 2oz canned
Juice of 2 large lemons
150ml/¼pt tahini (paste of ground sesame seeds)

4 tablespoons olive oil
2 garlic cloves (crushed)
Salt and pepper

- Drain the chickpeas, place in saucepan and cover with cold water. Bring to the boil and simmer gently for 2 hours or until tender.
- Drain the chickpeas, reserving a little of the liquid. Put them in a blender and gradually add the reserved liquid and the lemon juice, blending well after each addition, to form a smooth purée.
- Add the tahini paste, olive oil and garlic. Season to taste. Blend again until smooth.
- Serve with warm pitta bread and olives.

Thai spring rolls

SERVES 6

INGREDIENTS:

4–6 dried Chinese mushrooms (soaked)
50g/2oz bean thread noodles (soaked)
2 tablespoons vegetable oil
2 garlic cloves (chopped)
2 red chillies (seeded and chopped)
225g/8oz minced pork
50g/2oz chopped cooked prawns
2 tablespoons fish sauce
1 carrot (finely shredded)

50g/2oz bamboo shoots (chopped)
50g/2oz beansprouts
2 spring onions (chopped)
1 tablespoon chopped fresh coriander
2 tablespoons flour
24 x 15cm/6in square spring roll wrappers
Vegetable oil for frying

- Drain and chop the mushrooms. Drain the noodles and cut into 5cm/2in lengths.
- Heat the oil in a wok, add the garlic and chillies and fry for 30 seconds. Add the pork and stir until the meat is browned.
- Add the noodles, mushrooms and prawns. Season with fish sauce. Tip into a bowl.
- Mix in the carrot, bamboo shoots, beansprouts, spring onions and coriander for the filling.
- Put the flour in a small bowl and mix with a little water to make a paste.
- Place a spoonful of filling in the centre of a spring roll wrapper. Turn the bottom edge over to cover the filling, then fold in the sides. Brush the flour paste mixture over the top edge and seal. Repeat with all 24 wrappers.
- Heat the oil in a wok. Slide in the spring rolls a few at a time and fry until crisp and golden brown. Remove with a slotted spoon and drain on kitchen paper.

Smoked trout with cucumber & cumin

SERVES 4

INGREDIENTS:

½ large cucumber
Salt
1 tablespoon cumin seeds

250g/9oz smoked trout fillets
150g/5oz crème fraîche

- Peel the cucumber, cut it in half lengthways and scoop out the seeds with a teaspoon. Cut the flesh into thin strips, place in a colander and sprinkle with salt. Leave for 30 minutes.
- Dry-fry the cumin seeds in a frying pan until toasted. Flake the trout into large pieces.
- Rinse the cucumber under the cold tap, drain and pat dry with kitchen paper.
- Place in a bowl, sprinkle the toasted cumin seeds over the top and mix in the crème fraîche.
- Serve at room temperature, with trout pieces on top of the cucumber mixture.

Vegetable samosas

SERVES 5

INGREDIENTS:

100g/4oz carrots (finely diced)
100g/4oz potatoes (finely diced)
50g/2oz green beans (finely sliced)
2 tablespoons vegetable oil
2 shallots (finely chopped)
2 garlic cloves (crushed)
2 tablespoons hot curry paste

2 tablespoons mango chutney
50g/2oz frozen peas (defrosted)
2 tablespoons chopped fresh coriander
¼ teaspoon salt
250g/9oz filo pastry
Vegetable oil for deep-frying

- Cook the carrots and potatoes in separate pans of boiling, salted water until they are tender. Add the sliced beans to the pan of carrots after 4 to 5 minutes. Drain the cooked vegetables and set them aside.
- Heat the oil in a heavy-based frying pan, add the shallots and garlic and then fry, stirring frequently, for 5 minutes or until softened. Stir in the curry paste and

mango chutney and cook for 1 minute.

- Stir in the cooked vegetables together with the peas, coriander and salt and cook for a further 2 minutes. Leave the filling to cool before making the samosas.
- Cut the filo pastry into 20 strips, each measuring 10 x 30cm (4 x 12in).
- Divide the filling into 10 portions. Place 2 strips of filo pastry on top of each other and place a portion of filling at one end.
- Carefully fold a corner of the pastry over to the opposite edge to form a triangle enclosing the filling. Seal the edges with a little water. Repeat with the remaining pastry and filling to form 10 samosas.
- Heat the oil in a saucepan. Fry the samosas in 3 batches until they are crisp and golden.
- Remove with a slotted spoon and drain on kitchen paper. Serve hot or cold.

Onion rings

SERVES 5

INGREDIENTS:

350ml/12fl oz plain flour
4 tablespoons cornmeal
4 tablespoons onion powder
2 teaspoons salt
350ml/12fl oz milk

1 large egg
125ml/4fl oz water
8 large onions
Vegetable oil for deep-frying

- Combine the flour, cornmeal, onion powder, salt, milk, egg and water in a large mixing bowl and stir well until there are no lumps.
- Slice the onions across to make rings about 1cm/$\frac{1}{2}$in thick.
- Dip the rings into the batter.
- Heat the oil in a large saucepan.
- Drop coated rings into the oil and fry until golden brown.
- Drain on kitchen paper and serve.

Soft pretzels

SERVES 8

INGREDIENTS:

700g/1½lb plain flour
1 tablespoon sugar
2 teaspoons salt
2 teaspoons baking powder

2 teaspoons active dry yeast
2 tablespoon butter
225ml/8fl oz warm milk

- Put a large pot of water on to boil. Preheat the oven to 200°C/400°F/Gas mark 6.
- Punch down the dough and divide into 8 equal pieces. Roll or cut each piece into a rope 45cm/18in long, and twist each rope into a pretzel shape.
- Slide pretzels into water with a slotted spoon or broad spatula and boil each one until they float to the top. Remove them immediately to a lightly greased baking sheet.
- Bake pretzels in the oven for 15 minutes or until golden. Brush the pretzels very lightly with melted butter as they emerge from the oven. Serve warm.

Nettle broth

SERVES 6

INGREDIENTS:

50g/2oz butter
275g/10oz potatoes (chopped)
100g/4oz onion (chopped)
100g/4oz leeks (chopped)
Salt and pepper

1.2 litres/2pt chicken stock
150g/5oz young nettles (washed and chopped)
150ml/¼pt cream or creamy milk

- Melt the butter in a heavy-bottomed saucepan. When it foams, add the potatoes, onions and leeks and toss them in the butter until well coated. Season with salt and pepper.
- Cover and sweat on a gentle heat for 10 minutes or until the vegetables are soft.
- Add the stock and boil until the vegetables are just coloured.
- Add the chopped nettle leaves and simmer for a few minutes, being careful not to overcook. Add the cream or milk and liquidize. Serve hot.

Dolmades

SERVES 4

INGREDIENTS:

1 tablespoon olive oil
100g/4oz minced beef
2 tablespoons pine nuts
1 onion (chopped)
1 tablespoon chopped fresh coriander
1 teaspoon ground cumin
1 tablespoon tomato purée

Salt and pepper
8 vine leaves

For the tomato sauce:
150ml/¼pt passata
150ml/¼pt beef stock
2 teaspoons caster sugar

- For the filling, heat the oil in a pan. Add the minced beef, pine nuts and onion.
- Cook for 5 minutes until brown and sealed.
- Stir in the fresh coriander, cumin and tomato purée. Cook for a further 3 minutes and season well.
- Lay the vine leaves shiny side down on a work surface. Place some of the filling in the centre of each leaf and fold the stalk end over the filling. Roll up the parcel towards the tip of the leaf and place in a lightly greased flameproof casserole dish, seam side down.
- For the sauce, mix together the passata, stock and sugar and pour over each vine leaf. Cover and cook on a moderate heat for a few minutes. Reduce the heat and cook for a further 30 minutes. Serve hot.

Prawn cocktail

SERVES 4

INGREDIENTS:

4 tablespoons mayonnaise
4 tablespoons single cream
2 teaspoons tomato purée
2 teaspoons lemon juice
Dash of Worcestershire sauce
Dash of dry sherry

Salt and pepper
225g/8oz cooked and peeled prawns
(cooked)
A few lettuce leaves (shredded)
Lemon slices to garnish

→

- Put the mayonnaise, cream, tomato purée, lemon juice, Worcestershire sauce and sherry in a small bowl and mix together. Season to taste.
- Add the prawns and stir well until coated.
- To serve, place the shredded lettuce in 4 glasses and top with the prawn mixture. Garnish each prawn cocktail with lemon slices.

Mozzarella sticks

SERVES 4

INGREDIENTS:

450g/1lb brick mozzarella
2 eggs (beaten)
50ml/2fl oz water
350ml/12fl oz white breadcrumbs
½ teaspoon garlic salt

1 teaspoon mixed spice
150ml/¼pt flour
75ml/3fl oz cornflour
Vegetable oil for deep-frying

- Cut the mozzarella cheese into finger-size sticks.
- Beat the eggs with water and set aside. Mix the breadcrumbs, garlic salt and mixed spice and set aside. Blend the flour with the cornflour.
- Heat the vegetable oil. Dip the cheese sticks in flour, then in the egg, then in the breadcrumb mixture. Place carefully in the hot oil and fry for a few seconds until golden. When golden, remove from the hot oil and drain. Serve hot.

Courgette fritters

SERVES 6

INGREDIENTS:

100g/4oz self-raising flour
2 eggs (beaten)
50ml/2fl oz milk
300g/11oz courgettes (grated)

2 tablespoons chopped fresh thyme leaves
Salt and pepper
1 tablespoon vegetable oil

- Sift the flour into a large bowl and make a well in the centre. Add the eggs to the well and gradually draw in the flour with a wooden spoon.
- Slowly add the milk to the mixture, stirring constantly to form a thick batter.
- Add the courgettes and thyme to the batter, plus salt and pepper to taste, and mix thoroughly.

- Heat the oil in a large, heavy-based frying pan. Place the batter in the oil, 1 tablespoon for each fritter and cook, in batches, for 3 minutes on each side.
- Remove the fritters with a slotted spoon and drain on kitchen paper. Serve hot.

Breaded mushrooms

SERVES 4

INGREDIENTS:

34225g/8oz mushrooms
3 tablespoons grated Parmesan cheese
Pinch of garlic salt

Pinch of ground black pepper
1 tablespoon chopped fresh parsley
4 tablespoons white breadcrumbs

- Preheat the oven to 240°C/475°F/Gas mark 9.
- Remove the stems from the mushrooms and reserve. Then wipe with damp kitchen paper to clean.
- Combine the cheese with the breadcrumbs. Add the garlic salt and black pepper.
- Roll the mushrooms in the cheese mixture. Place on a greased non-stick baking tray.
- Bake in the oven for 8 to 10 minutes or until browned.

Devilled eggs with caviar

SERVES 4

INGREDIENTS:

20 eggs (hard-boiled)
6 tablespoons mayonnaise
Salt and pepper

2 tablespoons finely chopped fresh dill
100g/4oz caviar

- Peel the hard-boiled eggs and cut in half lengthways.
- Remove the yolks and chop them finely. Place in a bowl and add the mayonnaise, salt and pepper and dill. Blend until smooth.
- Fill each half-egg with the yolk mixture and serve garnished with grains of caviar.

Crab sticks

SERVES 2-4

INGREDIENTS:

2 tablespoons vegetable oil
1 onion (finely chopped)
2 red chillies (seeded and finely chopped)

2 garlic cloves (crushed)
250g/9oz crab sticks
2 teaspoons soy sauce
1 teaspoon sesame oil

- In a frying pan, a wok or a saucepan heat the oil and fry the onion for a few minutes. Add the chillies and garlic and continue to fry, stirring, for 1 minute.
- Tip in the crab sticks and cook for 2 minutes, until they have broken up, then fold in the soy sauce and sesame oil. Serve immediately.

Melon & strawberries

SERVES 4

INGREDIENTS:

¼ honeydew melon
½ Cantaloupe melon
150ml/¼pt rosé wine

3 teaspoons rose water
175g/6oz small strawberries (washed and hulled)

- Scoop out the seeds from both melons with a spoon. Carefully remove the peel.
- Cut the melon flesh into thin strips and place in a bowl. Pour over the wine and rose water. Mix together, cover and leave to chill in the refrigerator for at least 2 hours.
- Halve the strawberries and mix in with the melon. Allow to stand at room temperature for about 15 minutes before serving.

Layered prawns

SERVES 6

INGREDIENTS:

*350g/12oz fresh prawns in
their shells
225g/8oz cream cheese
125ml/4fl oz sour cream
¼ teaspoon onion salt*

*Dash of ground black pepper
50ml/2fl oz chilli sauce
1½ teaspoons Worcestershire sauce
¾ teaspoon lemon juice
½ teaspoon horseradish sauce*

- Bring a saucepan of water to the boil and add the prawns. Cook for 4 minutes.
- Drain well and rinse with cold water. Peel the prawns. Chop two-thirds of the prawns, leaving the remaining prawns whole. Cover and chill.
- Beat the cream cheese until creamy. Add the sour cream, onion salt and black pepper, beating until smooth.
- Spread the mixture onto a serving platter, shaping into a 12.5cm/5in circle.
- Cover and chill for at least 30 minutes.
- Combine the chilli sauce, Worcestershire sauce, lemon juice and horseradish in a small bowl. Stir well, and spread over the cream cheese round. Sprinkle the chopped prawns over the chilli sauce mixture and top with the whole prawns.
- Chill before serving.

Stuffed peppers

SERVES 2-4

INGREDIENTS:

*2 green peppers
1 egg (hard-boiled and finely chopped)
75g/3oz Cheddar cheese (grated)*

*2 medium-sized tomatoes
3 tablespoons mayonnaise
2 slices of bread (toasted)*

- Boil the peppers gently in a saucepan of water for 20 minutes or until tender.
- Remove the peppers from the water, and halve and deseed them.
- Mix the chopped eggs, cheese and tomatoes in a small bowl. Add the mayonnaise and stir well.
- Fill the pepper halves with the egg mixture and place on the slices of toast.
- Place under the grill until lightly browned. Serve hot.

Greek spinach & cheese pie

SERVES 8

INGREDIENTS:

150ml/¼pt olive oil
1 medium onion (finely chopped)
2 teaspoons ground cumin
2 garlic cloves (crushed)

450g/1lb chopped spinach
100g/4oz feta cheese (crumbled)
100g/4oz cream cheese
400g/14oz filo pastry

- Preheat the oven to 190°C/375°F/Gas mark 5.
- Heat 2 tablespoons olive oil in a frying pan, add the onion and cook gently, stirring frequently, for about 10 minutes until softened. Sprinkle in the cumin and stir for 2 minutes, then stir in the garlic and spinach. Remove the pan from the heat and stir in the cheeses until evenly mixed.
- Brush the inside of a 30 x 23cm/12 x 9in baking dish with olive oil. Place a sheet of pastry in the dish, letting the edges hang over the side. Brush the pastry in the dish with oil and continue until half the pastry is used.
- Spread the cheese mixture over the pastry. Use the remaining pastry to cover the mixture, spreading oil over individual sheets as before. Trim and seal the edges. Cut through the layers with a sharp knife to divide the pie into 16 segments.
- Bake in the oven for 30 minutes. Leave to cool for 10 minutes before serving.

Mini mushroom quiches

SERVES 6

INGREDIENTS:

4 slices wholewheat bread (crusts removed)
2 teaspoons butter
225g/8oz mushrooms (wiped with damp kitchen paper and finely chopped)

1 garlic clove (minced)
Salt and pepper
4 eggs
100g/4oz Emmental cheese (grated)

- Preheat the oven to 190°C/375°F/Gas mark 5.
- Roll each slice of bread with a rolling pin until flat, halve each slice and place on a greased muffin tray, pressing each slice into the cake mould. Bake at a low heat until crisp.

- In a small frying pan, melt the butter over medium heat. Add the mushrooms, garlic, salt and pepper and fry, stirring regularly, for 3 to 5 minutes or until tender.
- Break the eggs in a bowl, piercing the yolks with a small sharp knife. Pour the eggs over the bread cups, dividing the mixture evenly. Top with the mushroom mixture and sprinkle with the cheese.
- Bake in the oven for 15 minutes, or until the eggs are just set.

Succotash

SERVES 4-6

INGREDIENTS:

4 tablespoons vegetable oil
500g/1lb 2oz lean smoked bacon rashers (cut into squares)
1 large onion (finely sliced)
3 garlic cloves (finely chopped)
1 red pepper (deseeded and chopped)
1 green pepper (deseeded, chopped)

900g/2lb canned red kidney beans
1.4kg/3lb sweetcorn kernels
350ml/12fl oz water
3 tomatoes (diced)
150g/5oz Parmesan cheese (grated)

- Heat the oil in a heavy-based saucepan and brown the bacon over a high heat.
- Lower the heat and add the onion, garlic, peppers, beans, sweetcorn and water.
- Stir well.
- Simmer over a low heat for 15 minutes, then add the tomatoes. Continue to simmer for a further 20 minutes or until the sauce has reduced.
- Sprinkle with the cheese and serve hot.

Onion soup

SERVES 4-6

INGREDIENTS:

2 tablespoons butter
1 tablespoon oil
3 large onions (finely sliced)
1 teaspoon soft brown sugar
1 tablespoon plain flour
600ml/1pt vegetable stock

2 tablespoons medium sherry
2 teaspoons Worcestershire sauce
8 slices of a baguette
1 tablespoon wholegrain mustard
100g/4oz Gruyère cheese (grated)

→

- Heat the butter and oil in a large pan and add the onions and brown sugar.
- Cook gently for about 20 minutes, stirring occasionally, until the onions start to turn golden brown.
- Stir in the flour and cook for a further 2 minutes. Pour in the vegetable stock, then add the sherry and Worcestershire sauce. Cover and simmer gently for 25 to 30 minutes.
- Preheat the grill and, just before serving, toast the bread lightly on both sides.
- Spread one side of each slice with the mustard and top with the grated cheese.
- Grill the toasts until bubbling and golden. Ladle the soup into soup dishes and place 2 croûtons on top of each. Serve at once.

Carrot & coriander soup

SERVES 6

INGREDIENTS:

175g/6oz onion (diced)
50g/2oz butter
500g/1lb 2oz carrots (sliced)
1 garlic clove (finely chopped)
Handful of fresh coriander (chopped)

1.2 litres/2pt chicken or
vegetable stock
1 teaspoon caster sugar
150ml/¼pt whipping cream

- Sweat the onion in the butter until soft. Add the carrots to the pan and cook, stirring from time to time, for a further 5 minutes.
- Add the garlic and most of the coriander. Pour the stock over the top, add the sugar and bring to the boil. Lower the heat and simmer for 30 minutes.
- Put the contents of the pan into a food processor or blender and blend to a smooth purée.
- Pour back into a clean pan and add the whipping cream. Taste and adjust the seasoning, then heat the soup through gently, stirring.
- Scatter the reserved coriander leaves before serving.

Melon in wine

SERVES 4

INGREDIENTS:

2 small cantaloupe melons
175ml/6fl oz dry sparkling wine

3 tablespoons orange marmalade
½ bunch mint (chopped)

- Halve the melons lengthways and scoop out the seeds. Remove the flesh and cut into small cubes. Place the cubes in a bowl.
- In a separate small bowl whisk together the wine, marmalade and mint. Pour the mixture over the melon flesh and stir gently.
- Divide the mixture between the melon shells. Cover with clingfilm, place in the refrigerator and leave to marinate for 4 to 6 hours. Serve cold.

Mixed bhajias

SERVES 4

INGREDIENTS:

175g/6oz gram flour
1 teaspoon bicarbonate of soda
2 teaspoons ground coriander
1 teaspoon garam masala
1½ teaspoon ground turmeric
1½ teaspoon chilli powder
2 tablespoons chopped fresh coriander
1 small onion (halved and sliced)
1 small leek (sliced)

100g/4oz cauliflower (cooked)
12 tablespoons cold water
Vegetable oil for deep-frying

For the sauce:
150ml/¼pt natural yogurt
2 tablespoons chopped fresh mint
½ teaspoon ground turmeric
1 garlic clove (crushed)

- Sift the flour and bicarbonate of soda into a mixing bowl, add the spices and coriander and mix thoroughly.
- Divide the mixture between 3 separate small bowls. Stir the onion in one bowl, the leek into another and the cauliflower into the third. Add 4 tablespoons of water to each bowl and mix each to form a smooth paste.
- Heat the oil for deep-frying in a wok. Using 2 tablespoons, form the mixture into rounds and cook each in the oil until browned. Remove with a slotted spoon and drain on kitchen paper.
- Mix all the sauce ingredients together and pour into a small serving bowl. Serve with the warm bhajias.

Sesame seed prawn toasts

SERVES 4

INGREDIENTS:

225g/8oz uncooked peeled prawns
(finely chopped)
25g/1oz lard
1 tablespoon cornflour
1 egg white (lightly beaten)
½ spring onion (finely chopped)

½ teaspoon finely chopped root ginger
1 tablespoon dry sherry
100g/4oz white sesame seeds
6 slices white bread (remove crusts)
Vegetable oil for deep-frying

- In a mixing bowl, mash the prawns and the lard together with a fork to form a smooth paste.
- In a small bowl mix the cornflour with a teaspoon of water, using a small metal spoon make a paste.
- Add the egg white, spring onions, root ginger, sherry and cornflour paste to the prawns and lard.
- Spread the sesame seeds evenly on a large plate or tray. Spread the prawn paste thickly on one side of each slice of bread. Press the bread, spread side down, on to the seeds.
- Heat the oil in a wok until medium-hot and fry 2 slices of the sesame bread at a time, spread side down, for 2 minutes. Remove and drain on kitchen paper.
- Serve hot.

Cheesy potato skins

SERVES 4

INGREDIENTS:

3 medium baking potatoes (scored
into quarters)
1 teaspoon vegetable oil
50g/2oz lean smoked back bacon
(roughly chopped)
175g/6oz brown cap mushrooms
(roughly chopped)

100g/4oz cream cheese
2 tablespoons milk
1½ teaspoons wholegrain mustard
50g/2oz Cheddar cheese (grated)

- Preheat the oven to 200°C/400°F/Gas mark 6.

- Place the potatoes in the oven in a baking dish for 1 hour or until cooked.
- Heat the oil in a frying pan and fry the bacon until cooked. Add the mushrooms and fry until the excess moisture has evaporated.
- Blend the cream cheese, milk, mustard and half the Cheddar in a bowl.
- When the potatoes are cooked, quarter them and scrape out the inside, leaving a thin layer of potato on the skin. Put the potato to one side. Put the skins on a baking tray and return to the oven for 5 minutes.
- Mash the potato and stir into the cheese mixture with the bacon and mushrooms.
- Pile the mixture into the potato skins, sprinkle the remaining cheese over the top.
- Return to the oven for 10 minutes or until golden brown.

French anchovy flan

SERVES 6

INGREDIENTS:

25g/1oz butter
25g/1oz lard
100g/4oz plain flour
Pinch of salt
2 tablespoons water
450g/1lb onions (finely sliced)
2 garlic cloves (crushed)

6 tablespoons vegetable oil
225g/8oz tomatoes
2 tablespoons tomato purée
1 teaspoon chopped fresh thyme
Salt and freshly ground black pepper
16 black pitted olives
3 anchovy fillets

- Preheat the oven to 200°C/400°F/Gas mark 6.
- Cut the butter and lard into pieces and add these to the flour in a large bowl with the salt. Mix until the mixture resembles fine breadcrumbs. Add the water and mix until it forms a smooth dough. Cover and chill for 15 minutes.
- When the dough is cool, roll out and use to line a 20cm/8in plain flan ring. Bake in the preheated oven for 20 minutes.
- For the filling, fry the onions and garlic in the oil in a large saucepan for 10 minutes or until very soft but not brown.
- Place the tomatoes in a bowl of just-boiled water for 30 seconds. Remove the skin and seeds. Slice the tomatoes, add to the pan and continue cooking for 10 minutes until the liquid has evaporated. Stir in the tomato purée and thyme and season with salt and pepper.
- Turn the mixture into the flan case. Brush with a little oil and cook in the preheated oven for 20 minutes.
- When the flan is cooked, garnish with olives and strips of anchovy fillet. This dish can be served either hot or cold.

Naan bread

SERVES 8

INGREDIENTS:

1 teaspoon sugar	*1 tablespoon ghee*
1 teaspoon fresh yeast	*1 teaspoon salt*
150ml/¼pt warm water	*50g/2oz unsalted butter*
200g/7oz plain flour	*1 teaspoon poppy seeds*

- Put the sugar and yeast in a small bowl or jug together with the warm water and mix thoroughly until the yeast has completely dissolved. Set aside for 10 minutes.
- Place the flour in a large mixing bowl, making a well in the centre. Add the ghee and salt and pour in the yeast mixture. Mix thoroughly to form a dough, adding more water if required.
- Place the dough on a floured work surface and knead until smooth. Return to the bowl, cover and set aside to rise for 1½ hours.
- Preheat the grill to very hot. Turn the dough out on to a floured surface and knead for a further 2 minutes. Break off small balls and pat them into rounds about 12.5cm/5in in diameter and 1cm/½in thick.
- Place the rounds on a greased sheet of aluminium foil and grill for 7 to 10 minutes, turning twice and brushing with butter and sprinkling with poppy seeds.
- Serve immediately.

Prawn crackers

SERVES 4

INGREDIENTS:

250g/9oz peeled raw prawns	*Vegetable oil for deep-frying*
250g/9oz tapioca flour	
Salt and pepper	

- Liquidize the prawns in a blender until they form a smooth paste. Transfer the prawn paste into a bowl and mix in the tapioca flour, salt and pepper. Mix well to form a stiff dough.
- Divide the dough into 3 equal portions. Roll up each portion then place the rolls on a greased plate. Place the rolls on a stand in a pan of boiling water or

in a steamer, and steam for 40 to 45 minutes over a high heat.
- Leave the rolls to cool, then wrap in a clean tea towel and chill well in the refrigerator.
- Use a very sharp knife to slice thinly.
- Heat the oil in a deep wok and deep-fry the crackers in batches until crisp.
- Remove from wok and drain on kitchen paper. Serve hot or cold.

Sour curried seafood soup

SERVES 4–6

INGREDIENTS:

1 tablespoon tamarind pulp
150ml/¼pt boiling water
3 tablespoons vegetable oil
1 onion (finely chopped)
2 garlic cloves (crushed)
2.5cm/1in piece of root ginger (peeled and grated)
2 teaspoons ground coriander
2 teaspoons ground cumin
1 teaspoon ground turmeric
1 teaspoon chilli powder

½ teaspoon black mustard seeds
¼ teaspoon ground fenugreek
2 teaspoons Madras curry powder
1.2 litre/2pt fish stock
3 tomatoes (cut into wedges)
1 teaspoon salt
1 tablespoon lemon juice
250g/9oz skinless halibut (cut into bite-size pieces)
100g/4oz cooked and peeled prawns
2 tablespoons chopped fresh coriander

- Soak the tamarind pulp in the boiling water for 10 minutes, then strain the pulp through a sieve. Discard the pulp and reserve the liquid.
- Heat the oil in a saucepan, add the onion, garlic and ginger and fry over a gentle heat, stirring, for about 5 minutes or until softened but not coloured.
- Add the ground coriander, cumin, turmeric, chilli powder, mustard seeds, fenugreek and curry powder and cook gently, stirring, for a further 2 minutes.
- Add the fish stock and reserved tamarind liquid, stir well, then simmer gently for 10 minutes. Add the salt and lemon juice and simmer for a further 4 minutes.
- Stir the fish into the soup and cook gently for 4 minutes, until the fish is just cooked. Add the prawns and the chopped coriander and heat through gently for 2 minutes. Taste and add a little more salt, if necessary, and serve immediately.

Garlic breadsticks

SERVES 4

INGREDIENTS:

2 baguettes   150ml/¼ pt olive oil
2 garlic cloves (crushed)

- Preheat the oven to 200°C/400°F/Gas mark 6. Cut the baguettes into 3 lengthways, then halve each segment, creating 12 breadsticks. Place the sticks on a baking tray.
- Mix the garlic and oil in a small bowl, then spread over the breadsticks.
- Bake for 15 to 20 minutes or until golden brown. Can be served hot or cold.

Butterfly prawns

SERVES 2-4

INGREDIENTS:

16 raw tiger prawns (shelled, with tails intact)
Juice of 2 limes
1 teaspoon cardamom seeds
2 teaspoons ground cumin
2 teaspoons ground coriander

½ teaspoon ground cinnamon
1 teaspoon ground turmeric
1 garlic clove (crushed)
1 teaspoon cayenne pepper
2 tablespoons oil

- Cut the prawns in half lengthways down to the tail and flatten out to form a symmetrical shape.
- Thread a prawn on to 2 skewers with the tail in the middle. Thread another 3 prawns on to the same 2 skewers in the same way. Repeat until you have 4 sets of 4 prawns on each 2 skewers.
- Lay the skewered prawns on a non-metallic dish and sprinkle the lime juice over them.
- Combine the spices and the oil in a small bowl, then coat the prawns well with the mixture. Cover and chill the prawns for 2 hours.
- Cook on an aluminium foil-lined grill pan under a hot grill for 6 minutes, turning halfway through. Serve immediately.

Crispy seaweed

SERVES 4

INGREDIENTS:

1.1kg/2½lb pak choi
Groundnut oil for deep-frying

1 teaspoon salt
1 tablespoon caster sugar

- Rinse the pak choi leaves under cold running water, then dry thoroughly with kitchen paper.
- Roll each pak choi leaf up and slice through thinly with a small, sharp knife or use a food processor. Make sure the leaves are finely shredded.
- Heat the groundnut oil in a large wok or frying pan. Carefully add the shredded pak choi to the wok and fry for about 30 seconds, or until they shrivel up and become crispy. You may need to do this in batches.
- Remove the crispy 'seaweed' from the wok with a slotted spoon and drain on paper towels. Transfer to a large bowl, toss with salt and sugar and serve immediately.

Chicken & bacon kebabs

SERVES 4

INGREDIENTS:

2 corn on the cob
8 thick rashers back bacon
6 brown cap mushrooms (wiped with damp kitchen paper and halved)
2 small chicken fillets

2 tablespoons sunflower oil
1 tablespoon lemon juice
1 tablespoon maple syrup
Salt and pepper

- Cook the corn in a saucepan of boiling water until tender, then drain and cool.
- Stretch the bacon rashers with the back of a knife. Cut each rasher in half and wrap a piece around each mushroom.
- Cut both the corn and chicken into 8 equal pieces. Mix together the oil, lemon juice, syrup and seasoning and brush over the chicken.
- Thread the corn, bacon-wrapped mushrooms and chicken pieces alternately on skewers and brush all over with the lemon dressing.
- Grill for 8 to 10 minutes, turning once and basting occasionally with any extra dressing. Serve hot.

Chicken noodle soup

SERVES 4-6

INGREDIENTS:

*1 sheet of dried egg noodles from a
250g/9oz pack
1 tablespoon vegetable oil
4 skinless, boneless chicken thighs
(diced)
1 bunch spring onions (sliced)
2 garlic cloves (chopped)
1cm/¹/₂ in piece root ginger (peeled
and finely chopped)*

*900ml/1¹/₂ pt chicken stock
200ml/7fl oz coconut milk
3 teaspoons Thai red curry paste
3 tablespoons peanut butter
2 tablespoons soy sauce
1 small red pepper (chopped)
50g/2oz frozen peas*

- Put the noodles in a shallow dish and soak in boiling water, or as per instructions on the package.
- Heat the oil in a large wok. Add the diced chicken and fry for 5 minutes, stirring, or until lightly browned. Add the white part of the spring onions, the garlic and ginger and fry for a further 2 minutes, stirring.
- Stir in the chicken stock, coconut milk, red curry paste, peanut butter and soy sauce. Bring to the boil, stirring, then simmer for 8 minutes, stirring occasionally.
- Add the red pepper, peas and green spring onion tops and cook for 2 minutes.
- Add the drained noodles. Serve hot.

Mussels in white wine

SERVES 4

INGREDIENTS:

*50g/2oz butter
1 large onion (finely chopped)
2 garlic cloves (crushed)
350ml/12fl oz dry white wine
150ml/¹/₄ pt water
2 tablespoons lemon juice*

*Salt and pepper
3.6 litres/6pt fresh mussels (cleaned)
1 tablespoon plain flour
4 tablespoons double cream
3 tablespoons chopped fresh parsley
Salt and pepper*

- Melt half the butter in a large saucepan. Add the onion and garlic and fry gently until soft. Add the wine, water and lemon juice, and season well. Bring

to the boil, then cover and simmer for 5 minutes.
- Add the mussels to the pan, cover and simmer for a further 5 minutes, shaking the pan frequently, until all the mussels have opened. Discard any mussels that have not opened. Remove the empty half shell from each mussel.
- Blend the remaining butter with the flour and whisk into the soup, a little at a time. Simmer gently for 3 minutes.
- Add the cream and half the parsley to the soup and reheat gently. Adjust the seasoning. After dishing up the soup, sprinkle with the remaining parsley and serve immediately.

Chicken satay

SERVES 6

INGREDIENTS:

4 boneless chicken breasts (skinned)

For the marinade:
1 small onion (finely chopped)
1 garlic clove (crushed)
2cm/1in piece root ginger (peeled and grated)
2 tablespoons soy sauce
2 teaspoons chilli powder
1 teaspoon ground coriander

2 teaspoons brown sugar
1 tablespoon lemon juice
1 tablespoon vegetable oil

For the sauce:
300ml/½ pt coconut milk
4 tablespoons peanut butter
1 tablespoon fish sauce
1 teaspoon lemon juice

- Using a sharp knife, trim any fat away from the chicken, then cut the flesh into thin strips, about 7.5cm/3in long.
- To make the marinade, place all the ingredients in a shallow dish and mix well.
- Add the chicken strips and turn in the marinade until well coated. Cover with clingfilm and leave overnight in the refrigerator.
- To make the sauce, mix the coconut milk with the peanut butter, fish sauce and lemon juice in a saucepan. Bring to the boil and simmer for 3 minutes.
- Remove the meat from the marinade and thread the pieces on to wooden skewers. Grill the chicken satays for 10 minutes, turning and brushing occasionally with the marinade, until cooked through.
- Transfer the sauce to a serving bowl and serve with the cooked satays.

Mozzarella, avocado & tomato salad

SERVES 4

INGREDIENTS:

2 ripe avocados
125ml/4fl oz vinaigrette
175g/6oz Mozzarella cheese (sliced)

4 medium tomatoes (thinly sliced)
Basil leaves, to garnish

- Halve the avocados lengthways and carefully remove the stones. Peel and cut them into slices.
- Arrange slices of Mozzarella, tomato and avocado on 4 individual serving plates. Spoon the vinaigrette dressing over the top.
- Garnish with the basil leaves.

Chinese pickled vegetables

SERVES 4

INGREDIENTS:

100g/4oz carrot (cubed)
100g/4oz mooli (cubed)
100g/4oz drained canned water
chestnuts (quartered)
4 tablespoons rice vinegar

For the dip:
3 mild red chillies
50g/2oz pickled ginger
1 teaspoon tomato purée

- Mix the carrots, mooli and water chestnuts together in a bowl with the rice vinegar. Cover and set aside for 3 hours, stirring occasionally.
- Halve and deseed the chillies, then use a pestle and mortar to pound them to a paste with the pickled ginger. Mix in the tomato purée and place in a small serving bowl.
- Drain the vinegar-soaked vegetables and serve with a bowl of dip at room temperature.

Vichyssoise

SERVES 4

INGREDIENTS:

50g/1oz butter
300g/11oz leeks (sliced)
150g/5oz onion (finely chopped)
300g/11oz potatoes (peeled and diced)

900ml/1½pt chicken stock
Salt and pepper
4 tablespoons natural yogurt
1 tablespoon chopped fresh chives

- Melt the butter in a large saucepan, add the leeks and onion and stir well. Cover the pan and sweat the vegetables over a low heat for 5 minutes until soft.
- Add the potatoes and chicken stock and bring to the boil. Cover and simmer for about 30 minutes or until the potatoes are very soft. Season with salt and pepper.
- Pour the soup into a blender and purée until smooth. Pour into a bowl and leave to cool, then cover and chill in the refrigerator overnight.
- Stir well before serving. Ladle into chilled bowls and top with a tablespoon of natural yogurt and a sprinkling of chives. Serve chilled.

Feta cheese tartlets

SERVES 4

INGREDIENTS:

8 slices white bread
100g/4oz butter (melted)
100g/4oz feta cheese (cut into small cubes)
4 cherry tomatoes (cut into small wedges)
8 black olives (pitted and halved)

8 quail's eggs (hard-boiled)
2 tablespoons olive oil
1 tablespoon wine vinegar
1 teaspoon wholegrain mustard
Pinch of caster sugar
Salt and pepper

- Preheat the oven to 190°C/375°F/Gas mark 5.
- Remove the crusts from the bread. Trim the bread into squares and flatten each slice with a rolling pin. Brush with melted butter then arrange in bun or muffin trays. Press a piece of aluminium foil into each slice to secure in place. Bake for 10 minutes, or until crisp and browned.
- Mix together the feta cheese, tomatoes and olives. Shell the eggs and quarter them. Mix together the olive oil, vinegar, mustard and sugar. Season with salt and pepper.

→

←
- Remove the bread cases from the oven, discard the foil and leave to cool.
- Just before serving, fill the bread cases with the cheese and tomato mixture.
- Arrange the eggs on the top and spoon the dressing over. Serve immediately.

Vegetable fritters

SERVES 4

INGREDIENTS:

100g/4oz wholemeal flour
Pinch of salt
Pinch of cayenne pepper
4 teaspoons olive oil
175ml/6fl oz cold water
100g/4oz broccoli florets
100g/4oz cauliflower florets
50g/2oz mangetout
1 large carrots (cut into batons)
1 red pepper (seeded and sliced)
2 egg whites (beaten)
Vegetable oil for deep-frying

For the sauce:
150ml/¼pt pineapple juice
150ml/¼pt vegetable stock
2 tablespoons white wine vinegar
2 tablespoons brown sugar
2 teaspoons cornflour
2 spring onions (chopped)

- Sift the flour and salt into a mixing bowl and add the cayenne pepper. Make a well in the centre and gradually beat in the oil and cold water to make a smooth batter.
- Put the vegetables in a pan of boiling water and simmer for 5 minutes, then drain well.
- Whisk the egg whites until they form peaks and gently fold them into the flour batter.
- Heat the vegetable oil in a deep-fryer until a cube of bread browns in 30 seconds.
- Dip the vegetables into the batter, turning to coat them well. Drain off any excess batter. Fry in batches until golden. Remove with a slotted spoon and drain on kitchen paper.
- Place all of the sauce ingredients in a pan and bring to the boil, stirring, until thickened and clear. Serve with the fritters.

Minestrone soup

SERVES 8

INGREDIENTS:

250g/9oz dried borlotti beans (soaked overnight)
250g/9oz soup pasta
100ml/3½fl oz olive oil
1.4kg/3lb assorted vegetables (courgettes, French beans, broccoli,

leeks, potatoes, peas, carrots and onions)
3 garlic cloves (thinly sliced)
Salt and pepper
3 celery sticks

- Drain the soaked beans and place in a saucepan. Cover with fresh water and bring to the boil. Boil vigorously for 10 minutes, then drain. Cover with fresh cold water, bring back to the boil and simmer for about 1½ hours.
- Cook the soup pasta in plenty of rapidly boiling salted water until half done.
- Drain and reserve. Add 1 tablespoon olive oil and turn to coat.
- Cut the vegetables into 1cm/½in chunks or rounds as appropriate.
- Put the remaining olive oil in a large saucepan and sweat the onion, garlic, carrots and celery for 5 minutes, stirring from time to time. Add the remaining vegetables, except the broccoli and French beans. Cover with cold water. Bring to the boil, turn down the heat and simmer until the vegetables are just cooked.
- Add the drained borlotti beans, season to taste with salt and pepper and cook for a further 5 minutes. Remove from the heat, leave to cool and then refrigerate overnight.
- To serve, reheat the soup gently, stirring in the half-cooked pasta, French beans and broccoli florets. Simmer for a final 5 minutes. Serve warm.

Bacon-wrapped prawns

SERVES 6

INGREDIENTS:

24 uncooked large prawns (peeled)
24 canned whole water chestnuts (drained)
12 smoked bacon slices (cut in half)
75g/3oz butter

250g/9oz cream cheese
125ml/4fl oz mayonnaise
125ml/4fl oz sour cream
3 tablespoons horseradish sauce
1 tablespoon fresh lemon juice

- Wrap 1 prawn around a water chestnut, then wrap both in a half-rasher of

→

bacon and secure with a toothpick. Repeat with all prawns, water chestnuts and bacon.

- Melt 40g/1/2oz butter in a heavy large frying pan over a high heat. Add half of the prawn wraps and cook until the bacon browns. Transfer to a large dish and repeat with the remaining butter and prawns.
- Beat the cream cheese in a medium-sized bowl until smooth. Add the mayonnaise, sour cream, horseradish source and lemon juice and blend thoroughly.
- Spoon the sauce over the prawn wraps.
- Grill under a medium heat until golden brown. Serve immediately.

Fried wontons

SERVES 6

INGREDIENTS:

30 wonton wrappers
1 egg (beaten)
Vegetable oil for deep-frying

For the filling:
2 tablespoons vegetable oil
1 tablespoon grated root ginger
2 garlic cloves (finely chopped)
225g/8oz firm bean curd
6 spring onions (finely chopped)
2 teaspoons sesame oil

1 tablespoon soy sauce
Salt and pepper

For the dipping sauce:
2 tablespoons soy sauce
1 tablespoon sesame oil
1 tablespoon rice vinegar
1/2 teaspoon chilli oil
1/2 teaspoon honey
2 tablespoons water

- To make the filling, heat the vegetable oil in a frying pan, add the root ginger and garlic, and fry for 30 seconds. Crumble in the bean curd and stir-fry for a few minutes. Add the spring onions, sesame oil and soy sauce. Stir well and season.
- Make the dipping sauce by combining all the ingredients in a bowl and mixing well.
- Brush the edges of a wonton wrapper lightly with beaten egg. Spoon 1 teaspoon of the filling on to the centre of the wrapper, then fold the wrapper over to make a triangle. Press the edges firmly to seal. Repeat with all of the wonton wrappers.
- Heat the oil in a deep-fryer or large saucepan. Carefully add the wontons, in batches, and cook for a few minutes, until golden brown. Remove with a slotted spoon and drain on kitchen paper. Serve immediately with dipping sauce.

Scotch broth

SERVES 6-8

INGREDIENTS:

1.1kg/2½lb neck of lamb (cubed)
1.8 litres/3pt water
1 large onion (chopped)
50g/2oz pearl barley
Bouquet garni
1 large carrot (chopped)

1 turnip (chopped)
3 leeks (chopped)
½ small white cabbage (shredded)
Salt and pepper

- Put the lamb and water into a large saucepan and bring to the boil. Skim off any grey foam, then stir in the onion, pearl barley and bouquet garni.
- Bring the soup back to the boil, then partly cover the pan and simmer gently for 1 hour.
- Add the remaining vegetables and the seasoning. Bring to the boil again, partly cover and simmer for 35 minutes.
- Use a spoon to remove surplus fat from the top of the soup. Discard the bouquet garni and serve hot.

Spinach roulade

SERVES 4

INGREDIENTS:

500g/1lb 2oz small spinach leaves
2 tablespoons water
4 eggs (separated)
½ teaspoon ground nutmeg
Salt and pepper

For the filling:
175g/6oz small broccoli florets
25g/1oz Parmesan cheese (grated)
175g/6oz Mozzarella cheese (grated)

- Preheat the oven 220°C/425°F/Gas mark 7.
- Wash the spinach and pack, while still wet, into a large saucepan. Add the water, cover and cook over a high heat for 5 minutes, until reduced and soft. Drain thoroughly, leave to cool, then chop finely and pat dry.
- Mix the spinach with the egg yolks, nutmeg and seasoning. Whisk the egg whites until very frothy but not too stiff, and fold into the spinach mixture.
- Grease and line a Swiss roll tin. Spread the mixture in the tin and smooth the surface. Bake in the oven for about 15 minutes, until firm and golden.

$\rightarrow$

←

- Add the broccoli florets to a saucepan of lightly salted boiling water and simmer for 5 minutes. Drain and keep warm.
- Sprinkle the Parmesan on to a sheet of baking parchment. Turn out the cooked spinach mixture on to the Parmesan and peel away the lining paper. Sprinkle with Mozzarella and top with broccoli.
- Hold one end of the baking parchment and roll up the spinach base like a Swiss roll. Slice to serve.

Hot & sour soup

SERVES 4

INGREDIENTS:

6 dried Chinese mushrooms (soaked in warm water)
100g/4oz chicken
50g/2oz sliced bamboo shoots (drained)
600ml/1pt chicken stock

1 tablespoon dry sherry
1 tablespoon soy sauce
1 tablespoon rice vinegar
1 tablespoon cornflour
1 teaspoon water

- Squeeze the soaked mushrooms dry and discard the hard stalks. Thinly shred the mushrooms, chicken and bamboo shoots.
- Bring the stock to the boil in a wok and add the shredded ingredients. Bring back to the boil and simmer for 1 minute.
- Add the sherry, soy sauce and vinegar. Bring back to the boil. Mix the cornflour with the water to form a paste and stir into the liquid until it has thickened. Serve hot.

Bruschetta

SERVES 4

INGREDIENTS:

8 slices of ciabatta bread
2 garlic cloves (halved)
Salt and freshly ground black pepper

Extra-virgin olive oil
8 tomatoes (sliced)
8 basil leaves

- Toast the bread lightly and rub with garlic while still hot. Season with salt and lots of pepper, and pour enough oil on each slice to soak thoroughly.

- Divide the tomato slices evenly between the pieces of bread.
- Top each bruschetta with a fresh basil leaf.

Pork dim sum

SERVES 8

INGREDIENTS:

1 tablespoon vegetable oil
100g/4oz lean pork mince
1 garlic clove (crushed)
½ onion (finely chopped)
1 tablespoon finely chopped bamboo
shoots
2 red chillies (finely chopped)
2 teaspoons soy sauce

1 tablespoon oyster sauce
2 teaspoons tomato purée
1 teaspoon sesame oil
100g/4oz self-raising flour
Salt
25g/1oz lard
1 tablespoon caster sugar
2 teaspoons sesame seeds

- Heat the oil in a frying pan. Add the pork, garlic, onion, bamboo shoots and chillies and stir-fry for 5 minutes. Add the soy sauce, oyster sauce and tomato purée and cook for 5 minutes, stirring occasionally. Stir in the sesame oil and leave to cool.
- Sift the flour and a few pinches of salt into a mixing bowl. Rub in the lard finely.
- Add about 4 tablespoons of water and mix to form a soft dough.
- Divide the dough into 24 portions. Form each portion into a ball and roll out on to a lightly floured surface to an 7.5cm/3in round. Put a teaspoon of pork mixture into the centre of each round. Dampen the dough edges and gather together, sealing well by twisting together to form a pouch.
- Cook in a steamer over simmering water for about 15 minutes. Serve hot.

Cheesy garlic bread

SERVES 4-6

INGREDIENTS:

100g/4oz butter (melted)
4 garlic cloves (crushed)
¼ teaspoon dried oregano

1 baguette (halved lengthways)
3 tablespoons grated Parmesan cheese

←
- In a small bowl, combine the butter, garlic and oregano. Spread the mixture on the cut sides of the bread.
- Sprinkle the bread with Parmesan cheese and place on an ungreased baking sheet. Grill under a high heat for 3 minutes or until golden brown. Slice and serve hot.

Roquefort, leek & walnut tarts

SERVES 6

INGREDIENTS:

375g/13oz ready-rolled puff pastry
2 eggs
50g/2oz butter
400g/14oz trimmed leeks (sliced)

2 tablespoons chopped fresh chives
100g/4oz Roquefort cheese (sliced into 6 pieces)
75g/3oz walnuts (chopped)

- Preheat the oven to 200°C/400°F/Gas mark 6.
- Cut the puff pastry into 6 squares. Using a small sharp knife, score another square 1cm/½in in from the edge of each to make a frame.
- Put the squares on a greased baking tray. Beat 1 egg lightly and brush over each pastry case. Bake for 10 minutes or until well risen and slightly golden.
- Scoop out the pastry from the inner square, leaving a thin layer at the bottom.
- Melt the butter in a frying pan, add the leeks and cook until soft. Beat the remaining egg and add it to the leeks along with the chives.
- Fill each pastry case with the leek mixture. Top with a slice of Roquefort and sprinkle with walnuts. Return to the oven and bake for 10 to 15 minutes or until golden and heated thoroughly. Serve warm.

Prawns steamed in banana leaves

SERVES 4

INGREDIENTS:

2 garlic cloves (chopped)
1 shallot (chopped)
5cm/2in piece of fresh galangal
(peeled and chopped)
1 stalk of lemon grass (finely
chopped)
3 kaffir lime leaves (chopped)
1 teaspoon dried red chilli flakes
2 teaspoons chilli oil

1 tablespoon fish sauce
1 tablespoon lime juice
¼ teaspoon caster sugar
25g/1oz creamed coconut (chopped)
75ml/3fl oz boiling water
24 uncooked prawns (peeled, with
tails left intact)
4 large pieces of banana leaf

- Place the garlic, shallot, galangal, lemon grass, kaffir lime leaves, chilli flakes, chilli oil, fish sauce, lime juice and sugar in a food processor or blender and blend to produce a thick paste.
- Place the creamed coconut in a bowl and pour the boiling water over. Stir to dissolve the coconut, then add to the spice paste. Mix well.
- Place the prawns in a bowl and add the coconut spice mixture. Stir to coat the prawns evenly. Lay the 4 pieces of banana leaf on a flat surface. Place 6 prawns and a quarter of the coconut mixture in the centre of each leaf. Wrap up the leaves to enclose the prawns to form neat parcels.
- Steam the prawn parcels in a steamer over boiling water for 8 to 10 minutes.
- To serve, remove the prawns from the leaves and place on 4 serving plates. Pour the coconut sauce into a bowl and whisk briefly until smooth. Pour a little sauce over each portion and serve immediately.

Melon-ball salad

SERVES 4

INGREDIENTS:

1 watermelon
1 cantaloupe melon
1 honeydew melon
75ml/3fl oz chicken broth
50ml/2fl oz sherry vinegar
75ml/3fl oz lemon juice
4 garlic cloves (crushed)

¼ teaspoon salt
¼ teaspoon black pepper
2 tablespoons minced fresh tarragon
2 tablespoons minced fresh chervil
2 tablespoons minced fresh
lemon basil

- Cut melon balls from all 3 melons and drain in a colander.
- Make a salad dressing by stirring together in a mixing bowl the chicken broth, sherry vinegar, lemon juice, garlic, salt and pepper. Then add the tarragon, chervil and lemon basil.
- Dress the drained melon balls and let the dressing sink in for half an hour.
- Serve chilled.

Spanish stuffed eggs

SERVES 4

INGREDIENTS:

8 eggs
25g/1oz butter
25g/1oz flour
75ml/3fl oz dry sherry
125ml/4fl oz milk

100g/4oz cooked, sliced ham
(chopped)
100g/4oz breadcrumbs
Vegetable oil for deep-frying

- Hard-boil 6 of the eggs, cool them in cold water and shell. Halve, scoop out the yolks and reserve.
- Make a thick sauce by melting the butter in a heavy-based pan and stirring in the flour. Cook over a gentle heat, stirring, for 1 minute, then stir in the sherry and the milk. Beat to a thick paste. Lower the heat to minimum and, stirring frequently, cook for a further 10 minutes.
- Push the egg yolks through a sieve and stir them into the sauce along with the ham. Pour the mixture into a Swiss roll tin and leave to set.
- Fill the eggs with the mixture and press the halves back together.

- Beat the remaining eggs in a bowl and put some breadcrumbs in another bowl.
- Roll the stuffed eggs in flour, coat with beaten egg, then toss in the breadcrumbs. Repeat with each stuffed egg.
- Heat the oil and deep-fry the eggs for about 4 minutes, or until the coating is crisp and golden brown. Remove from the oil with a slotted spoon and drain on kitchen paper. Serve halved and warm.

Minted onion bhajias

SERVES 4

INGREDIENTS:

100g/4oz gram flour
¼ teaspoon cayenne pepper
½ teaspoon ground coriander
½ teaspoon ground cumin
1 tablespoon chopped fresh mint

4 tablespoons drained thick yogurt
75ml/3fl oz cold water
1 large onion (quartered and thinly sliced)
Vegetable oil for deep-frying

- Put the gram flour into a bowl, add the cayenne pepper, coriander, cumin and mint. Stir in the yogurt, water and onion and mix well.
- Fill a large frying pan a third full with the oil and heat until very hot. Drop heaped spoonfuls of the mixture, a few at a time, into the hot oil and use 2 forks to neaten the mixture into balls.
- Fry the bhajias until golden brown and cooked through, turning frequently.
- Remove with a slotted spoon and drain on kitchen paper. Serve hot.

Chicken liver pâté

SERVES 4

INGREDIENTS:

450g/1lb chicken livers
50g/2oz butter

2 eggs (hard-boiled)
1 medium onion

- Clean the livers thoroughly. Fry in large frying pan, over a medium-high heat, with the butter.
- In a blender or food processor, blend the livers, eggs, onion and any leftover butter from the frying. Place the mixture in a serving dish covered with aluminium foil with a weight on top. Chill overnight.

Potato wedges with chive & yogurt dressing

SERVES 4

INGREDIENTS:

4 large baking potatoes
3 tablespoons olive oil
1 teaspoon celery salt
½ teaspoon garlic salt

Salt and pepper
200g/7oz natural yogurt
1 bunch fresh chives

- Preheat the oven to 200°C/400°F/Gas mark 6.
- Scrub the potatoes and cut each lengthways into 6 pieces. Put the wedges in a large, non-stick roasting pan, add the oil and toss to coat. Mix together the salts and sprinkle over the potatoes.
- Roast the potatoes in the oven for 45 minutes, or until crisp and golden, turning them several times.
- Turn the cooked wedges into a warm serving bowl and season with salt and pepper. Spoon the yogurt into a small serving bowl, snip in most of the chives and stir well. Sprinkle the rest of the chives over the wedges and serve immediately.

Taramasalata

SERVES 6

INGREDIENTS:

225g/8oz smoked cod's roe
1 garlic clove (crushed)
50g/2oz white breadcrumbs
1 small onion (finely chopped)

Grated zest and juice of 1 lemon
150ml/¼pt olive oil
100ml/3½fl oz hot water
Pitta bread

- Skin the smoked cod's roe and break into pieces. Place in a blender or food processor and blend to form a purée. Add the garlic, breadcrumbs, onion, lemon zest and juice and blend for a few more seconds.
- Gradually add the oil and blend well after each addition until smooth. Blend in the hot water and pepper.
- Spoon into a serving dish and chill for at least 1 hour. Serve with pitta bread.

African chicken wings

SERVES 8

INGREDIENTS:

For the wings:
4 garlic cloves (crushed)
2 shallots (crushed)
1½ teaspoons salt
2 teaspoons paprika
1 teaspoon crumbled dried rosemary
½ teaspoon cayenne pepper
2 tablespoons vegetable oil
1.8kg/4lb chicken wings

For the sauce:
75ml/3fl oz peanut butter
50ml/2fl oz canned cream of coconut
(well stirred)
2 garlic cloves (chopped)
50ml/2fl oz water
50g/2oz chopped red pepper
1 teaspoon soy sauce

- Mix the garlic and shallots to form a paste with the salt.
- In a large bowl stir the garlic paste together with the paprika, rosemary, cayenne and oil. Mix well.
- Toss the chicken wings in the herb mix until they are completely covered. Let them marinate, covered and chilled, overnight.
- Preheat the oven to 220°C/425°F/Gas mark 7.
- Arrange the wings on the rack of an aluminium foil-lined large grill pan and bake in the upper third of the oven for 25 to 30 minutes or until they are golden.
- For the sauce, mix together all the ingredients in a blender or a food processor until the mixture is smooth.
- Transfer the sauce to a small bowl and serve with the chilled wings.

Spicy monkfish stew

SERVES 6

INGREDIENTS:

1 tablespoon olive oil
1 onion (finely sliced)
1 tablespoon tom yum soup paste
450g/1lb potatoes (cut into 2cm/³/₄in chunks)
400g/14oz can chopped tomatoes

600ml/1pt hot fish stock
Salt and pepper
450g/1lb monkfish (cut into 2cm/³/₄in chunks)
200g/7oz baby spinach

→

←

- Heat the oil in a large pan and fry the onion over a medium heat for 5 minutes, until golden.
- Add the tom yum paste and potatoes and stir-fry for 1 minute. Add the tomatoes and hot stock, season well with salt and pepper and cover. Bring to the boil then simmer, partially covered, for 15 minutes.
- Add the monkfish to the pan and continue to simmer for 10 to 12 minutes until the fish is cooked. Add the baby spinach leaves and stir through until wilted. Serve immediately.

Olive cheese balls

SERVES 6

INGREDIENTS:

225g/8oz Cheddar cheese (finely grated)
300g/11oz plain flour

75g/3oz butter (melted)
36 stuffed olives

- Mix together the grated cheese and flour, add the margarine and mix thoroughly to form a dough.
- Mould 1 teaspoon of dough around each olive and shape into a ball.
- Place the balls on a greased baking sheet. Cover, and chill for 1 hour.
- Preheat the oven to 200°C/400°F/Gas mark 6.
- Bake the balls for 15 to 20 minutes. Serve warm.

Chinese crispy spring rolls

SERVES 8

INGREDIENTS:

4 tablespoons vegetable oil
225g/8oz bean sprouts
100g/4oz leeks (shredded)
100g/4oz carrots (shredded)
100g/4oz bamboo shoots (sliced)
100g/4oz mushrooms (shredded)
1 teaspoon salt
1 teaspoon brown sugar

1 tablespoon soy sauce
1 tablespoon dry sherry
20 frozen spring roll skins (thawed)
1 tablespoon cornflour
1 teaspoon water
Flour for dusting
Vegetable oil for deep-frying

- Heat the 4 tablespoons of oil in a large wok and stir-fry the vegetables for about 1 minute. Add the salt, sugar, soy sauce and sherry and continue stirring for 2 minutes. Remove, drain the excess liquid and leave to cool.
- Cut each spring roll skin in half diagonally then place about 1 tablespoon of the vegetable mixture a third of the way down with the triangle pointing away from you. Lift the lower flap over the filling and roll it up immediately. Fold in both ends and roll once more. Mix the cornflour with the water to form a paste. Brush the upper edge of the spring roll with the paste and seal. Dust with flour. Repeat with all the skins.
- Heat the oil in a wok until hot and deep-fry the spring rolls in batches for 2 to 3 minutes or until golden and crisp. Remove with a slotted spoon and drain on kitchen paper. Serve hot.

Miniature seafood quiches

SERVES 4-8

INGREDIENTS:

2 prepared pie crusts	*2 eggs*
Butter for greasing	*125ml/4fl oz single cream*
100g/4oz Emmental cheese (grated)	*¼ teaspoon salt*
250g/9oz seafood spread	*2 tablespoons white wine*
2 onions (diced)	

- Preheat the oven to 190°C/375°F/Gas mark 5.
- Allow the pie crusts to stand at room temperature for 15 to 20 minutes. Grease 24 miniature muffin cups with butter. Unfold the pie crust and, using a 6cm/2½in cookie cutter, cut 12 circles. Repeat with the remaining pie crust. Press 1 circle of dough into each sprayed muffin cup.
- Divide the cheese evenly between the cups. Add 2 teaspoons of seafood spread to each. Top with some diced onion.
- Mix together the eggs, cream, salt and wine in a small bowl. Beat well and pour the mixture into the crusts.
- Bake for 25 to 30 minutes or until golden brown. Serve warm.

Cauliflower fritters

SERVES 8

INGREDIENTS:

600g/1¼lb cauliflower
50g/2oz chickpea flour
2 teaspoons ground cumin
1 teaspoon ground coriander
1 teaspoon ground turmeric
Pinch of cayenne pepper

½ teaspoon salt
50ml/2fl oz water
1 egg (lightly beaten)
1 egg yolk
Vegetable oil for deep-frying

- Cut the cauliflowers into bite-size florets.
- Sift the flour and spices into a bowl, then stir in ½ teaspoon salt and make a well in the centre.
- Combine the water with the whole egg and egg yolk and gradually pour into the well, whisking to make a smooth batter. Cover and leave for 30 minutes.
- Fill a deep, heavy-based pan a third full of oil and heat until a cube of bread browns in 15 seconds. Holding the florets by the stem, dip into the batter. Deep-fry in batches for 3 to 4 minutes. Remove with a slotted spoon and drain on kitchen paper. Serve hot.

Stuffed mushrooms

SERVES 4

INGREDIENTS:

3 large tomatoes
8 large mushrooms with stalks (wiped with damp kitchen paper)
1 small onion (grated)

25g/1oz butter
1 tablespoon chopped fresh parsley
Salt and pepper

- Preheat the oven to 190°C/375°F/Gas mark 5.
- Place the tomatoes in a bowl of just-boiled water for 30 seconds, then skin and chop.
- Remove the mushroom stalks. Chop the stalks and mix with the chopped tomatoes, grated onion, butter, parsley and seasoning.
- Put the mushroom tops on a large greased ovenproof dish. Fill each mushroom with the stuffing.
- Cover with aluminium foil and bake in the oven for about 30 minutes.

Garlic soup

SERVES 6

INGREDIENTS:

4 tablespoons oil
3 large onions (chopped)
16 garlic cloves (chopped)
150ml/¼pt white wine

350g/12oz potatoes (roughly chopped)
2 litres/3½pt vegetable stock
125ml/4fl oz whipping cream

- Heat the oil in a heavy-based pan, add the onions and garlic, then cover and cook over a low heat, stirring occasionally, for 20 to 30 minutes or until very soft.
- Add the wine and bring to the boil. Boil until the liquid has reduced by half.
- Add the potatoes and stock, bring to the boil and simmer, uncovered, for 45 minutes.
- Allow to cool slightly, then pour into a blender or food processor and blend until smooth. Add the cream and pour into the pan to reheat. Serve hot.

Tomato soup

SERVES 4

INGREDIENTS:

50g/2oz butter
700g/1½lb plum tomatoes (roughly chopped)
900ml/1½pt hot vegetable stock

50g/2oz ground almonds
150ml/¼pt milk
1 teaspoon sugar

- Melt the butter in a large saucepan. Add the tomatoes and cook for 5 minutes until the skins start to wrinkle. Add the stock to the pan, bring to the boil, cover and simmer for 10 minutes.
- Lightly toast the almonds under a medium grill until they are golden brown.
- Remove the soup from the heat, pour into a blender or food processor and blend until smooth. Pass the soup through a sieve to remove any tomato skin or pips.
- Place the soup back in the pan and reheat.
- Stir in the milk, almonds and sugar. Serve hot.

Turkey sticks with sour cream dip

SERVES 4

INGREDIENTS:

50g/2oz fine fresh breadcrumbs	1 egg (lightly beaten)
1/4 teaspoon paprika	3 tablespoons sour cream
Salt and pepper	1 tablespoon tomato sauce
350g/12oz turkey fillets (cut into strips)	1 tablespoon mayonnaise

- Preheat the oven to 190°C/375°F/Gas mark 5.
- Mix the breadcrumbs and paprika in a mixing bowl and season with salt and pepper. Dip the turkey strips into the beaten egg, then into the breadcrumbs, until thoroughly and evenly coated. Place on a baking sheet.
- Cook the turkey at the top of the oven for 20 minutes, until crisp and golden.
- Turn once during cooking.
- To make the dip, mix the sour cream, tomato sauce and mayonnaise together in a small bowl.

French onion soup

SERVES 6

INGREDIENTS:

1 tablespoon vegetable oil	2 tablespoons plain flour
50g/2oz butter	400g/14oz beef consommé
900g/2lb onions (sliced)	500ml/18fl oz water
1 teaspoon brown sugar	

- Heat the oil and butter in a large frying pan. Add the onion and brown sugar and cook, stirring frequently, over a medium heat until the onion is golden brown and softened.
- Add the flour and cook for a further 2 minutes.
- Remove from the heat and gradually stir in the beef consommé and water.
- Return to the heat, stirring constantly, until the soup boils and simmer until it thickens. Serve hot.

Salmon mousse

SERVES 8

INGREDIENTS:

350g/12oz salmon steaks
1 onion (sliced)
75g/3oz carrots (sliced)
10 black peppercorns
Salt and pepper
75ml/3fl oz white wine
125ml/4fl oz water

3 teaspoons gelatine
300ml/¹/₂pt milk
25g/1oz butter
2 tablespoons plain flour
75ml/3fl oz mayonnaise
150ml/¹/₄pt whipping cream
1 egg white

- Place the salmon steaks in a small shallow pan. Add half the onions and carrots, 5 peppercorns and a pinch of salt. Spoon the wine over the top, add the water and bring to the boil. Cover and simmer gently for 10 to 15 minutes.
- Remove the salmon steaks, reserving the liquid. Carefully ease off the skin. Using 2 forks, roughly flake the fish, removing any bones. Place the fish in a small bowl and put to one side.
- Boil the liquid until reduced by half and reserve.
- Spoon the remaining water into a small cup. Sprinkle the gelatine over the surface.
- Leave for 10 minutes.
- Bring the milk to the boil in a pan and add the remaining onion, carrot and peppercorns. Pour into a jug and leave to infuse for 10 minutes.
- Melt the butter and, off the heat, blend in the flour and strained milk. Season and bring to the boil again, then simmer for 3 minutes, stirring. Pour into a bowl and stir in the soaked gelatine.
- Stir the fish into the cool sauce with the reserved cooking juices. Spoon half at a time into a blender or food processor and blend for a few seconds. Pour into a large mixing bowl.
- Stir the mayonnaise gently into the salmon mixture. Lightly whip the cream and fold through the mousse. Whisk the egg white until stiff and fold lightly through the mousse until no traces of white are visible.
- Pour the mousse into an oiled soufflé dish, smooth the surface, cover and refrigerate for 2 hours.

Main courses

Taking inspiration from all over the world, this selection of classic main courses has something to suit every occasion. Meat, poultry and seafood dishes – including Coq au vin, Char siu pork and Sole Veronique – sit alongside pastas, pies and pizzas. From the foreign to the familiar family favourites, you can find delicious recipes in this chapter, including a wide vegetarian selection.

Sticky ginger chicken

SERVES 4

INGREDIENTS:

2 tablespoons lemon juice
2 tablespoons brown sugar
1 teaspoon grated root ginger

2 teaspoons soy sauce
Black pepper
8 chicken drumsticks (skinned)

- In a large bowl, mix together the lemon juice, sugar, ginger, soy sauce and pepper.
- With a sharp knife, slash the chicken drumsticks about 3 times through the thickest part, then toss the chicken in the glaze. Cook the chicken under a grill, or on a barbecue, turning occasionally and brushing with the glaze, until the chicken is golden and the juices run clear.
- Serve on a bed of lettuce with crusty bread.

Lamb with satay sauce

SERVES 4

INGREDIENTS:

450g/1lb lamb loin fillet (thinly sliced)
1 tablespoon mild curry paste
150ml/¼pt coconut milk
2 cloves garlic (crushed)
½ teaspoon chilli powder
½ teaspoon cumin

For the satay sauce:
1 tablespoon corn oil
1 onion (diced)
6 tablespoons crunchy peanut butter
1 teaspoon tomato purée
1 teaspoon lime juice
100ml/3½fl oz cold water

- Place the lamb in a large dish.
- Mix together the curry paste, coconut milk, garlic, chilli powder and cumin. Pour over the lamb, toss well, cover and marinate for 30 minutes.
- To make the satay sauce, heat the oil in a large wok and stir-fry the onion for 5 minutes, then reduce the heat and sweat the onions for a further 5 minutes. Stir in the peanut butter, tomato purée, lime juice and water.
- Thread the lamb on to wooden skewers, reserving the marinade. Grill the skewers under a hot grill for 6 to 8 minutes, turning once.
- Add the reserved marinade to the wok, bring to the boil and cook for 5 minutes.
- Serve the lamb skewers with the satay sauce.

Bouillabaisse

SERVES 4

INGREDIENTS:

16 black mussels
200g/7oz scallops
1.4kg/3lb assorted cod fillets
300g/11oz raw, peeled prawns
2 tablespoons oil

1 fennel bulb (thinly sliced)
1 onion (chopped)
5 tomatoes
1.2 litres/2pt fish stock (made from
stock cubes)

- Scrub the mussels with a stiff brush, discarding any that are broken or open. Slice any veins off the scallops and cut the cod into large bite-size pieces. Cover all the seafood and refrigerate.
- Heat the oil in a large saucepan over a medium heat and cook the fennel and onion until golden. Place the tomatoes in a bowl of just-boiled water for 30 seconds, then skin and chop them. Add them to the pan and cook for a further 3 minutes.
- Stir in the stock, bring to the boil and boil for 10 minutes. Reduce the heat and add the scallops, prawns, mussels and fish. Simmer until the mussels open. Serve hot.

Venison steaks

SERVES 4

INGREDIENTS:

4 venison steaks (each weighing
around 150g/5oz)
Salt and pepper
1 tablespoon olive oil
2 shallots (finely chopped)

300ml/½ pt beef stock
4 tablespoons port
1½ tablespoons redcurrant jelly
75g/3oz redcurrants (stalks removed)

- Season the steaks well with salt and pepper. Heat the oil in a non-stick frying pan and fry the steaks over a moderate heat for 3 to 5 minutes on each side, turning once. Remove the steaks from the pan and set them aside in a warm place.
- Lower the heat, add the shallots to the pan and cook gently until softened and browned. Add the stock, port and redcurrant jelly. Stir well, increase the heat and bring to the boil, then simmer until the sauce has reduced by almost half.
- Add the redcurrants and simmer until the sauce is syrupy.
- Spoon the sauce over the steaks and serve immediately.

Sweet & sour pork

SERVES 4

INGREDIENTS:

2 tablespoons vegetable oil
2 garlic cloves (finely sliced)
350g/12oz lean pork (sliced into thin strips)
1 small red onion (sliced)
2 tablespoons fish sauce
1 tablespoon granulated sugar

Black pepper
1 red pepper (seeded and diced)
½ cucumber (seeded and sliced)
2 plum tomatoes (cut into wedges)
100g/4oz pineapple (cut into small chunks)
2 spring onions (cut into short lengths)

- Heat the oil in a wok or large frying pan. Add the garlic and fry until golden, then add the pork and stir-fry for about 4 to 5 minutes. Add the onion and season with the fish sauce, sugar and pepper. Stir and cook for 3 to 4 minutes or until the pork is cooked.
- Add the rest of the vegetables, the pineapple and the spring onions. Continue to stir-fry for another 3 to 4 minutes.
- Serve hot.

Salt-crusted trout

SERVES 6

INGREDIENTS:

900g/2lb sea salt
6 tablespoons chopped tarragon

7 garlic cloves (unpeeled)
6 trout (heads and tails removed)

- Preheat the oven to 220°C/425°F/Gas mark 7.
- Line a roasting tin with aluminium foil and add enough salt to make a 1cm/½in layer.
- Scatter about half the tarragon over the salt and add the garlic. Press the trout down into the salt, scatter the remaining tarragon over the top, and cover completely with salt.
- Cook for 20 minutes until tender. Remove from the oven, crack the salt open, and carefully lift out the trout. Serve with rice and garnish with lemon wedges.

Basil-stuffed lamb roast

SERVES 10-12

INGREDIENTS:

For the roast:
*2.7kg/6lb leg of lamb (boned and
butterflied)*
1 teaspoon crushed dried rosemary

For the stuffing:
50ml/2fl oz olive oil
175g/6oz onion (chopped)
75g/3oz celery (chopped)

2 garlic cloves (minced)
2 eggs (beaten)
50g/2oz parsley (snipped)
3 tablespoons snipped fresh basil
¼ teaspoon crushed dried marjoram
¼ teaspoon pepper
1.4kg/3lb plain croûtons
4 tablespoons grated Parmesan cheese
125ml/4fl oz water

- Preheat the oven to 170°C/325°F/Gas mark 3.
- To make the stuffing, heat the oil in a pan and fry the onion, celery and garlic until tender but not brown.
- In a medium-sized mixing bowl, stir together the eggs, parsley, basil, marjoram and pepper. Then add the onion mixture and stir in the croûtons and cheese.
- Drizzle with water to moisten, tossing lightly. Set aside.
- Pound the meat to an even thickness and sprinkle with rosemary. Spread the stuffing over it, then roll up and tie the meat securely. Place the roast, seam side down, on a rack in a shallow roasting pan.
- Roast for 1½ to 2 hours. Leave to stand for 15 minutes before carving.

Sole Véronique

SERVES 4

INGREDIENTS:

12 sole fillets
250ml/9fl oz fish stock (made from
stock cubes)
50ml/2fl oz white wine
1 shallot (finely sliced)
1 bay leaf
6 black peppercorns

15g/¹/₂oz butter
3 teaspoons flour
125ml/4fl oz milk
50ml/2fl oz single cream
125g/4¹/₂oz seedless white
grapes (peeled)

- Preheat the oven to 180°C/350°F/Gas mark 4.
- Roll the fillets into coils with the skin on the inside. Secure with toothpicks and place in a well-greased ovenproof dish.
- Combine the stock, wine, shallot, bay leaf and peppercorns in a jug and pour over the fish. Cover with greased aluminium foil and bake for 15 minutes, or until the fish flakes when tested with a fork. Carefully lift the fish out of the liquid with a slotted spoon, place in another dish, cover and keep warm.
- Pour the cooking liquid into a saucepan and boil for about 2 minutes, or until reduced by half, then strain.
- In a clean pan, melt the butter, add the flour and stir for 1 minute, or until pale and foaming. Remove from the heat and gradually stir in the milk, cream and cooking liquid. Return to the heat and stir until the mixture boils and thickens.
- Add the grapes, then stir until heated through. Serve the sauce over the fish.

Beef hash

SERVES 6

INGREDIENTS:

2 tablespoons oil
3 spring onions (chopped)
1 garlic clove (finely chopped)
1 small red chilli (seeded and chopped)
900g/2lb minced steak

3 large tomatoes
100g/4oz seedless raisins
Salt and pepper

- Heat the oil in a large, deep frying pan and add the spring onions, garlic and chilli. Cook for 2 minutes over a moderate heat or until the spring onions have softened but not coloured. Add the meat and cook until it is browned all over.
- Place the tomatoes in a bowl of just-boiled water for 30 seconds and skin. Chop and add to the frying pan with the raisins, salt and pepper and simmer uncovered for 25 minutes or until cooked.
- Serve hot with plain boiled rice.

Rabbit with parsley sauce

SERVES 4

INGREDIENTS:

100ml/3½fl oz soy sauce
5 drops Tabasco sauce
½ teaspoon ground white pepper
1 tablespoon sweet paprika
1 teaspoon dried basil
1.4kg/3lb rabbit (cut into pieces)
3 tablespoons olive oil

75g/3oz plain flour
1 large onion (finely sliced)
250ml/9fl oz dry white wine
250ml/9fl oz chicken stock
2 garlic cloves (finely chopped)
4 tablespoons chopped fresh parsley
2 teaspoons salt

- Combine the soy sauce, Tabasco sauce, white pepper, paprika and basil in a medium-sized bowl. Add the rabbit pieces and turn them over in the mixture so they are coated thoroughly. Leave to marinate for at least 1 hour.
- Heat the oil in a flameproof casserole dish. Coat the rabbit pieces lightly in the flour, shaking off the excess. Brown the rabbit pieces in the hot oil for about 5 to 6 minutes, turning them frequently. Remove with a slotted spoon and set aside on a plate or dish. Preheat the oven to 180°C/350°F/Gas mark 4.
- Add the onion to the casserole dish and cook over a low heat for 8 to 10 minutes, until softened. Increase the heat, add the wine, and stir well to mix in all the cooking juices.
- Return the rabbit and any juices to the casserole dish. Add the stock, garlic, parsley and salt. Mix well and turn the rabbit to coat with the sauce. Cover and place in the oven. Cook for about 1 hour, until the rabbit is tender, stirring occasionally. Serve with mashed potatoes or rice.

Steak, kidney & mushroom pie

SERVES 4

INGREDIENTS:

2 tablespoons vegetable oil
100g/4oz bacon (chopped)
1 onion (chopped)
500g/1lb 2oz chuck steak (diced)
2 tablespoons plain flour
100g/4oz lamb's kidneys

Bouquet garni
400ml/14fl oz beef stock
100g/4oz button mushrooms
Salt and pepper
225g/8oz ready-made puff pastry
Beaten egg (to glaze)

- Preheat the oven to 170°C/325°F/Gas mark 3.
- Heat the oil in a heavy-based pan, add the bacon and onion and cook, stirring, until lightly browned. Toss the steak in the flour, add to the pan in batches and cook, stirring, until browned.
- Toss the kidneys in the flour and add to the pan with the bouquet garni. Cook until browned.
- Transfer to a casserole dish, then pour in the stock, cover and cook for 2 hours.
- Stir in the mushrooms, season, then leave to cool.
- Preheat the oven to 220°C/425°F/Gas mark 7. Roll out the pastry to 2cm/1in larger than the top of a 1.2 litre/2pt pie dish. Cut off a strip and fit around the dampened rim of the dish. Brush with water.
- Tip the meat mixture into the dish. Lay the pastry over the dish and press the edges together to seal. Knock up the edges with the back of a knife. Make a small slit in the pastry, brush with the beaten egg and bake for 20 minutes.
- Lower the oven to 180°C/350°F/Gas 4 and bake for a further 20 minutes.

Duck with Cumberland sauce

SERVES 4

INGREDIENTS:

4 duck portions
Salt and pepper
Grated zest and juice of 1 lemon
Grated zest and juice of 1 large orange

4 tablespoons redcurrant jelly
4 tablespoons port
Pinch of ground ginger
1 tablespoon brandy

- Preheat the oven to 190°C/375°F/Gas mark 5.
- Place a wire rack in a roasting tin. Prick the duck portions all over with a fork and sprinkle with salt and pepper. Place on the rack and cook in the oven for 45 to 50 minutes, until the juices run clear.
- Simmer the lemon and orange juices and zests together in a saucepan for 5 minutes. Stir in the redcurrant jelly until melted, then stir in the port. Bring to the boil, add ginger and season to taste.
- Transfer the duck to a serving plate, ensuring it is kept warm. Pour away the fat from the roasting tin, leaving the cooking juices. With the roasting tin over a low heat, stir in the brandy and bring to the boil. Stir in the port sauce and serve with the duck.

Persian lamb

SERVES 4-6

INGREDIENTS:

2 tablespoons chopped fresh mint
225ml/8fl oz natural yogurt
2 garlic cloves (crushed)
¼ teaspoon ground black pepper
6 lean lamb chops
2 tablespoons lemon juice

For the tabbouleh:
250g/9oz couscous
500ml/18fl oz boiling water
2 tablespoons olive oil
2 tablespoons lemon juice
½ onion (finely chopped)
4 tomatoes (chopped)
25g/1oz coriander (chopped)
2 tablespoons chopped fresh mint
Salt and pepper

- For the marinade, combine the mint, yogurt, garlic and pepper.
- Put the chops into a non-porous dish and rub all over with the lemon juice.
- Pour the marinade over the chops, cover and marinate for 2 to 3 hours.
- To make the tabbouleh, put the couscous into a heatproof bowl and pour the boiling water over it. Leave for 5 minutes. Drain and put into a sieve. Steam over a pan of barely simmering water for 8 minutes. Toss in the oil and lemon juice. Add the onion, tomatoes and herbs. Season and set aside.
- Cook the lamb over a medium hot barbecue for 15 minutes, turning once. Serve with the tabbouleh.

Spaghetti Bolognese

SERVES 4

INGREDIENTS:

1 tablespoon olive oil
1 onion (finely chopped)
2 garlic cloves (chopped)
1 carrot (chopped)
1 celery stick (chopped)
50g/2oz streaky bacon (diced)
350g/12oz lean minced beef

400g/14oz canned chopped tomatoes
2 teaspoons dried oregano
125ml/4fl oz red wine
2 tablespoons tomato purée
Salt and pepper
700g/1½lb fresh spaghetti

- Heat the oil in a large frying pan. Add the onions and fry for 3 minutes. Add the garlic, carrot, celery and bacon and sauté until just beginning to brown.
- Add the beef and cook over a high heat until all of the meat is brown.
- Stir in the tomatoes, oregano and red wine and bring to the boil. Reduce the heat and leave to simmer for about 45 minutes.
- Stir in the tomato purée and season with salt and pepper.
- Cook the spaghetti in a large saucepan of salted, boiling water until tender.
- Drain thoroughly. Transfer to a serving plate and top with Bolognese sauce.
- Serve hot.

Coronation chicken

SERVES 8

INGREDIENTS:

½ lemon
2.3kg/5lb chicken
1 onion (quartered)
1 carrot (quartered)
8 black peppercorns (crushed)
1 teaspoon salt

For the sauce:
1 small onion (chopped)
15g/½oz butter
1 tablespoon curry paste

1 tablespoon tomato purée
125ml/4fl oz red wine
Bay leaf
Juice of ½ lemon
2-3 teaspoons apricot jam
300ml/½pt mayonnaise
125ml/4fl oz whipping cream (whipped)
Salt and freshly ground black pepper

- Put the lemon in the posterior of the chicken, then place the chicken in a saucepan that it just fits. Add the vegetables, peppercorns and salt to the pan.
- Add sufficient water to come two-thirds of the way up the chicken, bring to the boil, then cover and cook gently for about 1½ hours until the chicken juices run clear.
- Transfer the chicken to a large bowl, pour the cooking liquid over it and leave to cool. When cold, skin and bone the chicken, then chop.
- To make the sauce, take a frying pan and fry the onion in the butter until soft.
- Add the curry paste, tomato purée, wine, bay leaf and lemon juice, then cook for 10 minutes. Add the jam, then sieve and leave to cool.
- Beat the mixture into the mayonnaise. Fold in the cream, then add seasoning to taste.

Pot roast of venison

SERVES 4–5

INGREDIENTS:

1.8kg/4lb boned joint of venison
75ml/3fl oz olive oil
8 black peppercorns (lightly crushed)
12 juniper berries (lightly crushed)
250ml/9fl oz red wine
100g/4oz streaky bacon (chopped)
2 onions (finely chopped)

2 carrots (chopped)
150g/5oz large mushrooms (sliced)
1 tablespoon plain flour
250ml/9fl oz chicken stock
2 tablespoons redcurrant jelly
½ teaspoon salt and pepper

- Put the venison in a bowl, add half the oil, the peppercorns, juniper berries and wine. Cover and leave in a cool place for 24 hours, turning the meat occasionally.
- Preheat the oven to 170°C/325°F/Gas mark 3.
- Remove the venison from the bowl and pat dry, reserving the marinade. Heat the remaining oil in a shallow pan, then brown the venison evenly. Transfer to a plate.
- Stir the bacon, onions, carrots and mushrooms into the pan and cook for about 5 minutes. Stir in the flour and cook for 2 minutes, then remove from the heat and stir in the marinade, stock, redcurrant jelly and seasoning. Return to the heat, bring to the boil, stirring, then simmer for 2 to 3 minutes.
- Transfer the venison and sauce to a casserole dish, cover and cook in the oven, turning the joint occasionally, for 3 hours until tender.

Pheasant with mushrooms

SERVES 6

INGREDIENTS:

2 pheasants
Salt and pepper
2 thin sheets of pork fat
25g/1oz butter
1 tablespoon oil
3 shallots (sliced)

8 flat-cap mushrooms (wiped with
damp kitchen paper and thickly sliced)
300ml/½pt dry white wine
1 sprig thyme
300ml/½pt double cream

- Preheat the oven to 230°C/450°F/Gas mark 8.
- Season the pheasants inside and out with salt and pepper. Tie the pork fat over the breasts and roast for 30 to 45 minutes in roasting trays, turning occasionally.
- Remove from the oven and leave to cool. Strip off the pheasant meat and tear into bite-size pieces.
- Warm the butter and oil in a deep frying pan and sauté the shallots until tender, without browning. Raise the heat and add the mushrooms. Fry until the mushrooms are tender. Add the wine, thyme and cooked pheasant.
- Bring up to the boil and let it bubble until almost all the liquid has evaporated.
- Add the cream and ½ teaspoon salt and pepper. Bring back to the boil and simmer for 4 to 5 minutes to reduce the sauce.
- Serve hot with baked potatoes or rice.

Steak teriyaki

SERVES 2

INGREDIENTS:

2 sirloin steaks
Vegetable oil
2 tablespoons dry sherry

2 tablespoons soy sauce
2 tablespoons sweet sherry
1 teaspoon sugar

- Cover the base of a heavy frying pan with a thin film of oil and place over a high heat. When it is very hot, place the steaks in the pan. Turn after 3 minutes, then spoon over the dry sherry. Cover the pan for a final 2 minutes.
- Transfer the steaks to a warm plate and cover to keep warm.

- Add the remaining ingredients to the pan and boil until reduced by half.
- Return the steaks to the pan with any juices, and cook for 1 minute, turning once.

Braised steak & green pepper

SERVES 6

INGREDIENTS:

2 tablespoons plain flour
½ teaspoon salt
¼ teaspoon freshly ground pepper
700g/1½lb lean steak (cut into strips)
1 tablespoon vegetable oil
400ml/14fl oz beef stock

225ml/8fl oz canned tomatoes
with juice
1 medium onion (sliced)
1 garlic clove (finely chopped)
1 large green pepper (cut into strips)
1½ teaspoons Worcestershire sauce

- Mix the flour, salt and pepper and coat the steak strips with mixture.
- Heat the oil in a large frying pan. Brown the meat on all sides and drain off any fat.
- Add the broth, tomato juice (reserving the tomato flesh for later), onion and garlic. Cover and simmer for about 1 hour until the meat is tender.
- Add the tomato, green pepper strips and Worcestershire sauce. Stir-fry for 4 to 5 minutes. Serve with rice.

Partridge with cabbage

SERVES 4

INGREDIENTS:

1 white cabbage
1½ tablespoons olive oil
2 partridges
100g/4oz lardons
2 large carrots (sliced)
1 large onion (sliced)

2 garlic cloves (chopped)
2 bay leaves
4 juniper berries (crushed)
500ml/18fl oz chicken stock

- Preheat the oven to 170°C/325°F/Gas mark 3.
- Quarter the cabbage and cut out the tough stem. Shred the leaves finely and pile into a bowl. Pour over enough boiling water to cover, leave for 1 minute then drain thoroughly. Make a bed of cabbage in the bottom of a casserole dish.
- Heat the olive oil in a frying pan and brown the partridges all over. Place in

→

the casserole dish. Fry the lardons in the same fat then add the carrots and onion and fry until golden brown. Scoop into the casserole dish. Add the garlic, bay leaves and juniper berries, and pour in enough stock to come about halfway up the dish. Cover and cook in the oven for 2 hours.

Chicken & beef satay

SERVES 4

INGREDIENTS:

2cm/³/₄in piece of tamarind pulp
100ml/3¹/₂fl oz hot water
2 boneless chicken breast fillets
350g/12oz flash-fry steak
1 teaspoon coriander seeds
1 teaspoon cumin seeds
1 onion (chopped)
1 tablespoon soy sauce
2 garlic cloves (crushed)
2 tablespoons vegetable oil
1 teaspoon ground turmeric

1 teaspoon five-spice powder
Salt

For the peanut sauce:
100g/4oz smooth peanut butter
100g/4oz creamed coconut (crumbled)
300ml/¹/₂pt water
4 teaspoons lemon juice
1 tablespoon soy sauce
1 tablespoon brown sugar
1 teaspoon chilli powder

- Soak the tamarind pulp in the hot water for a few minutes, then squeeze the pulp to extract as much liquid as possible. Discard the pulp and set tamarind liquid aside.
- Prepare the satay by using a sharp knife to cut the chicken and the steak into small chunks. Place in deep baking tray and set aside.
- Heat a small frying pan, add the coriander and cumin and fry over the dry heat for 1 to 2 minutes, stirring constantly. Remove from the heat and pound to a fine powder with a pestle and mortar.
- Put the pounded spices in a blender or food processor with the onion, tamarind liquid, soy sauce, garlic, vegetable oil, turmeric, five-spice powder and a pinch of salt. Blend for a few seconds, then pour over the meat. Cover and leave to marinate for 4 hours, turning the meat occasionally.
- Thread the meat on skewers. Place under a grill or on a barbecue and grill for 10 to 15 minutes, turning frequently and basting with any extra marinade.
- To make the peanut sauce, put the peanut butter, coconut, water, lemon juice, soy sauce, sugar and chilli powder in a clean pan and bring slowly to the boil.
- Lower the heat and simmer gently for 5 minutes until the coconut has dissolved and the sauce thickens. Adjust the seasoning to taste.
- Serve the satay sticks hot on a platter with a small bowl of peanut sauce.

Grilled marinated lamb

SERVES 4

INGREDIENTS:

1 green chilli (seeded and finely chopped)
1 small bunch of fresh mint (finely chopped)
1 garlic clove (finely chopped)

½ bunch spring onions (chopped)
Juice of 2 limes
Salt and pepper
450g/1lb lamb fillet (cut into large cubes)

- Mix together the chilli, mint, garlic and spring onions in a bowl. Add the lime juice and season with salt and pepper. Mix well, add the lamb cubes and toss to ensure they are thoroughly coated in the marinade. Cover the bowl with clingfilm and refrigerate overnight.
- Preheat the grill to a high heat. Thread the lamb onto metal skewers and grill for 8 to 10 minutes, turning once. Serve hot, on a bed of rice.

Barbecued beef ribs

SERVES 4

INGREDIENTS:

2.3kg/5lb beef short ribs

600ml/1pt barbecue sauce

- Place the ribs in a flat pan or dish. Pour the sauce over the ribs, turning so as to coat both sides. Pierce the meat with a large fork and leave to marinate for 3 hours, turning once.
- Remove the ribs from the marinade and brush off excess sauce to avoid burning.
- Grill the ribs under a hot grill for 15 minutes, turning occasionally and brushing with marinade. Serve on a bed of rice.

Glazed lamb cutlets

SERVES 4

INGREDIENTS:

12 lean lamb cutlets
150g/5oz redcurrant jelly
100ml/3½fl oz dry sherry
2 tablespoons orange juice

2 tablespoons green peppercorns (finely chopped)
150ml/¼pt olive oil
Redcurrants, to garnish

- Trim the cutlets of any excess fat. Place in a large dish.
- In a small saucepan, melt the redcurrant jelly with the sherry, orange juice and green peppercorns. Whisk in the olive oil. Set aside to cool. Pour over the lamb.
- Cover and marinate overnight in the refrigerator, turning once.
- Place the cutlets and marinade in a grill pan. Cook under a hot grill, basting frequently, and turning frequently, for about 5 minutes on each side.
- Drain the cutlets from the cooking juices. Pat dry with kitchen paper. Cool the cutlets and refrigerate the juices. After skimming off any fat, pour the juices over the chops and garnish with redcurrants.

Irish stew

SERVES 6

INGREDIENTS:

1.8kg/4lb lamb shoulder
3 onions (thickly sliced)
700g/1½lb carrots (cut into chunks)
900g/2lb potatoes (peeled and halved)

1 bay leaf
2 teaspoons Worcestershire sauce
Salt and pepper
Water or vegetable stock to cover

- Trim most of the fat off the meat and reserve. Cut the meat into large chunks.
- In a heavy-based pan, render down the fat over a low heat. Discard the solid bits. Brown the meat in the fat and set aside, then brown the onions and carrots in the same fat. Drain off any excess fat.
- Return the meat to the pan with the potatoes, bay leaf, Worcestershire sauce, salt, pepper and water or stock to cover. Simmer for 2 to 3 hours until the meat is tender and potatoes are soft, stirring occasionally. Skin off the fat and serve hot.

Chicken with sage & lemon

SERVES 4

INGREDIENTS:

4 skinless, boneless chicken breasts
Salt and pepper

2 tablespoons finely shredded fresh sage
Grated zest and juice of 2 lemons

- Preheat the oven to 200°C/400°F/Gas mark 6. Cut 4 pieces of aluminium foil large enough to wrap each chicken breast.
- Place a chicken breast in the centre of each piece of foil and season generously with salt and pepper. Sprinkle with a quarter of the sage and lemon zest, then drizzle some lemon juice over the top. Wrap the foil around the chicken to make a parcel and fold over the edges to seal. Repeat with the remaining chicken and ingredients.
- Place the chicken parcels on a baking sheet and bake in the oven for 15 minutes or until the chicken has cooked through and the juices run clear.
- To serve, unwrap the chicken and place on warm plates. Drizzle with the remaining lemon juice. Serve with rice.

Seafood medley

SERVES 4

INGREDIENTS:

2 tablespoons white wine
1 egg white (lightly beaten)
1/2 teaspoon five-spice powder
1 teaspoon cornflour
300g/11oz raw peeled prawns (deveined)
100g/4oz prepared squid (cut into rings)

100g/4oz cod fillets (cut into strips)
Vegetable oil for deep-frying
1 green pepper (seeded and cut into strips)
1 carrot (cut into thin strips)
4 baby corn cobs (halved lengthways)

- Mix the wine, egg white, five-spice powder and cornflour in a large bowl. Add the prawns, squid and cod and stir to coat evenly. Remove with a slotted spoon, reserving any leftover cornflour mixture.
- Heat the oil in a wok and deep-fry the prawns, squid and cod for 2 to 3 minutes.
- Remove from the wok with a slotted spoon and set aside.
- Pour off all but 1 tablespoon of oil from the wok and return to the heat. Add the pepper, carrot and corn cobs and stir-fry for 4 to 5 minutes.

→

← • Return the prawns, squid and cod to the wok with any remaining cornflour mixture. Heat through, stirring, and serve with rice.

Coq au vin

SERVES 4

INGREDIENTS:

4 tablespoons flour
1.4kg/3lb chicken (cut into 8 pieces)
1 tablespoon olive oil
4 tablespoons butter
20 button onions
75g/3oz bacon (without rind, diced)
20 button mushrooms (wiped with
damp kitchen paper)

2 tablespoons brandy
1 bottle red Burgundy
Bouquet garni
1 teaspoon brown sugar
Salt and pepper
15g/½oz butter (softened)

- Place 3 tablespoons of the flour in a large plastic bag and shake each chicken piece in it until lightly coated.
- Heat the oil and butter in a large flameproof casserole dish. Add the onions, bacon and mushrooms and sauté for 3 to 4 minutes. Remove with a slotted spoon and set aside. Add the chicken pieces to the hot oil and cook for about 5 to 6 minutes until browned on all sides.
- Pour in the brandy and (standing well back from the pan) carefully light it with a match, then shake the pan gently until the flames subside. Pour in the wine, then add the bouquet garni, sugar and seasoning.
- Bring to the boil, cover and simmer for 1 hour, stirring occasionally.
- Return the reserved onions, bacon and mushrooms to the casserole dish, cover, and cook for 30 minutes. Transfer the chicken, vegetables and bacon to a warmed dish. Remove the bouquet garni and boil rapidly for 2 minutes to reduce the liquid slightly.
- Cream the butter and remaining flour. Whisk this into the liquid in the casserole dish, a teaspoon at a time, until the liquid has thickened slightly. Pour over the chicken.

Salmon fillet

SERVES 4

INGREDIENTS:

3 sprigs dried thyme
5 fresh rosemary branches
8 bay leaves
900g/2lb salmon fillet

1 fennel bulb (cut into 8)
2 tablespoons lemon juice
2 tablespoons olive oil

- Make a base on a hot barbecue with the dried thyme, rosemary branches and bay leaves, overlapping them so that they cover a slightly bigger area than the salmon. Carefully place the salmon on top of the herbs. Arrange the fennel around the edge of the fish.
- Combine the lemon juice and oil and brush the salmon with it. Cover the salmon loosely with a piece of aluminium foil to keep it moist.
- Cook for about 20 to 30 minutes, basting frequently with the lemon juice mixture.
- Remove the salmon from the barbecue, cut into slices and serve with the fennel.

Honey-glazed goose

SERVES 6

INGREDIENTS:

5.4kg/12lb goose

For the marinade:
3 tablespoons clear honey
1 teaspoon chopped fresh thyme
1 teaspoon chopped fresh coriander

4 tablespoons soy sauce
3 garlic cloves (crushed)
1 teaspoon grated root ginger
1 teaspoon five-spice powder
1 teaspoon ground coriander
Pinch of ground cinnamon

- Rinse the goose inside and out and dry with kitchen paper. Remove the wing tips, neck and gizzard. Truss and place in a non-metallic dish.
- Mix together all the marinade ingredients in a large jug and pour over the goose. Cover and leave overnight, turning and basting occasionally.
- Preheat the oven to 220°C/425°F/Gas mark 7.
- Remove the goose from the marinade and pat dry. Weigh the bird, transfer to a rack in a roasting tin and cover with aluminium foil. Roast for 20 minutes, then reduce the temperature to 200°C/400°F/Gas mark 6 and roast for 15 minutes per 450g/1lb.
- Serve with roast potatoes and vegetables.

Liver with wine sauce

SERVES 4

INGREDIENTS:

500g/1lb 2oz lamb's liver (sliced)
Salt and pepper
Flour for coating
1 tablespoon olive oil
25g/1oz butter
1 garlic clove (crushed)
100g/4oz lean bacon rashers (cut into narrow strips)

1 onion (chopped)
1 celery stick (finely sliced)
150ml/¼pt red wine
150ml/¼pt beef stock
Pinch of allspice
1 teaspoon Worcestershire sauce
1 teaspoon chopped fresh sage
4 tomatoes

- Wipe the liver with kitchen paper, season with salt and pepper then coat lightly in flour, shaking off any excess.
- Heat the oil, butter and garlic in a pan and fry the liver until well sealed on both sides and just cooked through. Remove the liver from the pan, cover and keep warm.
- Add the bacon to the fat left in the pan, with the onion and celery. Fry gently until soft.
- Add the red wine, beef stock, allspice, Worcestershire sauce, sage and ¼ teaspoon salt and pepper to taste. Bring to the boil and simmer for 3 to 4 minutes.
- Place the tomatoes in a bowl of just-boiled water for 30 seconds and skin. Cut each tomato into 8 and take out the seeds. Add to the sauce and continue to cook for 2 to 3 minutes.
- Serve the liver on a little of the sauce, with the remainder spooned over. Serve with new potatoes.

Honey & orange chicken

SERVES 4

INGREDIENTS:

4 boneless chicken breasts
1 tablespoon vegetable oil
4 spring onions (chopped)
1 garlic clove (crushed)

3 tablespoons clear honey
4 tablespoons fresh orange juice
1 orange (peeled and segmented)
2 tablespoons soy sauce

- Preheat the oven to 190°C/375°F/Gas mark 5.
- Place the chicken breasts in a shallow roasting tin and set aside.
- Heat the oil in a small pan and fry the spring onions and garlic for 2 minutes until softened. Add the honey, orange juice, orange segments and soy sauce to the pan, stirring well until the honey has dissolved.
- Pour over the chicken and bake, uncovered, for about 45 minutes, until the chicken is cooked basting once or twice. Serve with baked potatoes and a side salad.

Chicken, leek & parsley pie

SERVES 4-6

INGREDIENTS:

For the pastry:
275g/10oz plain flour
Pinch of salt
200g/7oz butter (diced)
2 egg yolks

For the filling:
3 chicken breasts
1 small onion (sliced)
50g/2oz butter

2 leeks (finely sliced)
50g/2oz Cheddar cheese (grated)
25g/1oz Parmesan cheese
(finely grated)
3 tablespoons chopped fresh parsley
2 tablespoons wholegrain mustard
1 teaspoon cornflour
300ml/¹/₂pt double cream
Salt and pepper
Beaten egg (to glaze)

- To make the pastry, first sift the flour and salt. Blend together the butter and egg yolks in a blender or food processor until creamy. Add the flour and process until the mixture is just coming together. Add about 1 tablespoon cold water and process for a few seconds more. Turn out on to a lightly floured surface and knead lightly. Wrap in clingfilm and chill for about 1 hour.
- Poach the chicken breasts with the onion in a large saucepan of boiling water until the chicken is tender. Leave to cool in the liquid.
- Preheat the oven to 200°C/400°F/Gas mark 6.
- Divide the pastry into 2 pieces, one slightly larger than the other. Roll out the larger piece on a lightly floured surface and use to line a 18 x 28cm/7 x 11in baking dish. Prick the base with a fork and bake for 15 minutes. Leave to cool.
- Lift the cooled chicken from the poaching liquid and discard any skin and bones. Cut the chicken flesh into strips, then set aside.
- Melt the butter in a frying pan and fry the leeks over a low heat, stirring occasionally, until soft. Stir in the Cheddar, Parmesan and parsley. Spread half the leek mixture over the cooked pastry base, leaving a border all the way around. Cover the leek mixture with the chicken strips, then top with the remaining leek mixture.

→

←

- Mix together the mustard, cornflour and cream in a small bowl. Add seasoning to taste. Pour over the filling.
- Moisten the edges of the cooked pastry base. Roll out the remaining pastry and use to cover the pie. Brush with beaten egg and bake for 30 to 40 minutes until golden and crisp. Serve hot.

Cajun blackened chicken

SERVES 4

INGREDIENTS:

4 skinless, boneless chicken breasts
2 tablespoons olive oil

For spice mixture:
1 tablespoon cumin seeds
1 tablespoon dried oregano

1 tablespoon dried basil
½ tablespoon sea salt
½ tablespoon garlic salt
1 tablespoon ground white pepper
1 tablespoon ground black pepper
1 tablespoon cayenne pepper

- Make the spice mixture using a pestle and mortar. Grind the cumin seeds to a powder with the oregano and basil. Mix with all the salt and pepper.
- Coat the chicken breasts with the spice mixture and set aside for at least 10 to 15 minutes.
- Heat the oil in a non-stick frying pan and pan-fry the chicken breasts for about 5 minutes on each side or until cooked through. Serve hot.

Irish breakfast

SERVES 4

INGREDIENTS:

4 pork sausages
1 tablespoon vegetable oil
2 tomatoes
Salt and pepper
Knob of butter

4 thick slices white pudding
4 thick slices black pudding
4 smoked back bacon rashers
4 smoked streaky bacon rashers
4 eggs

- Preheat the oven to 180°C/350°F/Gas mark 4.
- Prick the sausages and fry in oil over a medium heat until golden all over. Drain and keep hot.
- Cut the tomatoes in half, put on to a heatproof plate and season with salt and pepper. Place a little blob of butter on each tomato, cover loosely with greaseproof paper and cook in the oven for 5 to 10 minutes.
- Fry the puddings gently on both sides and drain on kitchen paper. Cut the rinds off the rashers and fry until just crisp in a very hot pan.
- Finally heat a little bacon fat or butter in a clean pan, crack the eggs and cook on a gentle heat as desired.
- Divide everything between 4 plates and serve immediately.

Ceviche

SERVES 4

INGREDIENTS:

450g/1lb haddock fillets
1 teaspoon coriander seeds
1 teaspoon black peppercorns
Juice of 6 limes
1 teaspoon salt
2 tablespoons olive oil

Bunch of spring onions
(finely chopped)
4 tomatoes (chopped)
Tabasco sauce to taste
2 tablespoons chopped fresh coriander
1 avocado to finish

- To skin the haddock fillets, put them skin-side down on a board, dip your fingers in salt, then grip the tail end of the skin. Using a sharp knife, flake off the flesh of the fish by working away from you with a sawing action.
- Wash the fillets, then pat them dry with kitchen paper. Cut them diagonally into thin, even strips and place in a bowl.
- Crush the coriander seeds and peppercorns to a fine powder with a pestle and mortar. Mix with the lime juice and salt, then pour over the fish. Cover and chill in the refrigerator for 24 hours, turning the fish occasionally.
- The next day, heat the oil in a pan, add the spring onions and fry gently for 5 minutes. Add the tomatoes and Tabasco sauce to taste and toss together briskly over the heat for 1 to 2 minutes. Remove from the heat and leave to cool for 20 to 30 minutes.
- To serve, drain the fish from the marinade, discarding the marinade. Combine the fish with the spring onion, tomato mixture and the chopped coriander. Halve the avocado, peel it and remove the stone. Slice the flesh widthways. Arrange the slices around the edge of a serving bowl and pile the ceviche in the centre. Serve chilled.

Caribbean pork stir-fry

SERVES 4-6

INGREDIENTS:

100g/4oz dried shrimps
50ml/2fl oz groundnut oil
225g/8oz pork (cubed)
3 spring onions (finely chopped)
3 garlic cloves (crushed)
½ teaspoon dried shrimp paste
2 red chillies (seeded and finely chopped)

100g/4oz white cabbage (finely sliced)
100g/4oz beansprouts
1 tablespoon white sugar
3 tablespoons soy sauce
225g/8oz rice noodles (cooked as instructed on the packet)
1 leek (finely sliced)

- Soak the dried shrimps in cold water for 2 hours. In a wok or cast-iron frying pan, heat the groundnut oil to smoking point, then stir-fry the pork for 2 minutes or until brown. Add the shrimps, onion, garlic, shrimp paste and chillies and stir-fry for another 2 minutes.
- Add the cabbage, beansprouts, sugar and soy sauce and stir-fry on a medium heat for another minute. Finally, mix in the noodles and fry for a further 2 minutes, stirring constantly.

Beef daube

SERVES 6-8

INGREDIENTS:

25g/1oz butter
1 large onion (cut into wedges)
2 celery sticks (chopped)
1 green pepper (cored, seeded and chopped)
450g/1lb sirloin steak (trimmed and cut into strips)
1kg/2½lb lean braising steak (cubed)
50g/2oz plain flour (seasoned with salt and pepper)

600ml/1pt beef stock
2 garlic cloves (crushed)
150ml/5fl oz red wine
2 tablespoons red wine vinegar
2 tablespoons tomato purée
½ teaspoon Tabasco sauce
1 teaspoon chopped fresh thyme
2 bay leaves
½ teaspoon Cajun spice mix

- Heat the butter in a large, heavy-based casserole dish. Add the onion wedges and cook until browned on all sides. Remove with a slotted spoon and set aside.

- Add the celery and pepper to the pan and cook until softened. Remove the vegetables with a slotted spoon and set aside.
- Coat the meat in the seasoned flour, add to the pan and sauté until browned on all sides. Add the stock, garlic, wine, vinegar, tomato purée, Tabasco sauce and thyme and heat gently.
- Return the onions, celery and pepper to the pan. Tuck in the bay leaves and sprinkle with Cajun seasoning.
- Bring to the boil, transfer to the oven and cook for 3 hours or until the meat and vegetables are tender. Serve with French bread.

Quails with bacon & juniper

SERVES 4

INGREDIENTS:

4 quails
3 tablespoons juniper berries
1 teaspoon black peppercorns
1 tablespoon chopped fresh sage
50g/2oz unsalted butter (slightly softened)
8 rashers of smoked streaky bacon

For the rosti:
450g/1lb potatoes (peeled)
1 bunch spring onions (finely chopped)
1 red pepper (seeded and finely diced)
3 tablespoons vegetable oil

- Preheat the oven to 200°C/400°F/Gas mark 6.
- Wash and dry the quails. Place in a roasting tin.
- Crush the juniper berries and black peppercorns together in a mixing bowl, then mix with the sage leaves and butter to form a paste. Spread evenly over the quails and place 2 rashers of bacon over each quail. Roast for 25 to 30 minutes in the oven until cooked through.
- To make the rosti, cook the potatoes in salted boiling water for 15 minutes, drain and allow to cool.
- Coarsely grate the potatoes into a large mixing bowl, add the chopped spring onions and red pepper, and mix well. Divide the mixture into 8 and shape into rounds.
- Heat the oil in a frying pan and cook the rosti rounds for 2 to 4 minutes on each side until golden brown and crisp. Keep warm.
- Serve each quail on 2 rosti rounds and spoon any juices over.

Mixed game pie

SERVES 4

INGREDIENTS:

450g/1lb mixed game meat (off the bone)
1 small onion (halved)
2 bay leaves
2 carrots (halved)
4 black peppercorns
1 tablespoon vegetable oil
75g/3oz streaky bacon (rinded and
chopped)

1 tablespoon plain flour
2 tablespoons sweet sherry
2 teaspoons ground ginger
Grated zest and juice of ½ orange
350g/12oz ready-made puff pastry
Egg and milk to glaze
Salt and pepper

- Place the game meat in a deep pan with half an onion, the bay leaves, carrots and black peppercorns. Cover with water and bring to the boil. Simmer until reduced to about 300ml/½pt, then strain the stock.
- Cut the game meat into bite-sized pieces. Chop the remaining onion and, in a frying pan, fry in the oil until softened. Then add the bacon and meat and fry quickly to seal. Sprinkle on the flour and stir until beginning to brown. Gradually add the stock, stirring as it thickens, then add the sherry, ginger, orange zest and juice, and seasoning. Simmer for 20 minutes.
- Transfer to a 900ml/1½pt pie dish and allow to cool slightly. Put a pie funnel in the centre of the filling to help hold up the pastry.
- Preheat the oven to 220°C/425°F/Gas mark 7. Roll out the pastry until slightly larger than the dish. Place over the top of the dish and brush with egg or milk.
- Bake for 15 minutes, then reduce the heat to 190°C/375°F/Gas mark 5 for a further 25 to 30 minutes. Serve hot.

Mushroom steak

SERVES 4

INGREDIENTS:

1 tablespoon vegetable oil
4 lean beef steaks
1 small onion (chopped)
175g/6oz mushrooms (wiped with
damp kitchen paper and sliced)

2 tablespoons Worcestershire sauce
125ml/4fl oz beef stock
3 teaspoons cornflour
2 tablespoons chopped fresh parsley

- Heat a heavy-based pan on a high heat. Brush oil onto both sides of the steaks.
- To seal, cook the steaks for 2 to 3 minutes on each side. Continue frying until cooked to your personal preference and remove from the heat.
- Add the onion and mushrooms to any pan juices and cook for 1 minute. Add the
- Worcestershire sauce, stock and cornflour. Bring to the boil, stirring constantly, until slightly thickened. Add the parsley and any juices from the steak. Serve with the steamed vegetables and mashed potatoes.

Duck vindaloo

SERVES 4

INGREDIENTS:

700g/1½lb boneless duck breasts
6 medium dried red chillies (seeded and chopped)
150ml/¼pt distilled malt vinegar
6 garlic cloves (chopped)
2cm/1in piece of fresh root ginger (grated)
1 teaspoon crushed mustard seeds

1 tablespoon ground coriander
1 tablespoon ground cumin
1 teaspoon ground turmeric
1 tablespoon vegetable oil
1 teaspoon salt
150ml/¼pt water
1 tablespoon soft brown sugar

- Slice the duck breasts diagonally into 2cm/1in thick slices and place them in a shallow non-metallic dish.
- Place the chillies, vinegar, garlic, ginger and mustard seeds in a blender or food processor and blend to a smooth paste. Stir the ground coriander, cumin and turmeric into the paste.
- Pour this spice mixture over the duck slices and mix until they are evenly coated. Cover and leave to marinate for 3 hours at room temperature or overnight in the refrigerator.
- Heat the oil in a heavy-based saucepan. Remove the duck from the marinade, reserving the marinade, and add the duck to the pan with the salt. Cook over a gentle heat for 5 minutes, then pour away any excess fat from the pan. Add the reserved marinade together with the water and stir well. Cover and simmer, stirring, for 30 minutes, or until the duck is tender.
- Stir in the sugar, increase the heat and cook the vindaloo over a medium-high heat for 6 to 8 minutes, stirring frequently to prevent it sticking. The sauce should be of a thick, coating consistency. Serve hot with basmati rice.

→

Fresh baked sardines

SERVES 4

INGREDIENTS:

2 tablespoons olive oil
2 large onions (sliced into rings)
3 garlic cloves (chopped)
2 large courgettes (cut into sticks)
3 tablespoons fresh thyme (stalks removed)

8 sardine fillets
75g/3oz Parmesan cheese (grated)
4 eggs (beaten)
150ml/¼pt milk
Salt and pepper

- Preheat the oven to 180°C/350°F/Gas mark 4.
- Heat 1 tablespoon of the oil in a frying pan. Add the onions and garlic and sauté for 2 to 3 minutes. Add the courgettes and cook for about 5 minutes or until golden. Stir 2 tablespoons of thyme into the mixture.
- Place half of the onions and courgettes in the base of a large ovenproof dish.
- Top with the sardine fillets and half the Parmesan cheese. Place the remaining onions and courgettes on top and sprinkle with the remaining thyme.
- Mix the eggs and milk together in a bowl and season to taste with salt and pepper. Pour the mixture over the vegetables and sardines in the dish. Sprinkle the remaining Parmesan cheese over the top.
- Bake in the oven for 20 to 25 minutes or until golden and set. Serve immediately.

Steak tartare

SERVES 4

INGREDIENTS:

4 x 175g/6oz lean rump steaks
4 egg yolks (in half shell)
1 red onion (finely chopped)
4 tablespoons small capers (rinsed)
8 small pickled gherkins (finely chopped)

4 tablespoon chopped fresh parsley
8 anchovy fillets (finely chopped)
Dijon mustard, to serve
Worcestershire sauce, to serve
Tabasco sauce, to serve

- Trim the steaks and chop finely with a sharp knife. Pile the meat from one steak in the centre of each plate. Nestle the egg yolk in its shell in the centre.
- Place little mounds of onion, capers, gherkins, parsley and anchovies around the meat. Serve straight away, with mustard and sauces to accompany.

Creamy orange chicken

SERVES 4

INGREDIENTS:

8 chicken thighs (skinned)
2 tablespoons vegetable oil
3 tablespoons brandy
300ml/¹/₂pt orange juice
3 spring onions (chopped)

2 teaspoons cornflour
2 teaspoons water
100ml/3¹/₂fl oz fromage fraîs
Salt and pepper

- Cook the chicken pieces in the oil in a heavy-based pan, turning until evenly browned. Stir in the brandy, orange juice and spring onions. Bring to a boil, then cover and simmer for 15 minutes, or until the juices run clear.
- Blend the cornflour with the water then mix into the fromage fraîs. Stir this into the sauce and stir over moderate heat until boiling.
- Adjust the seasoning and serve with boiled rice or pasta.

Duck breasts with orange

SERVES 4

INGREDIENTS:

4 duck breasts
Salt and pepper
1 tablespoon sunflower oil
2 oranges
150ml/¹/₂pt fresh orange juice

1 tablespoon port
2 tablespoons orange marmalade
15g/¹/₂oz butter
1 teaspoon cornflour

- Season the duck breast skin with salt and pepper. Heat the oil in a frying pan over a moderate heat and add the duck breasts, skin side down. Cover and cook for 3 to 4 minutes, until lightly browned. Turn the breasts over, lower the heat slightly, and cook uncovered for 5 to 6 minutes.
- Peel the skin and pith from the oranges. Working over a bowl to catch any juice, slice either side of the membranes to release the orange segments, then set aside with the juice.
- Remove the duck breasts from the pan with a slotted spoon, drain on kitchen paper and keep warm in the oven while making the sauce. Drain off the fat from the pan. Add the segmented oranges, all but 2 tablespoons of the orange

→

juice, the port and the orange marmalade to the pan. Bring to the boil and then reduce the heat slightly.
- Blend the cornflour with the reserved orange juice, pour into the pan and stir until slightly thickened. Add the duck breasts and cook gently for about 3 minutes. Serve hot with sauce.

Shepherd's pie

SERVES 4

INGREDIENTS:

2 tablespoon vegetable oil	1 bay leaf
1 onion (finely chopped)	3 teaspoons Worcestershire sauce
1 carrot (finely chopped)	1 tablespoon tomato purée
100g/4oz mushrooms (chopped)	675g/1½lb potatoes (boiled)
500g/1lb 2oz minced lamb	25g/1oz butter
300ml/½pt lamb stock	3 tablespoons hot milk
1 tablespoon plain flour	Salt and pepper

- Heat the oil in a saucepan, add the onion, carrot and mushrooms and cook, stirring occasionally, until browned. Stir the lamb into the pan and cook, stirring to break up the lumps, until lightly browned. Blend a few spoonfuls of the stock with the flour, then stir this mixture into the pan.
- Pour in the remaining stock and bring to a simmer, stirring constantly. Add the bay leaf, Worcestershire sauce and tomato purée, then cover the pan and cook very gently for 1 hour, stirring occasionally. Remove the lid from the pan towards the end of cooking to allow any excess water to evaporate, if necessary, but do not let it boil dry or stick to the pan.
- Preheat the oven to 190°C/375°F/Gas mark 5.
- Mash the potatoes with the butter, milk and seasoning. Add the seasoning to the mince mixture, then spoon into an ovenproof dish. Cover with an even layer of potato and make a pattern on the top with the prongs of a fork. Bake for 25 minutes, until golden brown. Serve hot.

Seekh kebab

SERVES 4

INGREDIENTS:

450g/1lb lean lamb (finely minced)
1 large onion (grated)
2 garlic cloves (crushed)
1 green chilli (seeded and chopped)
1 teaspoon ground cumin

½ teaspoon salt
½ teaspoon freshly ground black pepper
Grated zest and juice of 1 lemon
Vegetable oil

- Thoroughly blend all the ingredients except the oil in a bowl. Lightly cover and chill for 1 hour.
- Divide the meat mixture into 16 pieces and shape each piece into a tight oval shape. Place 4 meat rolls on a skewer and brush with vegetable oil. Repeat with all the meat.
- Barbecue or cook under the grill for 10 minutes, turning frequently. Serve with pitta bread and rice.

Country cider hotpot

SERVES 4

INGREDIENTS:

2 tablespoons flour
Salt and pepper
450g/1lb boneless rabbit pieces
25g/1oz butter
1 tablespoon vegetable oil
15 baby onions
4 lean smoked bacon rashers (chopped)

2 teaspoons Dijon mustard
450ml/¾pt cider
3 carrots (chopped)
2 parsnips (chopped)
12 ready-to-eat prunes (stoned)
1 fresh rosemary sprig
1 bay leaf

- Preheat the oven to 160°C/325°F/Gas mark 3.
- Place the flour and seasoning in a plastic bag, add the rabbit pieces and shake until coated. Remove from the bag and set aside.
- Heat the butter and oil in a flameproof casserole dish and add the onions and bacon. Fry for 4 minutes until the onions have softened. Remove the onions and bacon with a slotted spoon and reserve.

→

- Fry the seasoned rabbit pieces in the oil in the casserole dish until they are browned all over, then spread a little of the mustard over the top of each piece.
- Return the onions and bacon to the pan. Pour on the cider and add the carrots, parsnips, prunes, rosemary and bay leaf. Season well. Bring to the boil, then cover and transfer to the oven.
- Cook for about 1½ hours until tender. Remove the rosemary sprig and bay leaf and serve the rabbit hot, with creamy mashed potato if desired.

Corned beef dinner

SERVES 8

INGREDIENTS:

1.8kg/4lb corned beef brisket
350ml/12fl oz beer
1 small onion (whole)
1 bay leaf
½ teaspoon whole cloves
4 black peppercorns

2 celery sticks with leaves (chopped)
8 potatoes (halved)
8 large carrots (halved)
1 medium head green cabbage (quartered)

- Place the brisket in a deep pan and add cold water to just cover. Add the beer, onion, bay leaf, cloves, peppercorns and celery. Cover and bring to a boil.
- Immediately reduce the heat and simmer for about 4 hours until tender.
- About 30 minutes before the meat is done, remove and discard the onion and celery. Skim the excess fat from the liquid. Add the potatoes and carrots and simmer for 15 minutes.
- Add the cabbage quarters and simmer for an additional 15 minutes or until the vegetables are tender.

Roast pheasant

SERVES 4

INGREDIENTS:

1 large pheasant
50g/2oz butter
75g/3oz onions (chopped)
75g/3oz soft white breadcrumbs

1 tablespoon chopped fresh parsley
¼ teaspoon salt and pepper
Knob of butter

- Preheat the oven to 190°C/375°F/Gas mark 5.
- Gut the pheasant if necessary, then wash and dry well.
- To make the stuffing, melt the butter and sweat the onions in a pan until soft but not browned, then remove from the heat. Stir in the breadcrumbs and parsley, and season with salt and pepper. Allow the stuffing to cool.
- Stuff the pheasant loosely. Smear the breast and legs generously with butter.
- Roast the pheasant for about 1¼ hours. Test by pricking the leg at the thickest point; the juice should run clear. Serve with roast potatoes, gravy and cranberry sauce.

Guinea fowl with fennel

SERVES 4-6

INGREDIENTS:

4 garlic cloves (chopped)
2 tablespoons chopped rosemary leaves
Salt and pepper
2 guinea fowl (each cut into 8 pieces)
Olive oil, for drizzling

1 red onion (cut into 8)
3 fennel bulbs (cut into 8)
10 pancetta slices (cut into 1cm/½in pieces)
250ml/9fl oz white wine

- Preheat the oven to 200°C/400°F/Gas mark 6.
- Mix the garlic and rosemary with a pinch of salt and pepper in a small bowl.
- Put the guinea fowl into a separate bowl, drizzle with olive oil and add the garlic mixture. Make sure each piece is thoroughly coated.
- Place the guinea fowl in a roasting tin and add the red onion, fennel and pancetta. Drizzle with olive oil and roast for 30 minutes.
- Add the wine and roast for a further 20 minutes. Raise the heat for the last few minutes to brown and serve hot.

Pork chops with Marsala

SERVES 4

INGREDIENTS:

4 pork chops
2 tablespoons olive oil
A sprig of rosemary
200ml/7fl oz medium-sweet Marsala

4 strips of lemon zest
1 tablespoon lemon juice
Salt and pepper

→

←

- Pat the chops dry with kitchen paper. Put the olive oil in a large frying pan and then brown the chops slowly on both sides.
- Pour off the excess fat, turn the heat down and add all the remaining ingredients. Simmer, half-covered, for 20 minutes, turning the chops once.
- Discard the rosemary and lemon zest. Remove the chops from the pan and keep warm.
- Boil the juices remaining in the pan until they are reduced to a thin layer on the base. Taste and season, pour over the chops and serve.

Chicken & mushroom pie

SERVES 6

INGREDIENTS:

For the pastry:
225g/8oz plain flour
¼ teaspoon salt
100g/4oz cold butter (diced)
75g/3oz lard (diced)
100ml/3¼fl oz–125ml/4fl oz iced water

For the filling:
15g/½oz dried porcini mushrooms
50g/2oz butter
15g/½oz plain flour

250ml/9fl oz chicken stock
50ml/2fl oz single cream
Salt and pepper
1 onion (chopped)
2 carrots (sliced)
2 celery sticks (chopped)
50g/2oz button mushrooms (wiped with damp kitchen paper and quartered)
450g/1lb cooked chicken meat (cubed)
50g/2oz fresh peas
1 egg (beaten, to glaze)

- To make the pastry, sift the flour and salt into a bowl. With a pastry blender or 2 knives, cut in the butter and lard until the mixture resembles fine breadcrumbs. Sprinkle with the lesser quantity of iced water and mix until the dough holds together. If the dough is too crumbly, add more water, 1 tablespoon at a time.
- Gather the dough into a ball and flatten into a round. Place in a sealed polythene bag and chill for at least 30 minutes.
- Place the porcini mushrooms in a small bowl. Add hot water to cover and leave to soak for about 30 minutes, until soft. Lift out of the water with a slotted spoon and drain on kitchen paper.
- Preheat the oven to 190°C/375°F/Gas mark 5.
- Melt half of the butter in a heavy-based saucepan. Whisk in the flour and cook until bubbling, whisking constantly. Add the hot stock and cook over a medium heat, whisking, until the mixture boils. Cook for 2 to 3 minutes more,

then whisk in the cream. Season and set aside.

- Heat the remaining butter in a large frying pan. Add the onion and carrots and cook for about 5 minutes, until softened. Add the celery and mushrooms and cook for a further 5 minutes. Stir in the cooked chicken, peas and drained porcini mushrooms.
- Add the chicken mixture to the cream sauce and stir to mix. Turn into a 2.5 litre/4pt rectangular baking dish.
- Roll out the dough to about 4mm/¹/₈in thickness. Cut into a rectangle about 2cm/³/₄in bigger than the dish. Lay over the filling and seal the edge by pressing down with your fingertips. Cut several slits in the pastry to allow steam to escape and brush the top of the pastry with the beaten egg. Use any remaining pastry for decoration.
- Bake for about 30 minutes, until the pastry is browned. Serve hot from the dish.

Moroccan lamb kebabs

SERVES 6

INGREDIENTS:

3 garlic cloves (chopped)
1 onion (chopped)
¹/₂ teaspoon ground coriander
¹/₂ teaspoon ground cumin
¹/₂ teaspoon sweet paprika
¹/₂ teaspoon ground ginger

1kg/2¹/₂lb minced lamb
3 tablespoons chopped fresh mint
3 tablespoons chopped fresh coriander
Salt and pepper
12 large vine leaves
Olive oil

- Put the garlic, onion and spices in a blender or food processor and blend to form a paste. Add the lamb and herbs and blend again until mixed. Season with salt and pepper.
- Divide the mixture into 12 and, with damp hands, roll into large sausage shapes.
- Rinse and dry the vine leaves on kitchen paper. Wrap each sausage in a leaf and skewer through the middle, 2 per skewer. Brush generously with oil and place on a grill rack.
- Grill or barbecue under medium heat for 4 to 5 minutes on each side. Serve with rice.

Turkey meatloaf

SERVES 4

INGREDIENTS:

1 tablespoon olive oil
1 onion (chopped)
1 green pepper (seeded and finely chopped)
1 garlic clove (chopped)
450g/1lb minced turkey
50g/2oz fresh white breadcrumbs
1 egg (beaten)

50g/2oz pine nuts
12 sun-dried tomatoes in oil (drained and chopped)
75ml/3fl oz milk
2 teaspoons chopped fresh rosemary
1 teaspoon fennel seeds
½ teaspoon dried oregano
Salt and pepper

- Preheat the oven to 190°C/375°F/Gas mark 5.
- Heat the oil in a frying pan. Add the onion, green pepper and garlic and cook over a low heat for 8 to 10 minutes, stirring frequently, until the vegetables are just softened. Remove from the heat and leave to cool.
- Place the minced turkey in a large bowl. Add the onion mixture and all the remaining ingredients and mix thoroughly.
- Transfer to a 21 x 11cm/8 x 4in loaf tin, packing down firmly. Bake for 1 hour, until golden brown. Serve hot.

Chicken chow mein

SERVES 4

INGREDIENTS:

350g/12oz noodles
225g/8oz skinless, boneless chicken breasts
3 tablespoons soy sauce
1 tablespoon rice wine
1 tablespoon dark sesame oil
4 tablespoons vegetable oil

2 garlic cloves (finely chopped)
50g/2oz mangetouts (topped and tailed)
100g/4oz beansprouts
50g/2oz ham (finely shredded)
Salt and pepper
4 spring onions (finely chopped)

- Cook the noodles in a saucepan of boiling water until tender. Drain, rinse under cold water and drain well.
- Slice the chicken into fine shreds, about 5cm/2in in length. Place in a bowl and add 2 tablespoons of the soy sauce, the rice wine and the sesame oil.

- Heat half of the vegetable oil in a wok or frying pan over a high heat. When it starts smoking, add the chicken mixture. Stir-fry for 2 minutes, then transfer the chicken to a plate and keep it hot.
- Wipe the wok clean and heat the remaining oil. Stir in the garlic, mangetouts, beansprouts and ham, stir-fry for another minute and add the noodles.
- Continue to stir-fry until the noodles are heated through. Add the remaining soy sauce to taste and season with salt and pepper. Return the chicken and any juices to the noodle mixture, add the chopped spring onions and stir. Serve immediately.

Beef & pork ragú

SERVES 4

INGREDIENTS:

15g/1/2oz dried porcini mushrooms
225g/8oz boneless beef chuck (trimmed of all fat)
225g/8oz lean, boneless pork (trimmed of all fat)
50g/2oz butter
3 shallots (chopped)

1 celery stick (finely chopped)
1 carrot (finely chopped)
2 tablespoons chopped fresh parsley
1 tablespoon flour
175ml/6fl oz beef stock
150ml/1/4pt dry white wine
Salt and pepper

- Soak the porcini mushrooms in 250ml/9fl oz warm water for 30 minutes.
- Cut the beef and pork into 1cm/1/2in dice.
- Drain the porcini, reserving the liquid. Squeeze the water out of the porcini and chop. Strain the liquid.
- Melt the butter in a large pan over a medium-low heat. Add the shallots, celery, carrot and porcini mushrooms. Increase the heat to medium and sauté for about 5 minutes, or until lightly coloured. Stir in the parsley.
- Reduce the heat and add the meat. Brown it lightly on all sides. Stir in the flour, pour in the porcini liquid, meat broth and wine, and season with salt and pepper.
- Stir, cover and simmer for about 2½ to 3 hours, stirring occasionally, until the meat begins to disintegrate and the sauce thickens. Serve hot with fresh pasta.

Balti lamb tikka

SERVES 4

INGREDIENTS:

700g/1½lb lean lamb (cubed)
1 unripe papaya
3 tablespoons natural yogurt
1 teaspoon grated root ginger
1 teaspoon chilli powder
1 teaspoon crushed garlic

¼ teaspoon ground turmeric
2 teaspoons ground coriander
¼ teaspoon red food colouring
300ml/½pt corn oil
Salt

- Place the cubed lamb in a large mixing bowl.
- Peel the papaya, cut in half and scoop out the seeds. Cut the flesh into cubes, place in a blender or food processor and blend until pulped.
- Pour about 2 tablespoons of the papaya pulp over the lamb cubes and rub it in well with your fingers. Set aside to marinate for at least 3 hours.
- Mix together the yogurt, ginger, chilli powder, garlic, turmeric, ground coriander, red food colouring and 2 tablespoons of oil in a clean mixing bowl. Season with salt and set aside.
- Spoon the yogurt mixture over lamb and mix together well.
- Heat the remaining oil in a wok. When it is hot, lower the heat slightly and add the lamb cubes, a few at a time. Deep-fry the batches of lamb for 5 to 7 minutes or until the lamb is cooked and tender. Serve with rice and naan bread.

Sweet & sour chicken

SERVES 4

INGREDIENTS:

275g/10oz dried Chinese egg noodles
2 tablespoons vegetable oil
3 spring onions (chopped)
1 garlic clove (crushed)
2cm/¾in fresh root ginger (peeled and grated)
1 teaspoon hot paprika
1 teaspoon ground coriander
3 chicken breast fillets (sliced)

100g/4oz sugar snap peas (topped and tailed)
100g/4oz baby sweetcorn (halved)
225g/8oz fresh beansprouts
1 tablespoon cornflour
3 tablespoons soy sauce
3 tablespoons lemon juice
1 tablespoon sugar
Salt

- Bring a large saucepan of salted water to the boil. Add the noodles and cook according to the package instructions. Drain thoroughly, cover and keep warm.
- Heat the oil in a preheated wok. Add the spring onions and cook over a gentle heat. Mix in the garlic, ginger, paprika, coriander and chicken, then stir-fry for 3 to 4 minutes.
- Add the peas, baby sweetcorn and beansprouts, cover and cook briefly. Add the noodles.
- Combine the cornflour, soy sauce, lemon juice and sugar in a small bowl. Add to the wok and simmer briefly to thicken. Serve immediately.

Ocean pie

SERVES 4

INGREDIENTS:

500g/1lb 2oz cod fillet (skinned)
225g/8oz salmon steak
450ml/³/₄pt skimmed milk
1 bay leaf
Salt and pepper
900g/2lb potatoes (coarsely chopped)

50g/2oz peeled prawns
50g/2oz margarine
25g/1oz plain flour
3 tablespoons white wine
1 teaspoon chopped fresh dill
2 tablespoons drained capers

- Preheat the oven to 200°C/400°F/Gas mark 6.
- Put the cod and salmon into a saucepan with 300ml/¹/₂pt of the milk, bay leaf and seasoning. Bring to the boil, cover and simmer gently for 10 to 15 minutes until tender.
- Cook the potatoes in boiling salt water until tender (about 15 minutes).
- Drain the fish, reserving the cooking liquid. Flake the fish, discarding any bones, and place in a shallow ovenproof dish. Add the prawns.
- Melt half the margarine in a saucepan, add the flour and cook, stirring, for 1 minute. Gradually stir in the reserved cooking liquid and the wine and bring to the boil. Add the dill, capers and seasoning to taste and simmer until thickened. Pour over the fish and mix well.
- Drain the potatoes and mash them, adding the remaining margarine, seasoning and milk. Spread the mashed potatoes over the fish and cook in the oven for about 25 minutes, or until piping hot and browned. Serve immediately.

Peppered crabs

SERVES 4

INGREDIENTS:

3 spring onions (chopped)
1 red chilli (deseeded and chopped)
1 teaspoon cayenne pepper
3 garlic cloves (chopped)
1 tablespoon lime juice
4 teaspoons chilli sauce
1 tablespoon soy sauce

1 teaspoon sugar
1cm/½in fresh root ginger (peeled and finely chopped)
1 green chilli (deseeded)
8 crab meat portions (from 2 crabs)
50ml/2fl oz cold water

- Blend the spring onions, capsicum, cayenne pepper and garlic in a mixing bowl to create a smooth paste. Pour into a large frying pan or wok and stir-fry for 3 minutes.
- Add the lime juice, chilli sauce, soy sauce, sugar, ginger and chilli and stir well.
- Add the crab portions and leave for 1 minute, then pour in the water, cover and simmer for 15 minutes.
- Serve hot, with the sauce poured over the crab meat.

Pheasant with apples

SERVES 4

INGREDIENTS:

1 pheasant
2 small onions (quartered)
3 celery sticks (thickly sliced)
2 red apples (thickly sliced)
125ml/4fl oz chicken stock (see p.xx)

1 tablespoon clear honey
2 tablespoons Worcestershire sauce
Ground nutmeg
Salt and pepper

- Preheat the oven to 180°C/350°F/Gas mark 4.
- Sauté the pheasant without fat in a non-stick pan, turning occasionally until golden. Remove and keep hot.
- Sauté the onions and celery in the pan to brown lightly. Spoon into a casserole dish and place the pheasant on top. Tuck the apple slices around it.
- Spoon over the stock, honey and Worcestershire sauce. Sprinkle with nutmeg, salt and pepper, cover and bake for 1½ hours or until tender. Serve hot with roast potatoes.

Poached guinea fowl

SERVES 4

INGREDIENTS:

1.4kg/3lb guinea fowl
1 teaspoon salt
4 carrots (quartered)
2 celery sticks (halved)
1 bunch spring onions (halved)

2cm/1in piece fresh root ginger (peeled and sliced)
2 bay leaves
10 black peppercorns

- Put the guinea fowl into a large pan with the salt. Cover with water and bring to the boil, skimming the scum from the surface now and then. Add the carrots, celery, spring onions, ginger, bay leaves and peppercorns and leave to simmer for 45 minutes or until the juices run clear when the thigh is pierced with a skewer.
- Lift the guinea fowl on to a plate and leave to cool slightly. Strain the remaining stock into a large shallow pan, bring back to the boil and boil rapidly for about 10 minutes, until reduced and well flavoured.
- Remove the skin from the guinea fowl and then cut into joints. To do this, first cut off the legs and cut them in half at the joint. Carefully cut the breast meat away from the bones in 2 large pieces and then cut each one across into 2 smaller pieces.
- Serve hot with potatoes.

Skate with black butter

SERVES 4

INGREDIENTS:

175g/6oz butter (chopped)
900g/2lb small skate wings

600ml/1pt fish stock
75ml/3fl oz malt vinegar

- To clarify the butter, melt it in a pan over a low heat without stirring. Remove from the heat and cool slightly. Skim the foamy mixture from the surface. Pour off the clear yellow liquid and reserve. Discard the milky sediment left in the pan.
- Pat the skate with kitchen paper. Cut fillets from either side of the cartilage with a sharp knife, cutting close to the cartilage. Place skin side down on a chopping board and, using a sawing motion, cut along the length of the wing. Cut into similar-sized pieces.
- Place the stock and vinegar in a large pan and bring to the boil. Add the skate and poach for 8 minutes. Drain well and pat dry with kitchen paper.

→

←

- Melt a little butter in a frying pan and cook the skate for 1 to 2 minutes each side or until tender. Place on a serving dish and keep warm.
- Heat the clarified butter in a pan until brown and foaming. Pour over the skate.

Fried chicken in batter

SERVES 4

INGREDIENTS:

8 chicken thighs (skinned and boned)
2 garlic cloves (finely chopped)
Juice of 2 lemons
Vegetable oil for deep-frying

For the batter:
100g/4oz plain flour

2 eggs
200ml/7fl oz lager
2 tablespoons olive oil
1 teaspoon salt
2 teaspoons dried oregano
½ teaspoon chilli flakes
½ teaspoon black pepper

- Put the chicken thighs in a deep dish, add the garlic, pour over the lemon juice and toss to coat. Cover with clingfilm and refrigerate overnight.
- Remove the chicken from the refrigerator and allow it to come to room temperature before cooking.
- To make the batter, in a mixing bowl mix the flour, eggs, lager, olive oil, salt, oregano, chilli flakes and black pepper. Whisk until smooth and leave to stand for 1 hour at room temperature.
- Heat the oil for deep-frying and stir the batter. Wipe the marinade from the chicken and pat dry with kitchen paper, then coat in the batter. Fry the chicken in 2 batches, for about 8 minutes each, turning once. Serve hot.

Pan-fried pigeon

SERVES 4

INGREDIENTS:

2 teaspoons olive oil
8 pigeon breasts

For the plum sauce:
250g/9oz canned plums in syrup
1 tablespoon clear honey

1 tablespoon soy sauce
1 teaspoon Worcestershire sauce
½ teaspoon Tabasco sauce
¼ teaspoon ground cardamom
Salt and pepper

- To make the sauce, put all the ingredients, except the salt and pepper, in a small saucepan and bring to the boil over a moderate heat. Simmer for 5 minutes, then remove from the heat and leave to cool.
- Once the sauce has cooled, pour it into a blender or food processor and blend until completely smooth. Check the seasoning, adding salt and pepper if necessary, and transfer to a small bowl. Cover and chill in the refrigerator.
- Heat the oil in a non-stick frying pan and pan-fry the pigeon breasts for 3 to 4 minutes on each side until tender.
- To serve, slice the pigeon breasts and drizzle with plum sauce.

Smoked fish with white sauce

SERVES 6-8

INGREDIENTS:

900g/2lb haddock fillets
225ml/8fl oz milk
225ml/8fl oz water

For the white sauce:
600ml/1pt milk
1 onion (halved)

1 bay leaf
Pinch of white pepper
50g/2oz butter
40g/1½oz plain flour
Salt and freshly ground black pepper
1–2 tablespoons chopped fresh parsley

- For the white sauce, combine the milk in a small pan with the onion, bay leaf and white pepper. Heat slowly to a simmer, then remove from the heat and allow to stand for 3 minutes before straining into a jug. Melt the butter in a pan over a low heat, stir in the flour and cook for 1 minute, or until pale and foaming.
- Remove from the heat and gradually stir in the milk.
- Return to the heat and stir constantly until the sauce boils and thickens. Reduce the heat and simmer for 2 minutes. Remove from the heat and season to taste with salt and pepper. Stir in the chopped fresh parsley.
- Cut the haddock fillets into serving-sized pieces and place in a large frying pan.
- Cover with the milk, combined with the water. Bring to the boil, reduce the heat to low and gently cook the fish until it flakes easily at the thickest part when tested with a fork. Lift out of the pan with a slotted spoon. Drain on kitchen paper and place on serving plates. Top with the white sauce.

Laksa

SERVES 4

INGREDIENTS:

100ml/3½fl oz tablespoons vegetable oil
225g/8oz pressed tofu (cubed)
2 red onions (finely chopped)
3 garlic cloves (finely chopped)
4 Brazil nuts (finely grated)
2 teaspoons ground cumin
1 tablespoon ground coriander
½ teaspoon ground turmeric
1 red chilli (deseeded and chopped)
1 green chilli (deseeded and chopped)

½ teaspoon shrimp paste
2 tablespoons Thai red curry paste
1.2 litres/2pt coconut milk
1 tablespoon soft brown sugar
Salt and pepper
350g/12oz cooked chicken breasts (shredded)
100g/4oz beansprouts
1 tablespoon chopped fresh coriander
225g/8oz dried egg noodles

- Heat two tablespoons of the oil in a wok. Fry the tofu in the oil, in two batches, turning it frequently. Cook each batch for 5 minutes, until crisp and golden, then remove with a slotted spoon, drain on kitchen paper and set aside.
- Heat 2 more tablespoons of oil in the wok, add the onions and garlic and fry over a gentle heat, stirring frequently, for 5 minutes until softened.
- Add the Brazil nuts, cumin, coriander, turmeric and the red and green chillies and the shrimp and curry pastes to the wok. Stir well to mix and fry for further 2 minutes.
- Stir in the coconut milk and sugar and season generously with salt and pepper.
- Bring to the boil, then reduce the heat and simmer gently for 6 minutes. Taste and adjust the seasoning if necessary.
- Heat the remaining oil in a frying pan, add the chicken and stir-fry for 6 minutes, until golden. Add the beansprouts and chopped coriander and stir-fry for a further 1 minute.
- Place the noodles in a bowl and pour boiling water over them to cover completely. Allow to stand for 5 minutes, and then drain well.
- To serve, divide the noodles between 4 large soup bowls. Place a quarter of the fried tofu and a quarter of the chicken and beansprout mixture on top of each portion of noodles. Ladle hot curry sauce over the top and serve immediately.

Roast beef & Yorkshire pudding

SERVES 6-8

INGREDIENTS:

1.8kg/4lb joint of beef
Salt and pepper
Splash of red wine
300ml/¹/₂pt reduced beef stock

For the Yorkshire pudding:
175g/6oz plain flour
1 teaspoon salt
300ml/¹/₂pt cold milk
150ml/¹/₄pt oz cold water
3 eggs (beaten)
60g/2¹/₂oz beef dripping

- To prepare the Yorkshire pudding batter, sift the flour into a mixing bowl with the salt.
- In another large bowl, mix together the milk with the water and whisk with the beaten eggs. Add this to the flour in a thin stream, whisking to a smooth batter.
- Leave to stand for 60 minutes at room temperature.
- Preheat the oven to 240°C/475°F/Gas mark 9.
- Season the joint of beef heavily with salt and pepper, rubbing it in all over.
- Sit the joint on a rack in a roasting pan and put to roast for 25 minutes, then lower the temperature to 200°C/400°F/Gas mark 6 and continue cooking for a further 25 minutes. It is important not to open the oven door for more than a few seconds at any time from start to finish.
- Remove the meat from the oven and allow to rest on its rack for about 30 minutes in a warm place, covered with aluminium foil. Increase the oven setting to 230°C/450°F/Gas mark 8.
- While the meat is resting, cook the Yorkshire pudding. Put the beef dripping into a metal pan at least 6.5cm/2¹/₂in deep and place in the oven until smoking hot.
- Give the batter a final whisk and pour into the fat. Bake for 25 to 30 minutes, when the pudding will be well risen with a crisp, golden crust.
- Make a gravy by pouring off the fat from the roasting pan. Put the pan over a high heat and deglaze it with a splash of red wine. Add the stock and boil fiercely, scraping the stuck-on sediment with a wooden spoon. Taste and adjust the seasoning if necessary.

Stuffed crabs

SERVES 6

INGREDIENTS:

6 cooked medium blue swimmer crabs
50g/2oz butter
2 garlic cloves (finely chopped)
½ red pepper (finely chopped)
½ green pepper (finely chopped)
1 small onion (finely chopped)
1 celery stick (finely chopped)

½ red chilli (finely chopped)
¼ teaspoon celery salt
¼ teaspoon dried thyme
175ml/6fl oz canned condensed seafood bisque
75g/3oz fresh breadcrumbs

- Preheat the oven to 200°C/400°F/Gas mark 6.
- Pull away the crab legs and claws, crack open and extract the meat from the legs.
- Reserve 2 front claws on each crab. Lift the flap on the underside of the crab and prise off the top shell. Remove the soft organs and pull off the gills. Scrub the crab back shells and set aside. Shred the crab meat, picking out the shell fragments.
- Melt the butter in a pan and add the chopped garlic, peppers, onion, celery and chilli. Cook, stirring over a medium heat, for about 5 minutes.
- Add the celery salt, thyme and bisque and cook for 3 minutes. Add the crab meat with half the breadcrumbs. Stir until combined and season to taste.
- Spoon the mixture into the crab shells, smooth the tops and press the remaining crumbs over the surface. Bake the crabs on a baking tray for about 15 minutes, or until heated through and golden, adding the extra claws close to the end of cooking to warm through.

New England clam chowder

SERVES 2

INGREDIENTS:

2 tablespoons vegetable oil
3 rashers of smoked back bacon (diced)
1 medium onion (finely chopped)
500ml/18fl oz milk

1 large potato (diced)
600ml/1pt water
½ teaspoon salt
10 fresh clams in their shells (washed)

- Heat the oil in a saucepan and brown the bacon. Remove the bacon from the oil and set aside. Sauté the onion in the oil for 3 to 4 minutes over a medium heat.

- Add half the milk, all the potato, the water and the salt, then lower the heat and boil for about 10 minutes, until the potato is soft.
- Add the remaining milk and the clams. Cover and cook for another 5 to 10 minutes until the clams are cooked and the shells open. Discard any unopened clams. Sprinkle some bacon on each helping and serve hot.

Chicken fajitas

SERVES 4

INGREDIENTS:

2 red peppers (deseeded and cut into strips)
1 habañero chilli (finely chopped)
2 onions (thinly sliced)
3 tablespoons sunflower oil
3 teaspoons cumin seeds

3 teaspoons coriander seeds
½ teaspoon salt
1 teaspoon freshly ground black pepper
4 skinless chicken breast fillets (cut into strips)
12 flour tortillas

- Sweat the peppers, chilli and onions over a low heat in the oil for 5 minutes, or until soft.
- Put the cumin seeds, coriander seeds, salt and pepper into a dry pan over a very low heat and toast them for 2 to 3 minutes, stirring. Grind to a powder with a pestle and mortar and sprinkle over the frying vegetables. Turn up the heat and add the chicken to the pan, tossing to cook for 3 to 4 minutes.
- Serve with tortillas, guacamole, sour cream and refried beans.

Pork spare ribs

SERVES 6

INGREDIENTS:

1 tablespoon soy sauce
300ml/½pt sherry
1 teaspoon brown sugar

½ teaspoon ground ginger
1 garlic clove (crushed)
3 racks pork ribs

- Mix the soy sauce, sherry, brown sugar, ginger and garlic in a mixing bowl.
- Marinate the ribs in the mixture, in a covered dish, overnight.
- Preheat the oven to 220°C/425°F/Gas mark 7.
- Cook in the oven for 1 hour, turning after 30 minutes. Serve hot with rice.

Fish & chips

SERVES 4

INGREDIENTS:

Vegetable oil for deep-frying
4 large cod fillets
8 large potatoes (peeled and cut into chips)

For the batter:
150g/5oz plain flour
2 tablespoons olive oil
1½ egg whites
Sea salt

- To make the batter, sieve the flour into a mixing bowl and make a well in the centre. Pour in the olive oil, stir, and add enough water to make a batter about the consistency of double cream. Allow to stand for at least 1 hour.
- Just before frying, whisk the egg whites to a stiff peak and fold into the batter, adding a good pinch of sea salt.
- Heat the oil in a deep frying pan over a high heat or to 180°C/350°F. Dip the fish pieces into the batter one at a time, then fry until crispy and golden. Dip the chips in the oil until brown. Drain both the fish and chips on kitchen paper and serve hot.

Veal chops

SERVES 4

INGREDIENTS:

4 garlic cloves (finely chopped)
4 tablespoons finely chopped sage leaves
Zest of 1 lemon (grated)

Salt and pepper
4 veal loin chops
2 tablespoons olive oil
Juice of ½ lemon

- Preheat a barbecue or grill.
- Mix the garlic, sage and lemon zest together in a small bowl with salt and pepper.
- Put the chops in a mixing bowl, and add the olive oil and lemon juice. Add the garlic mixture, turn the chops over and marinate for 1 hour.
- Brush most of the garlic and herb off the chops and pat dry with kitchen paper before cooking.
- Put the chops on the barbecue or grill and allow to brown lightly. Turn the chops frequently so that they cook evenly and brown on both sides. Cook for 10 to 15 minutes. Serve hot with mashed potatoes.

Char siu pork

SERVES 4

INGREDIENTS:

1.1kg/2½lb shoulder of pork (cut into strips)
Salt and pepper
2 tablespoons sunflower oil (plus more for greasing)
1 tablespoon soy sauce

2 tablespoons rice wine
100g/4oz shallots (finely chopped)
3 garlic cloves (finely chopped)
5 tablespoons hoisin sauce
2 tablespoons honey

- Put the pork strips into a dish and season lightly. Dribble the oil, soy sauce and rice wine over the pork, then sprinkle with shallots and garlic. Spoon over the hoisin sauce, cover with clingfilm and refrigerate overnight.
- Preheat the oven to 180°C/350°F/Gas mark 4.
- Remove the pork from the refrigerator and allow it to come to room temperature
- Brush a roasting tin with oil. Lay the pork in it and dribble over a tablespoon of honey. Roast for 20 minutes and turn the pork over. Baste with the remaining honey and roast for another 10 minutes. Turn again and roast for a further 10 minutes. The exterior should be slightly charred and the meat should be cooked.
- Serve immediately with rice.

Smoked salmon tartare

SERVES 4

INGREDIENTS:

450g/1lb salmon fillet (diced)
100g/4oz smoked salmon (diced)
2 teaspoons English mustard
Juice of 1 lemon
1 tablespoon capers (rinsed, drained)

2 shallots (finely chopped)
Small bunch of chives (finely chopped)
Salt and pepper
150ml/¼pt double cream

- Put the salmon fillet and smoked salmon in a mixing bowl and add the mustard, lemon juice, capers, shallots and chives. Season with a little salt and lots of pepper and refrigerate for 2 to 4 hours.
- Whip the cream to soft peaks and fold the tartare into it. Serve with rice.

Thai green chicken curry

SERVES 4

INGREDIENTS:

2 tablespoons groundnut oil
2.5cm/1in piece of fresh root ginger
(finely chopped)
2 shallots (chopped)
4 tablespoons Thai green curry paste
600g/1½lb skinless, boneless chicken
thighs, cut into 5cm/2in pieces

300ml/½pt coconut milk
4 teaspoons fish sauce
1 teaspoon palm sugar or soft
brown sugar
3 kaffir lime leaves (shredded)
1 green chilli (deseeded and sliced)

- Heat the oil in a wok, adding the ginger and shallots. Fry over a gentle heat, stirring for about 3 minutes or until softened. Add the green curry paste and fry for a further 2 minutes.
- Add the chicken to the wok, stir to coat evenly in the spice mixture and fry for 3 minutes to seal the chicken. Stir the coconut milk into the curry, bring to the boil, then reduce the heat and cook the curry gently, stirring occasionally, for 10 minutes or until the chicken is cooked through and the sauce has thickened.
- Stir in the fish sauce, sugar, lime leaves and green chilli and cook the curry for a further 5 minutes. Taste and adjust the seasoning, if necessary and serve the curry immediately.

Minted racks of lamb

SERVES 4

INGREDIENTS:

4 x 4-cutlet racks of lamb
275g/10oz mint jelly

2 tablespoons white wine
3 tablespoons chopped fresh chives

- Preheat the oven to 200°C/400°F/Gas mark 6.
- Trim any excess fat from the lamb, leaving just a thin layer of fat. Clean any meat or sinew from the ends of the bones, using a small sharp knife. Cover the bones with aluminium foil. Place the lamb on a rack in a baking dish.
- Mix the mint jelly and white wine together in a small saucepan over a high heat. Bring to the boil for 4 minutes, or until the mixture is reduced and thickened.
- Cool slightly, and then stir in the chives. Brush the glaze over the racks of lamb.

- Bake for 15 to 20 minutes for rare, or 35 minutes for medium-rare, brushing with glaze every 10 minutes or so. Remove the aluminium foil from the bones and leave the lamb to stand for 5 minutes before serving with roast potatoes and steamed vegetables.

Prawn & spinach lasagne

SERVES 6

INGREDIENTS:

225g/8oz fresh egg lasagne (unrolled)
1½ teaspoons salt

For the filling:
900g/2lb fresh spinach (stems removed)
50g/2oz butter

1 large onion (finely chopped)
450g/1lb raw peeled prawns (deveined)
½ teaspoon salt
125ml/4fl oz plain tomato sauce
600ml/1pt béchamel sauce
50g/2oz Parmesan cheese (grated)

- Roll the lasagne as thinly as possible. With a knife, cut into sheets of 8 x 11cm/3½ x 4½in and let them rest on dry tea towels for at least 15 minutes.
- Bring a large saucepan of water to the boil. Add the salt and slip in the pasta, 2 or 3 pieces at a time, leaving to cook for 1 minute. Remove with a slotted spoon and immerse immediately in cold water. Lay the pasta on damp tea towels.
- Place the spinach in a large, deep pan with no water. Cook, tossing occasionally, for 5 to 10 minutes. Remove from heat, chop finely and set aside.
- Warm the butter in a frying pan and add the onion. Sauté over a medium heat for 4 minutes. Add the prawns and sauté quickly, stirring to cook evenly. Remove the pan from the heat and stir in the chopped spinach and salt.
- Preheat the oven to 200°C/400°F/Gas mark 6.
- Combine the tomato and béchamel sauces. Select a 25 x 35cm/10 x 14in baking dish. Smear a very thin layer of sauce on the bottom of the baking dish. Carefully place a layer of the pasta over the sauce, to cover the entire area.
- Smear a thin layer of sauce over the pasta. Spoon some of the spinach and prawn mixture over it, and sprinkle with some Parmesan. Repeat the process of layering, ending with a layer of pasta, topped with sauce and cheese.
- Bake for about 20 minutes, or until the sauce forms a light golden crust.
- Remove the dish from the oven and leave to stand for 10 minutes before serving.

Four seasons pizza

SERVES 4

INGREDIENTS:

1 large pizza base (ready-made)
175ml/6fl oz tomato sauce
25g/1oz chorizo sausage (sliced thinly)
25g/1oz button mushrooms (wiped with damp kitchen paper and sliced thinly)
50g/2oz artichoke hearts (sliced thinly)
25g/1oz mozzarella (sliced thinly)

3 anchovies (halved lengthways)
2 teaspoons capers, rinsed and drained
4 pitted black olives (sliced)
4 fresh basil leaves (shredded)
Olive oil for drizzling
Salt and pepper

- Preheat the oven to 200°C/400°F/Gas mark 6.
- Place the pizza base on a large, greased baking tray. Spread the tomato sauce over the base, almost to the edge.
- Put the sliced chorizo on one quarter of the pizza, the sliced mushrooms on another, the artichoke hearts on a third, and the mozzarella and anchovies on the fourth.
- Dot all over with the capers, olives and basil leaves. Drizzle with a little olive oil and season. Do not put any salt on the anchovy section.
- Bake in the oven for 18 to 20 minutes, or follow the instructions for the pizza base, until the crust is golden and crisp. Serve immediately.

Kung po chicken

SERVES 4

INGREDIENTS:

250g/9oz chicken meat (boned and skinned)
1/4 teaspoon salt
1/2 egg white
1 teaspoon cornflour
1 medium green pepper (cored and seeded)
4 tablespoons vegetable oil

1 spring onion (cut into short sections)
A few small slices of fresh root ginger
5 dried red chillies (soaked, seeded and shredded)
2 tablespoons yellow bean sauce
1 teaspoon rice wine
100g/4oz roasted cashew nuts
A few drops of sesame oil

- Cut the chicken into small cubes about the size of sugar lumps. Place the chicken in a small bowl and mix with the salt and egg white. Mix a few drops

of water with the cornflour to form a paste, and add to the bowl.
- Cut the green pepper into cubes about the same size as the chicken pieces.
- Heat the oil in a wok, add the chicken, spring onion and ginger and stir-fry for 1 minute, then add the chillies with the yellow bean sauce and wine. Blend well and stir-fry for another minute. Finally stir in the cashew nuts and sesame oil.
- Serve hot with boiled rice.

Hawaiian poke salad

SERVES 4-6

INGREDIENTS:

450g/1lb tuna steaks (cut into small cubes)
1 large onion (finely chopped)
6 spring onions (sliced)

2 small red chillies (cut into fine strips)
75ml/3fl oz soy sauce
1 tablespoon sesame oil
Lettuce leaves for serving

- Put the fish, onion, spring onion, chillies, soy sauce and sesame oil in a bowl.
- Cover and refrigerate for 4 hours.
- Line a serving platter with lettuce leaves. Top with the marinated fish.

Chicken chop suey

SERVES 4

INGREDIENTS:

4 tablespoons soy sauce
2 teaspoons brown sugar
500g/1lb 2oz skinless, boneless chicken breasts
3 tablespoons vegetable oil
2 onions (quartered)

2 garlic cloves (crushed)
350g/12oz beansprouts
3 teaspoons sesame oil
1 tablespoon cornflour
3 tablespoons water
450ml/³/₄pt chicken stock

- Mix the soy sauce and sugar together in a small bowl, stirring until the sugar has dissolved.
- Trim any fat away from the chicken and cut into thin strips. Place the meat in a shallow dish and spoon the soy mixture over it, turning to coat. Marinate in the refrigerator for 20 minutes.
- Heat the oil in a wok and stir-fry the chicken for 2 to 3 minutes, until golden

→

brown. Add the onions and garlic and cook for a further 2 minutes. Add the beansprouts, cook for 4 to 5 minutes, and then add the sesame oil.

- Mix the cornflour and water to form a smooth paste. Pour the stock into the wok, add the cornflour paste and bring to the boil, stirring until the sauce is thickened and clear. Serve hot.

Tangy pork chops

SERVES 4

INGREDIENTS:

1 tablespoon dry mustard
6 tablespoons brown sugar
4 large pork chops

175ml/6fl oz lemon juice
Salt and pepper

- Preheat the oven to 180°C/350°F/Gas mark 4.
- Mix the mustard and sugar and dust over the chops. Pour lemon juice over, cover and cook in the oven for 20 minutes.
- Take the lid off, raise the temperature to 190°C/375°F/Gas mark 5 and cook for a further 20 minutes, or until the chops look browned. Serve hot.

Salmon fishcakes

SERVES 4

INGREDIENTS:

350g/12oz potato
350g/12oz cooked fresh salmon (flaked)
225g/8oz smoked salmon (roughly chopped)
1 tablespoon lemon juice

Freshly ground black pepper
75g/3oz butter (melted)
3 tablespoons chopped fresh dill
2 eggs (beaten)
225g/8oz dried white breadcrumbs
Vegetable oil for frying

- Cut the potatoes into small cubes and boil until tender, then mash. Mix the fresh and smoked salmon in a large bowl with the mashed potato, lemon juice, pepper to taste, butter and dill. Add just enough beaten egg to bind the mixture together so it is firm. Cool, then refrigerate for 1 hour until very firm.
- Shape the mixture into 16 cakes about 2.5cm/1in thick. Brush with some of the remaining beaten egg and coat with breadcrumbs. Chill for 30 minutes until firm.

- Coat the cakes with egg and crumbs once more. Chill again until firm.
- Shallow fry the cakes in batches for 3 to 4 minutes on each side, or until golden brown. Drain on kitchen paper and keep warm in the oven. Serve with chips.

Baked stuffed lobster

SERVES 4

INGREDIENTS:

50ml/2fl oz vegetable oil
1 large onion (finely chopped)
4 garlic cloves (finely chopped)
250ml/9oz tomato purée
150ml/¼ pt red wine
225g/8oz cooked canned clams (with their juice)

450g/1lb dried white breadcrumbs
1½ teaspoons dried oregano
1 teaspoon garlic salt
1 tablespoon grated Parmesan cheese
1 tablespoon chopped parsley
3–4 medium or large lobsters (halved, intestines removed)

- Preheat the oven to 200°C/400°F/Gas mark 6.
- Heat the oil and sauté the onion and garlic in a frying pan over a medium heat for about 5 minutes, or until they are translucent. Add the tomato purée and cook for 3 minutes, then add the wine and the clams and their juice. Cook for 5 minutes.
- In a large mixing bowl, mix together the breadcrumbs, oregano, garlic salt, Parmesan and parsley. Make a well in the middle and pour in the sauce. Stir and mix into a very soft dough. Cover and set aside.
- Place each lobster on a chopping board and stuff carefully with the prepared mixture, making sure the holes are well filled. Push the halves together to encase the stuffing. Repeat the exercise with the remaining lobsters and stuffing.
- Lightly grease a baking tray and place the lobsters on it. Bake in the oven for 45 to 60 minutes, checking halfway through. Serve with crisp green salad.

Chargrilled lemon tuna

SERVES 8

INGREDIENTS:

3 large lemons
2 garlic cloves (crushed)
100ml/3½fl oz olive oil

Freshly ground black pepper
900g/2lb fresh tuna (cut into short strips)

→

←

- Take 2 of the lemons, finely grate the zest from one of them and squeeze the juice from them both. Mix with the garlic and oil and season well with pepper.
- Lay the tuna strips in a shallow dish, pour the marinade over them and turn the tuna to coat. Cover and leave for at least 30 minutes.
- Roll up the tuna strips and thread on a skewer, securing the ends. Repeat until you have 8 skewers with tuna. Cut the remaining lemon into 8 wedges and push one wedge on each skewer. Put in a container, pour the remaining marinade over the top, and chill until needed.
- Put the skewers under a hot grill or on a barbecue and cook for 2 to 3 minutes on each side, brushing with the marinade. Serve hot with rice.

Stuffed cannelloni

SERVES 4-6

INGREDIENTS:

225g/8oz wild mushrooms (wiped with damp kitchen paper)
50g/2oz butter
1 small onion (finely chopped)
3 boneless chicken breasts (minced)
50g/2oz ham (thinly sliced)
Salt and pepper

1 egg (beaten)
1 egg yolk (beaten)
225ml/8fl oz béchamel
225g/8oz dried cannelloni
225ml/8fl oz tomato sauce
25g/1oz grated Parmesan cheese

- Slice the mushrooms thinly, and then chop finely.
- Melt the butter in a frying pan. Add the onion and sauté gently until wilted.
- Add the mushrooms, minced chicken, ham, salt and pepper. Sauté gently until the chicken is lightly coloured, stirring frequently, for about 5 minutes. Remove from the heat and allow to cool.
- Preheat the oven to 200°C/400°F/Gas mark 6.
- Blend the egg and egg yolk and 3 tablespoons of béchamel sauce with the chicken mixture.
- Half-cook the pasta in plenty of boiling salted water. Leave to cool on damp tea towels and pat dry.
- Smear 2 to 3 tablespoons of tomato sauce on the base of a baking dish. Roll 1 to 2 tablespoons of filling into tubes with the cannelloni. Repeat and place all stuffed tubes side by side in the dish.
- Spoon the remaining tomato sauce over the cannelloni and spoon the béchamel over that. Sprinkle with Parmesan.
- Bake the cannelloni in the middle of the oven for about 15 minutes, or until bubbly and golden. Allow to settle for 10 minutes before serving.

Chicken korma with green beans

SERVES 4

INGREDIENTS:

2 tablespoons vegetable oil
350g/12oz chicken breasts (skinless, boneless, cut into bite-size pieces)
1 onion (sliced)
2½ teaspoons korma curry powder
150ml/¼pt chicken stock
1 teaspoon tomato purée

2 teaspoons caster sugar
75g/3oz tomatoes (roughly chopped)
150ml/¼pt pint single cream
Salt
100g/4oz green beans (topped and tailed, cut into 2.5cm/1in lengths)
25g/1oz ground almonds

- Heat the oil in a saucepan, add the chicken and onion, and fry over a gentle heat, stirring occasionally for 6 minutes, or until the onion is soft and the chicken is lightly coloured. Stir in the curry powder and cook for a further 2 minutes.
- Add the stock, tomato purée, sugar, tomatoes, cream and a little salt. Stir to combine the ingredients, bring to the boil, then reduce the heat, cover the pan and simmer gently for 10 minutes, stirring occasionally.
- Stir the beans into the curry and cook, covered, for a further 15 to 20 minutes, stirring occasionally, until the chicken is cooked and the beans are tender. Stir the ground almonds into the curry and simmer for 1 minute to thicken the sauce. Taste and adjust the seasoning if necessary. Serve with rice.

Prawn gumbo

SERVES 4

INGREDIENTS:

900g/2lb raw prawns in their shells
50ml/2fl oz vegetable oil
6 rashers bacon (finely chopped)
2½ tablespoons flour
2 tablespoons vegetable oil (extra)
2 onions (finely chopped)
½ teaspoon cayenne pepper

1 red pepper (chopped)
1 green pepper (chopped)
16 okra (trimmed, halved lengthways)
1 bay leaf
850g/1¾lb canned tomatoes
Salt and pepper
1 teaspoon Tabasco sauce

→

- Peel the prawns, leaving the tails intact. Gently pull out the dark vein from each prawn back, starting at the head end. Cover and set aside.
- Heat the oil in a large saucepan, add the bacon and cook over a medium heat for 5 minutes. Stir in the flour and cook, stirring, until the flour turns nutty brown. Remove from the saucepan. This mixture will be used to thicken and flavour the gumbo.
- Heat the extra oil in the saucepan, add the onion, cayenne and peppers and cook, stirring, over a medium heat for 5 minutes, or until the onion is golden brown.
- Add the okra, bay leaf and tomatoes to the saucepan and bring to the boil.
- Reduce the heat and simmer for 30 minutes. You may need to add water if the mixture is too thick.
- Stir the prawns and the roux into the mixture and season to taste with salt and pepper and Tabasco sauce. Cook for 5 minutes, or until the prawns are cooked.

Pork with apples

SERVES 4

INGREDIENTS:

500g/1lb 2oz lean pork fillet
2 teaspoons sunflower oil
150ml/¼pt vegetable stock
150ml/¼pt dry rosé wine
1 tablespoon chopped thyme
1 tablespoon clear honey
2 green dessert apples (cored, sliced
and tossed in 1 tablespoon lemon juice)
175g/6oz fresh blackberries
Salt and pepper
2 teaspoons cornflour
4 teaspoons lemon juice

- Trim away any fat and silvery skin from the pork fillet and cut into 1cm/½in thick slices.
- Heat the oil in a non-stick frying pan, add the pork slices and fry for 4 to 5 minutes until browned all over. Using a slotted spoon, remove the pork and drain on kitchen paper. Reserve the pan juices.
- Pour the stock and wine into the pan with the juices and add the thyme and honey. Mix well, bring to a simmer and add the pork and apples. Continue to simmer, uncovered, for 5 minutes.
- Add the blackberries, season to taste and simmer for a further 5 minutes. Mix the cornflour with the lemon juice and add to the pan – stir until the sauce is thickened. Serve with boiled potatoes.

Warm chicken & feta salad

SERVES 4

INGREDIENTS:

4 boneless, skinless chicken breasts
4 garlic cloves (peeled)
2 tablespoons olive oil
3 tablespoons lemon juice
1 medium onion (cut into wedges)
175g/6oz French beans

Assorted salad leaves
200g/7oz feta cheese (cubed)
175g/6oz cherry tomatoes (halved)
50g/2oz black olives
1 red pepper (sliced)

- Place the chicken breasts in a shallow dish. Crush 1 of the garlic cloves and blend with 1 tablespoon olive oil and all the lemon juice. Pour over the chicken, cover and leave in the refrigerator for at least 30 minutes, turning at least once.
- Heat a frying pan until smoking hot. Drain the chicken and cook for 6 to 8 minutes on each side. Remove and allow to stand for 5 minutes.
- Heat the remaining oil in a heavy-based frying pan and sauté the rest of the garlic with the onion wedges. Cook, stirring occasionally, for 8 to 10 minutes.
- Cook the French beans in a pan of lightly salted water for 5 minutes. Drain and reserve.
- Arrange the salad leaves in a serving bowl with the feta cheese, cherry tomatoes, beans, black olives and red pepper. Place the onion mixture on top of the salad leaves, then add the chicken and serve drizzled with olive oil.

Chicken hotpot

SERVES 4-6

INGREDIENTS:

175g/6oz dried haricot beans
3 chicken legs
1 tablespoon vegetable oil
350g/12oz lean pork (diced)
1 small carrot (chopped)
1 onion (chopped)
2.4 litres/4pt water
1 garlic clove (crushed)
2 tablespoons tomato purée

1 bay leaf
2 chicken stock cubes
350g/12oz new potatoes (cubed)
2 teaspoons chilli sauce
2 tablespoons white wine vinegar
3 firm tomatoes (chopped)
225g/8oz Chinese leaves (shredded)
Salt and pepper

→

←

- Put the haricot beans in a bowl, cover with plenty of cold water and set aside to soak for 8 hours.
- Separate the chicken drumsticks from the thighs. Chop off the narrow end of each drumstick and discard.
- Heat the vegetable oil in a preheated wok, add the chicken, pork, carrot and onion, and then brown evenly.
- Drain the haricot beans and add to the wok with the water, garlic, tomato purée and bay leaf and stir to mix. Bring to the boil, lower the heat and simmer for 2 hours until the beans are almost tender.
- Crumble the chicken stock cubes into the wok, add the new potatoes and the chilli sauce, and then simmer for 15 to 20 minutes until the potatoes are cooked.
- Add the vinegar, tomatoes and Chinese leaves to the wok, then simmer for 1 to 2 minutes. Season to taste. Serve with rice.

Cantonese fried noodles

SERVES 4

INGREDIENTS:

350g/12oz egg noodles
3 tablespoons vegetable oil
700g/1½lb lean beef steaks (cut into thin strips)
150g/5oz green cabbage (shredded)
75g/3oz bamboo shoots
6 spring onions (sliced)

25g/1oz green beans (halved)
1 tablespoon soy sauce
2 tablespoons beef stock
1 tablespoon dry sherry
1 tablespoon brown sugar
2 tablespoons chopped fresh parsley

- Cook the noodles in a saucepan of boiling water for 2 to 3 minutes. Drain well, rinse under cold running water and drain thoroughly again.
- Heat 1 tablespoon of the oil in a preheated wok or frying pan until it is really hot. Add the noodles and stir-fry for 1 to 2 minutes. Drain the noodles and set aside until required.
- Heat the remaining oil in the wok. Add the beef and stir-fry for 2 to 3 minutes.
- Add the cabbage, bamboo shoots, spring onions and beans to the wok and stir-fry for 1 to 2 minutes.
- Add the soy sauce, beef stock, dry sherry and brown sugar to the wok, stirring well.
- Stir the noodles into the mixture in the wok, tossing to mix well. Transfer to serving bowls, garnish with parsley and serve immediately.

Roast monkfish

SERVES 4

INGREDIENTS:

2 lemons
Salt and pepper
Olive oil

2 rosemary sprigs
2 monkfish tails
8 anchovy fillets

- Preheat the oven to 220°C/425°F/Gas mark 7.
- Slice one lemon finely. Season and drizzle with oil.
- Heat an ovenproof tray and drizzle with olive oil. Place the rosemary sprigs on the tray and place the monkfish on top. Cover with lemon slices and the anchovies.
- Season with salt and pepper.
- Roast in the oven until cooked. To test, pierce with a pointed knife; the juices should be opaque. This should take about 20 to 30 minutes. Serve with lemon wedges.

Danish beef stew

SERVES 4

INGREDIENTS:

450g/1lb chuck steak
700g/1½lb potatoes
50g/2oz butter (plus extra to serve)
1 large onion (chopped)
600ml/1pt water

Salt and pepper
3 bay leaves
6 peppercorns
3 tablespoons chopped spring onions

- Cut the steak into 2.5cm/1in cubes. Peel the potatoes and cut into 2.5cm/1in cubes.
- Melt the butter in a large pan and add the chopped onion and meat. Cook gently, stirring, until the onion is tender but not browned.
- Add the water, a pinch of salt, bay leaves and peppercorns. Bring to the boil, cover and simmer for 1½ hours. Add the potatoes and continue simmering, half-covered, for a further 45 minutes, stirring, until the potatoes disintegrate to thicken the stew.
- Remove from the heat, sprinkle with the spring onions and season well. Serve with rye bread.

Moules marinière

SERVES 4

INGREDIENTS:

1.1kg/2½lb mussels
1 onion (finely chopped)
1 tablespoon olive oil
1 garlic clove (crushed)
200ml/7fl oz dry white wine

1 bay leaf
1 tablespoon fresh thyme leaves
2 tablespoons chopped fresh parsley
Salt and pepper

- Rinse the mussels well in cold water and scrape off any barnacles with a small, sharp knife. Discard any mussels that are open or do not close when tapped sharply against the work surface.
- In a deep, lidded saucepan, sweat the onion in the oil until softened. Add the garlic and stir for 1 minute, then add the wine, bay leaf, thyme and drained mussels. Stir well, cover tightly and cook rapidly for 5 to 10 minutes, or until the mussels have opened. Discard any that remain closed.
- Remove from the heat and add the parsley and seasoning.

Caesar salad

SERVES 4

INGREDIENTS:

4 thick slices white bread (crusts removed and cut into cubes)
3 rashers smoked bacon (chopped)
1 cos lettuce (leaves torn into pieces)
50g/2oz Parmesan cheese (grated, plus extra to garnish)

For the dressing:
4 anchovies in oil (drained)
1 egg
2 tablespoons lemon juice
1 garlic clove (crushed)
125ml/4fl oz olive oil
Salt and pepper

- Preheat the oven to 190°C/375°F/Gas mark 5.
- Spread the bread on a baking tray and bake for 15 minutes, until golden.
- Cook the bacon in a frying pan over a medium heat until it is crisp. Drain on kitchen paper.
- Put the lettuce leaves in a serving bowl with the bread cubes, bacon and Parmesan cheese.

- For the dressing, process the anchovies, egg, lemon juice and garlic in a blender or food processor for 20 seconds, or until smooth. With the blender still rotating, add the olive oil in a thin stream until the dressing is thick and creamy. Season with salt and pepper and drizzle over the salad. Sprinkle with extra Parmesan and serve immediately.

Salmon & asparagus linguine

SERVES 4

INGREDIENTS:

150g/5oz asparagus (cut into 5cm/2in lengths)
2 eggs
Juice of ½ lemon
Salt and pepper

2 tablespoons chopped fresh dill
275g/10oz fresh linguine
175g/6oz smoked salmon trimmings (cut into strips)

- Cook the asparagus in boiling salted water for 2 to 5 minutes, or until just tender. Remove with a slotted spoon and drain on kitchen paper, keeping the water hot in the pan.
- Break the eggs into a round-bottomed bowl and add the lemon juice. Set the bowl over a separate pan of hot water, making sure the bottom of the bowl does not touch the water. Whisk the eggs until warmed, pale and very frothy. Season and stir in half the dill, then remove the bowl from the pan and set aside in a warm place.
- Top up the asparagus water with boiling water and bring back to the boil, then add the linguine. Boil for 7 to 8 minutes.
- Drain the linguine, reserving the water, and then return the linguine to the pan.
- Add the asparagus and salmon with 1 ladleful of the water and the lemon sauce.
- Toss and add more water if necessary.
- Season with the rest of the dill and serve immediately.

Meatloaf

SERVES 4

INGREDIENTS:

25g/1oz butter
450g/1lb minced beef
1 onion (chopped)
2 garlic cloves (crushed)
50g/2oz bulgur wheat (soaked)
25g/1oz Parmesan cheese
1 celery stick (trimmed and sliced)
2 tablespoons horseradish sauce

2 tablespoons tomato purée
2 tablespoons instant oatmeal
1 tablespoon chopped fresh thyme

For the relish:
2 tablespoons horseradish sauce
150ml/¼pt soured cream

- Grease and line the base of a 700g/1½lb loaf tin. Preheat the oven to 180°C/350°F/Gas mark 4.
- Melt the butter in a large pan and add the minced beef, onion and garlic. Cook for 7 minutes until brown and sealed.
- Place the mixture in a bowl and add the remaining ingredients. Mix well, season and spoon into the prepared tin. Cover with aluminium foil.
- Stand the loaf tin in a roasting tin and add 2.5cm/1in of water. Cook in the preheated oven for 1½ hours.
- Mix together the relish ingredients in a mixing bowl. Turn out the meatloaf and garnish with fresh thyme. Serve with fresh vegetables and relish.

Prawn jambalaya

SERVES 6

INGREDIENTS:

900g/2lb raw large prawns in their shells
2 onions (chopped)
2 celery sticks (chopped)
225ml/8fl oz dry white wine
1.2 litres/2pt water
50ml/2fl oz vegetable oil
200g/7oz spicy sausage (chopped)

1 red pepper (chopped)
400g/14oz canned chopped tomatoes
½ teaspoon cayenne pepper
½ teaspoon cracked black pepper
¼ teaspoon dried thyme
¼ teaspoon dried oregano
400g/14oz long-grain rice

- Peel the prawns and pull out the dark vein from each prawn back, starting at the head end. Reserve the shells. Refrigerate the prawn meat. Put the heads, shells and tails in a pan with 1 chopped onion, 1 chopped celery stick, the wine and the water. Bring to the boil, then reduce the heat and simmer for 20 minutes. Strain.
- Heat the oil in a large, heavy-based pan and cook the chopped sausage for 5 minutes, or until browned. Remove from the pan with a slotted spoon and set aside.
- Add the rest of the onion, celery and the red pepper to the pan and cook, stirring occasionally, for 5 minutes. Add the tomato, cayenne, black pepper and dried herbs and bring to the boil. Reduce the heat and simmer, covered, for 10 minutes.
- Return the sausage to the pan and add the rice and prawn stock. Bring back to the boil, reduce the heat and simmer, covered, for 25 minutes, until almost all the liquid has been absorbed and the rice is tender.
- Add the prawn meat to the pan and stir through gently. Cover and cook for another 5 minutes. Serve immediately.

Surf & turf

SERVES 4

INGREDIENTS:

For the patties:
225g/8oz minced beef
100g/4oz fresh wholemeal breadcrumbs
4 spring onions (sliced)
1 garlic clove (crushed)
1 teaspoon chilli powder
2 tablespoons oil
Salt and pepper

For the sauce:
25g/1oz plain flour
150ml/¼pt dry white wine
50ml/2fl oz vegetable stock
125ml/4fl oz double cream
100g/4oz tiger prawns in their shells

For the croûtes:
4 slices white bread
25g/1oz butter

- For the patties, mix the minced beef with the breadcrumbs, spring onions, garlic and chilli powder. Season well and form into four equal rounds.
- Heat the oil in a frying pan and cook the patties for about 7 minutes, turning them frequently. Remove the patties from the frying pan and keep to one side.
- For the sauce, add the flour to the frying pan and cook for 1 minute. Gradually pour in the wine, stock and cream, then add the prawns. Cook for 5 more minutes, stirring all the time.
- For the croûtes, stamp out 4 x 10cm/4in rounds from the sliced bread. Melt the butter in a frying pan and add the bread. Cook for 2 to 3 minutes, turning once. Remove and reserve. Place the patties on the croûtes and spoon the sauce on top.

Bratwurst in ale

SERVES 4-6

INGREDIENTS:

1.2 litres/2pt water
850g/1³/₄lb bratwurst
75g/3oz butter
2 bay leaves
450ml/³/₄pt light ale

1 large onion (peeled and chopped)
25g/1oz plain flour
Salt and pepper
Chopped fresh parsley

- Bring the water to the boil in a large saucepan. Prick the bratwurst all over and carefully lower it into the boiling water. Boil over a medium heat for about 5 to 7 minutes. Drain off the water and discard.
- Add half the butter to the sausage, increase the heat and brown the outside very quickly all over. Lower the heat and add the bay leaves and half the ale.
- Cover and simmer until the ale has reduced by half.
- In a frying pan, melt the remaining butter, fry the chopped onion until golden, then stir in the flour and continue stirring and cooking until the mixture turns light brown. Quickly blend in the remaining ale, stirring all the time, to form a light and creamy smooth sauce. Season with salt and pepper and add to the sausage mixture.
- Stir well to ensure the sausage is well coated with the sauce. Simmer on low heat until the sausage is cooked and the sauce thickens. Garnish with parsley and serve with cabbage and potatoes.

Mackerel in mustard sauce

SERVES 6

INGREDIENTS:

900ml/1¹/₂pt water
6 fresh mackerel (heads removed,
gutted and cleaned)
1 teaspoon salt

For the sauce:
2 egg yolks
1 teaspoon French mustard
2 teaspoons dried mixed herbs
175g/6oz butter

- To make the sauce, whisk the egg yolks in a bowl with the mustard and herbs.
- Bring the butter to the boil in a small pan and pour in onto the egg yolks, whisking continuously until the sauce thickens. Keep warm in a covered bowl.

- Bring the water to the boil and add the mackerel and the salt. Bring back to boiling point, cover and remove from the heat. After about 5 to 8 minutes, check to see if the mackeral is cooked. When it is, carefully remove it from the water, lift the fillet off the bone and place on a serving plate. Coat with the sauce.
- Serve with new potatoes.

Special fried rice

SERVES 4

INGREDIENTS:

50g/2oz peeled and cooked prawns
50g/2oz cooked ham
3 eggs
1 teaspoon salt
2 spring onions (finely chopped)

4 tablespoons vegetable oil
100g/4oz green peas
1 tablespoon soy sauce
1 tablespoon dry sherry
450g/1lb cooked rice

- Pat dry the prawns with kitchen paper. Dice the ham into small pieces, about the same size as peas.
- In a bowl, lightly beat the eggs with a pinch of salt and a few pieces of spring onion.
- Heat about half of the oil in a preheated wok, stir-fry the peas, prawns and ham for 1 minute, then add the soy sauce and sherry. Remove and keep warm.
- Heat the remaining oil in the wok and lightly scramble the eggs. Add the rice and stir to make sure that the grains are separated. Add the remaining salt and spring onions and the prawn mixture. Blend well and serve either hot or cold.

Dressed crab

SERVES 2

INGREDIENTS:

Shell and meat from 1 medium crab
Salt and pepper
1 tablespoon lemon juice

2 tablespoons fresh white breadcrumbs
1 egg (hard-boiled)
1 tablespoon chopped fresh parsley

- Using 2 forks, flake all the white meat from the crab, removing any shell or membrane. Season, adding about 1 teaspoon lemon juice.
- Pound the brown meat of the crab thoroughly and work in the breadcrumbs

→

←

- with the remaining lemon juice and seasoning.
- Using a spoon, put the white meat in both ends of the crab's empty shell, making sure it is well piled up with the inside edges kept neat. Then spoon the brown meat in a neat line down the centre, between the two sections of white crabmeat.
- Hold a blunt knife between the white and brown crabmeat and carefully spoon lines of parsley, sieved egg yolk and chopped egg white across the crab, moving the knife as you go to keep a neat edge. Serve on a bed of lettuce.

Lamb korma

SERVES 4

INGREDIENTS:

700g/1¹/₂lb boned leg of lamb (cubed)
¹/₂ teaspoon saffron threads
150ml/¹/₄pt natural yogurt
1 teaspoon salt
2 tablespoons ghee
¹/₄ teaspoon ground cardamom
¹/₂ teaspoon ground cinnamon
1¹/₂ teaspoons ground cumin
1¹/₂ teaspoons ground coriander
225ml/8fl oz coconut milk
2 tablespoons chopped fresh coriander
¹/₂ teaspoon caster sugar

For the blended mixture:
2 onions (chopped)
3 garlic cloves (chopped)
2.5cm/1in piece of fresh root ginger (chopped)
2 green chillies (deseeded and chopped)
50g/2oz ground almonds
150ml/¹/₄pt water

- Place the lamb in a bowl. Infuse the saffron in 2 tablespoons of boiling water for 10 minutes. Mix together the yogurt, saffron and its water and the salt. Pour over the lamb, cover and leave to marinate for 2 hours.
- Place the ingredients for the blended mixture in a blender or food processor and blend to produce a thick paste. Set aside.
- Heat the ghee in a saucepan, add the cardamom, cinnamon, cumin and coriander, and cook over a gentle heat for 1 minute. Stir in the blended mixture and cook, stirring frequently, for a further 5 minutes.
- Add the coconut milk, lamb and saffron yogurt, bring to the boil, then lower the heat. Cover the pan and cook very gently, stirring occasionally, for 45 minutes or until the lamb is tender and the sauce is thick.
- Stir in the coriander and sugar and serve hot.

Cannelloni

SERVES 4

INGREDIENTS:

8 cannelloni tubes
100g/4oz spinach

For the filling:
1 tablespoon oil
175g/6oz minced beef
2 garlic cloves (crushed)
25g/1oz plain flour
125ml/4 fl oz beef stock

1 small carrot (finely chopped)
1 small yellow courgette (chopped)
Salt and pepper

For the sauce:
25g/1oz butter
25g/1oz plain flour
225ml/8fl oz milk
50g/2oz Parmesan cheese (grated)

- Preheat the oven to 180°C/350°F/Gas mark 4.
- For the filling, heat the oil in a large pan. Add the minced beef and garlic. Cook for 5 minutes.
- Add the flour and cook for a further 1 minute. Slowly stir in the stock and bring to the boil.
- Add the carrot and courgette, season well and cook for 10 minutes.
- Spoon the mince mixture into the cannelloni tubes and place in an ovenproof dish.
- Blanch the spinach in boiling water for 3 minutes. Drain well and place on top of the cannelloni tubes.
- For the sauce, melt the butter in a pan. Add the flour and cook for 1 minute.
- Pour in the milk, add the grated cheese and season well. Bring to the boil, stirring all the time. Pour over the cannelloni and spinach and cook for 30 minutes in the preheated oven. Serve with tomatoes and a crisp green salad.

Lancashire hotpot

SERVES 6

INGREDIENTS:

12 lamb cutlets
6 lamb's kidneys (halved)
50g/2oz butter (melted)
1.1kg/2½lb potatoes (thinly sliced)
3 large onions (sliced)

225g/8oz flat-cap mushrooms (thickly sliced)
Salt and pepper
300ml/½pt water

→

←
- Preheat the oven to 220°C/425°F/Gas mark 7.
- Brown the cutlets and kidneys in a pan, using half the butter, over a high heat.
- Layer the potatoes, cutlets, kidneys, onions and mushrooms in a deep casserole, seasoning well between each layer. End with a layer of potatoes, neatly overlapping and covering the surface of the dish.
- Pour the water over. Brush the remaining butter over the top layer of potatoes and season well.
- Cover the casserole dish and place in the oven. Give it 20 to 25 minutes to heat through, then reduce the oven temperature to 150°C/300°F/Gas mark 2 and leave to cook for a further 2 hours.
- Remove the lid, raise the oven temperature back to 220°C/425°F/Gas mark 7 and cook for a final 20 to 30 minutes until the top layer of potato is browned.

Indian lamb stew

SERVES 4

INGREDIENTS:

3 tablespoons oil
450g/1lb lamb (cubed)
200ml/7fl oz coconut milk
3 onions (finely chopped)
3 tomatoes (chopped)
6 green chillies (deseeded and slit lengthways)
1/2 teaspoon salt
Juice of 1 lime
1 tablespoon fresh coriander leaves

For the spice paste:
10 garlic cloves
20 peppercorns
2 cinnamon sticks (about 5cm/2in each)
1 tablespoon freshly grated coconut
1 tablespoon coriander seeds
1/4 teaspoon poppy seeds
A pinch of ground cumin

- Place all the ingredients for the spice paste in a blender or food processor and blend for 2 to 3 minutes to make a fine paste. Set aside.
- Heat 1 tablespoon of the oil in a large pan. Add the lamb and stir-fry for 2 to 3 minutes. Stir in the spice paste, then add the coconut milk, two-thirds of the onions, the tomatoes, green chillies and salt. Mix well and simmer for 20 minutes, stirring frequently, until the lamb is cooked through.
- Add the lime juice and coriander leaves to the lamb and mix well. Return the mixture to the boil, simmer for 2 minutes, then remove the pan from the heat.
- In a frying pan, heat the remaining 2 tablespoons of oil and fry the rest of the onion until golden brown. Pour the contents of the frying pan into the lamb stew and stir through. Serve hot.

Chinese-style chicken

SERVES 4

INGREDIENTS:

¹/₂ cucumber (peeled and cut into matchsticks)
1 teaspoon salt
4 boneless chicken breasts
4 tablespoons soy sauce
Pinch of Chinese five-spice powder
1 tablespoon lemon juice
3 tablespoons sunflower oil
2 tablespoons sesame oil
1 tablespoon sesame seeds
2 tablespoons dry sherry

2 carrots (cut into matchsticks)
8 spring onions (shredded)
75g/3oz beansprouts

For the sauce:
4 tablespoons crunchy peanut butter
2 teaspoons lemon juice
2 teaspoons sesame oil
¹/₄ teaspoon hot chilli powder
1 spring onion (finely chopped)

- Place the cucumber matchsticks in a colander, sprinkle with the salt and cover with a plate with a weight on top. Set the colander in a bowl or on a deep plate to catch the drips and leave to drain for 30 minutes.
- Put the chicken portions into a large pan and just cover with water. Add 1 tablespoon of the soy sauce, the five-spice powder and lemon juice, cover and bring to the boil, then simmer for about 20 minutes.
- Lift out the poached chicken with a slotted spoon and leave until cool enough to handle. Remove and discard the skins and bash the chicken lightly with a rolling pin to loosen the fibres. Slice into thin strips and reserve.
- Heat the oils in a large frying pan or wok. Add the sesame seeds, fry for 30 seconds and then stir in the remaining 3 tablespoons of soy sauce and the sherry.
- Add the carrots and stir-fry for 2 to 3 minutes, until just tender. Remove from the heat and reserve.
- Rinse the cucumber well, pat dry with kitchen paper and place in a bowl. Add the spring onions, beansprouts, cooked carrots, pan juices and shredded chicken, and mix together. Transfer to a shallow dish. Cover and chill for about 1 hour, turning the mixture in the juices once or twice.
- To make the sauce, cream the peanut butter with the lemon juice, sesame oil and chilli powder, adding a little hot water to form a paste, then stir in the spring onion.
- Arrange the chicken mixture on a serving dish and serve with the peanut sauce.

Cajun chicken jambalaya

SERVES 4

INGREDIENTS:

1.4kg/2¹/₂lb fresh chicken
600ml/1pt water
1¹/₂ onions
1 bay leaf
4 black peppercorns
1 parsley sprig
2 tablespoons vegetable oil
2 garlic cloves (chopped)
1 green pepper (seeded and chopped)
1 celery stick (chopped)
225g/8oz long grain rice

100g/4oz chorizo sausage (chopped)
100g/4oz cooked ham (chopped)
400g/14oz canned chopped tomatoes
¹/₂ teaspoon hot chilli powder
¹/₂ teaspoon cumin seeds
¹/₂ teaspoon ground cumin
1 teaspoon dried thyme
100g/4oz cooked, peeled prawns
Dash of Tabasco sauce
Chopped fresh parsley, to garnish

- Place the chicken in a large flameproof casserole dish and pour over the water.
- Add the onion half, bay leaf, peppercorns and parsley sprig, and bring to the boil.
- Cover and simmer gently for about 1¹/₂ hours.
- When the chicken is cooked, lift it out of the stock, remove the skin and carcass and chop the meat. Strain the stock, leave to cool and reserve.
- Chop the remaining onion and heat the oil in a large frying pan. Add the onion, garlic, green pepper and celery. Fry for about 5 minutes, then stir in the rice, coating the grains with the oil. Add the sausage, ham and chopped chicken and fry for a further 2 to 3 minutes, stirring frequently.
- Pour in the tomatoes and 300ml/¹/₂pt of the reserved stock and add the chilli, cumin and thyme. Bring to the boil, then cover and simmer gently for 20 minutes, or until the rice is tender and the liquid absorbed.
- Stir in the prawns and Tabasco. Cook for a further 5 minutes, then season well and serve hot, garnished with chopped parsley.

Dover sole with capers

SERVES 4

INGREDIENTS:

Salt and pepper
Olive oil
4 Dover sole, skin removed

2 tablespoons capers, rinsed and drained
2 tablespoons finely chopped marjoram
2 lemons (cut into wedges)

- Preheat the oven to 220°C/425°F/Gas mark 7.
- Heat 2 flat oven trays, scatter them with salt and pepper and drizzle with the olive oil.
- Place the Dover sole on the trays.
- Scatter over the capers and marjoram, season and drizzle with olive oil.
- Put the trays in the oven and roast the fish for 10 to 15 minutes or until the flesh comes away easily from the bone when tested with a knife. Serve with lemon wedges.

Kleftiko

SERVES 4

INGREDIENTS:

4 lamb shanks
Salt and pepper
5 tablespoons olive oil
450g/1lb onions (thinly sliced)
4 garlic cloves (crushed and chopped)

300ml/^{1}/$_2$pt dry white wine
450g/1lb canned chopped plum tomatoes
1 bay leaf
1 teaspoon dried oregano

- Rub the lamb shanks with salt and pepper, then brown them all over in a frying pan in 3 tablespoons of the olive oil. Put into a casserole dish with a tight-fitting lid.
- Add some more olive oil to the frying pan and, over a low heat, sweat the onions until soft and translucent. Add the garlic and fry for 2 minutes, then transfer to the casserole dish, distributing around the shanks.
- Over a high heat, deglaze the pan with the wine, stirring and scraping, then pour over the lamb. Add the tomatoes with their liquid, the bay leaf and oregano.
- Bring to the boil, put on the lid and lower the heat to summer. After 1^1/$_2$ hours, test that the meat is done. If not, continue cooking until it is tender.
- Remove the shanks and keep warm on serving plates. Discard the bay leaf and transfer the tomato and onion mixture to a blender or food processor. Blitz briefly and pass through a sieve. Spoon the sauce around the shanks and serve.

Tuna with pak choi

SERVES 4

INGREDIENTS:

4 pieces of tuna fillet (each weighing 150–175g/5–6oz)
3 red chillies (thinly sliced)
2 garlic cloves (thinly sliced)
225ml/8fl oz red wine

Salt and pepper
1 tablespoon olive oil
300g/11oz pak choi (coarsely chopped)
100g/4oz button mushrooms (wiped with damp kitchen paper and halved)

- Place the pieces of tuna in a single layer on a non-metallic dish. Sprinkle the chillies and garlic over the tuna and pour over the wine. Cover and marinate in the refrigerator for 1 hour.
- Heat a ridged cast iron griddle pan until very hot. Lift the tuna out of the marinade, drain on kitchen paper and season with a little salt.
- Pour the marinade into a small pan, add salt and pepper to taste, then simmer for a few minutes until reduced by about half. Remove from the heat, cover and keep warm.
- Dip a wad of kitchen paper in oil and wipe it over the hot griddle pan. Place the tuna on the pan and chargrill it for 3 to 4 minutes.
- Heat the remaining oil in a wok or large, deep frying pan until very hot. Add the pak choi and mushrooms and stir-fry over a high heat for about 3 minutes. Season.
- To serve, cut the tuna fillets in half, mound the vegetables on warm plates and top with tuna and marinade. Serve hot.

Roast pork with sage

SERVES 4

INGREDIENTS:

50ml/2fl oz olive oil
25g/1oz butter
1 onion (finely chopped)
100g/4oz fresh white breadcrumbs
2 teaspoons chopped fresh sage
1 tablespoon chopped fresh parsley
2 teaspoons grated lemon zest
2½ tablespoons salted capers, rinsed

1 egg (beaten)
2 large pork fillets
8 large thin slices of streaky bacon
2 teaspoons plain flour
100ml/3½fl oz dry vermouth
300ml/½pt chicken stock
8 whole sage leaves

- Preheat the oven to 170°C/325°F/Gas mark 3.
- Heat 1 tablespoon oil and the butter in a frying pan, add the onion and cook for 5 minutes, or until lightly golden.
- For the stuffing, place the breadcrumbs, sage, parsley, lemon zest, ½ tablespoon capers and the cooked onion in a bowl. Add the egg and season well.
- Split each pork fillet in half lengthways and open out. Spread the stuffing down the length of one and cover with the other fillet.
- Stretch the bacon with the back of a knife and wrap each piece, slightly overlapping, around the pork to form a neat parcel. Tie with string at intervals. Place the pork in a baking dish and drizzle with 1 tablespoon oil. Bake for 1 hour.
- To test if the meat is cooked, insert a skewer in the thickest part. The juices should run clear. Remove the meat from the dish, cover with aluminium foil and leave to rest. Place the baking dish on the stove, add the flour and stir in well.
- Add the vermouth and allow to bubble for 1 minute. Add the stock and stir while cooking to remove all the lumps. Simmer for 5 minutes. Add the remaining capers to the sauce.
- In a small saucepan, heat the remaining oil and when very hot, fry the whole sage leaves until crisp. Drain on kitchen paper.
- Slice the pork into 1cm/½in slices. Spoon a little sauce over the pork and serve each portion with fried sage leaves on top.

Salad Niçoise

SERVES 4-6

INGREDIENTS:

4 eggs
450g/1lb baby new potatoes
225g/8oz green beans (topped and tailed)
6 artichoke hearts in oil (drained)
350g/12oz mixed salad leaves
4 tomatoes (cut into wedges)
400g/14oz canned tuna (drained and separated into chunks)
1 red pepper (cut into strips)
1 tablespoon capers, rinsed and drained

10 black olives
1 tablespoon chopped fresh tarragon

For the dressing:
1 garlic clove (crushed)
3 teaspoons Dijon mustard
2 anchovy fillets in oil (drained and finely chopped)
50ml/2fl oz white wine vinegar
125ml/4fl oz olive oil
Salt and pepper

- Fill a pan with cold water and gently add the eggs. Bring to the boil, then reduce the heat and simmer for 6 minutes. Drain and plunge the eggs in cold water to stop the cooking process. Peel and cut into wedges.
- Steam or boil the potatoes for 10 minutes. Drain, cool and cut into thick slices.

→

←

- Place the beans in a pan of boiling water, return to the boil for 2 minutes, then drain and rinse under cold water. Chill in a bowl of iced water. Halve or quarter the artichokes.
- Arrange the salad leaves on a serving platter or individual plates. Top with the potato, beans, tomato, artichoke, tuna, egg and red pepper. Sprinkle with the capers and olives.
- For the dressing, use a blender or food processor or whisk to mix the garlic, mustard, anchovies and vinegar until smooth. Gradually add the oil and blend until smooth. Season with salt and pepper and drizzle over the salad. Sprinkle with tarragon.

Tuscan chicken

SERVES 4

INGREDIENTS:

8 chicken thighs (skinned)
1 teaspoon olive oil
1 medium onion (sliced thinly)
2 red peppers (seeded and sliced)
1 garlic clove (crushed)
300ml/½pt puréed tomatoes

150ml/¼pt dry white wine
1 teaspoon dried oregano
400g/14oz canned cannellini beans
(drained)
3 tablespoons fresh breadcrumbs
Salt and pepper

- Cook the chicken in the oil in a heavy-based pan until golden brown. Remove and keep hot. Add the onion and peppers to the pan and gently sauté until softened but not brown. Stir in the garlic.
- Add the chicken, tomatoes, wine and oregano. Season well, bring to a boil, then cover the pan tightly.
- Lower the heat and simmer gently, stirring occasionally for 30 to 35 minutes or until the chicken is tender and the juices run clear.
- Stir in the cannellini beans and simmer for 5 minutes more, until heated through. Sprinkle with the breadcrumbs and cook under a grill until golden brown.

Glazed gammon

SERVES 8

INGREDIENTS:

1.4kg/3lb unsmoked gammon knuckle
end on the bone
1 teaspoon Dijon mustard

50g/2oz breadcrumbs
25g/1oz demerara sugar
75ml/3fl oz apple juice

- Preheat the oven to 160°C/325°F/Gas mark 3.
- Wrap the joint in aluminium foil, place in a roasting tin and cook for 3 hours, or until the juices run clear.
- Remove the joint from the oven and raise the heat to 190°C/375°F/Gas mark 5.
- With two large spatulas, place the joint on a chopping board, leaving the cooking liquid in the tin. Remove the skin, score the flesh and spread with the mustard. Mix together the breadcrumbs and sugar and press firmly over the joint.
- Place the joint back in the roasting tin and cover the exposed meat end with aluminium foil. Pour the apple juice around the joint. Bake for 30 to 40 minutes, or until golden brown. Baste the breadcrumbs several times during cooking, being careful not to dislodge them. Remove the joint from the oven and leave to cool before slicing.

Taglierini & seafood sauce

SERVES 4-6

INGREDIENTS:

225g/8oz raw prawns in their shells
1 tablespoon olive oil
50g/2oz butter
2 garlic cloves (finely chopped)
450g/1lb canned plum tomatoes
(drained and chopped)
125ml/4fl oz dry white wine

450g/1lb whole sea bass (gutted and
washed)
225g/8oz cod fillets
1/8 teaspoon saffron strands
Salt and pepper
450g/1lb fresh egg pasta (cut into
taglierini/fine noodles)

- Use a small knife to peel the shells off the prawns, remove the tails and the dark vein. Wash well, making sure all traces of the vein are removed. Dry well with a tea towel then dice and set aside.
- Warm the oil and 40g/1½oz butter in a deep, broad frying pan.
- Add the garlic and sauté for 3 to 4 minutes until softened. Add the tomatoes and

→

← simmer for 5 minutes over a medium heat.

- Stir in the wine. Allow it to evaporate for 2 minutes. Place the seabass and cod in the pan. Cook for 10 minutes over a medium heat, turning once. Remove the pan from the heat.
- Take the whole seabass out of the pan and remove its bones and skin. Flake the meat finely and return it to the pan.
- Warm the remaining butter in a small frying pan and add the prawns. Sauté for about 3 minutes. Add the prawns, saffron and salt to the sauce and heat through. Season with pepper and remove the heat.
- Meanwhile, bring a large saucepan of water to the boil. Add the pasta and 1½ tablespoons of salt. Let the water return to the boil and then cook for 15 seconds.
- Drain and toss with the sauce in the frying pan, then serve immediately.

Pan-fried chicken with red wine sauce

SERVES 6

INGREDIENTS:

25g/1oz butter
1 tablespoon oil
6 chicken breasts (about 14g/5oz each)
175g/6oz rindless streaky bacon (chopped)
225g/8oz button mushrooms (wiped with damp kitchen paper)

225g/8oz button onions
100ml/3½fl oz tablespoons brandy
350ml/12fl oz red wine
700ml/1¼pt chicken stock
4 tablespoons redcurrant jelly
Salt and pepper

- Preheat the oven to 150°C/300°F/Gas mark 2.
- Melt the butter and oil in a pan. Add the chicken breasts and cook in batches over a high heat for 3 minutes on each side or until golden. Remove from the pan and place in a baking dish in the oven to finish cooking while you make the sauce.
- Add the bacon, mushrooms and onions to the frying pan. Cook for 4 to 5 minutes or until golden. Remove from the pan and set aside. Add the brandy, wine, stock and redcurrant jelly. Bring to the boil and bubble furiously for 15 to 20 minutes or until the sauce is syrupy.
- Return the chicken, bacon, mushrooms and onions to the pan. Bring to the boil, season with salt and pepper and serve.

Piri piri prawns

SERVES 4

INGREDIENTS:

100ml/3½fl oz tablespoons oil
2 teaspoons dried chilli flakes
4 garlic cloves (crushed)
1 teaspoon salt

900g/2lb raw medium prawns in their
shells
75g/3oz butter
50ml/2fl oz lemon juice

- Place the oil, chilli flakes, garlic and salt in a large glass bowl and mix well.
- Peel the prawns, leaving the tails intact and removing the dark vein. Stir the prawns into the chilli mixture, cover and refrigerate for 3 hours, stirring and turning occasionally.
- Preheat the grill to very hot. Place the prawns in a single layer on a baking tray and brush with any of the remaining oil and chilli mixture. Grill for about 5 minutes, or until tender.
- Melt the butter with the lemon juice in a small pan and pour into a serving jug.
- Serve the prawns hot, drizzled with the lemon butter, with boiled rice.

Seafood chimichangas

SERVES 4-6

INGREDIENTS:

15g/½oz butter
1.4kg/3lb large raw peeled prawns
(de-veined)
100g/4oz spring onion tops (finely
chopped)
225g/80oz mushrooms

3 garlic cloves (finely chopped)
350g/12oz spinach (thinly sliced)
½ teaspoon salt
3 teaspoons lemon juice
6 thin tortillas
Vegetable oil for deep-frying

- Melt the butter in a heavy-based saucepan and sauté the prawns, spring onion tops, mushrooms, garlic, spinach, salt and lemon juice for about 7 to 10 minutes or until the vegetables go limp.
- Spread out the tortillas and divide the seafood mixture equally between them, spooning it over the middle of each one. Roll up each tortilla and tuck in the ends to form solid packages. Secure with wooden cocktail sticks.
- Heat the oil in a deep, heavy-based saucepan. Fry each chimichanga for about 3 minutes until golden, turning it over as it cooks to brown on all sides.

→

← • Remove from the oil and drain on paper towels. Serve hot with cheese, guacamole, soured cream and diced tomatoes.

Fresh tomato risotto

SERVES 4

INGREDIENTS:

6 plum tomatoes
Salt and pepper
2 tablespoons olive oil
5 tablespoons fresh basil leaves
1.5 litres/2½pt chicken stock
200g/7oz butter
1 red onion (chopped)

1 tablespoons fresh thyme leaves
1 garlic clove (chopped)
250g/9oz risotto rice
125ml/4fl oz extra-dry vermouth
4 tablespoons tomato sauce
75g/3oz Parmesan cheese (grated)

- Place the tomatoes in a bowl of just-boiled water for 30 seconds, skin and roughly chop. Put the tomatoes in a bowl, season and add the olive oil and basil.
- Bring the stock to a simmer in a saucepan.
- Melt half of the butter in a heavy-based pan, add the onion and cook until soft. Add the thyme and garlic. Add the rice and stir to coat each grain with the butter. Add the vermouth, stirring until it is absorbed, then add the tomato sauce. Season.
- Add the hot stock, ladle by ladle, only adding more when the last has been absorbed. Stir and continue adding the stock over a period of about 20 minutes, until the rice is cooked.
- Remove from the heat and stir in the tomatoes, the remaining butter and the Parmesan.

Sautéed chicken with herbs

SERVES 4

INGREDIENTS:

2–3 tablespoons olive oil
1 chicken (cut into 8 pieces)
3 garlic cloves (sliced)
2 shallots (finely chopped)

3 tablespoons dried herbs
Salt and pepper
Juice of ½ lemon

- Heat the oil in a heavy-based frying pan over a high heat. Brown the chicken pieces in the oil in 2 batches.
- When browned, reduce the heat to medium-high and place all the chicken in the pan. Cover the pan and leave to cook for about 10 minutes.
- Turn the chicken pieces, spooning their juices over them. Sprinkle the garlic, shallots, half the herbs, salt and pepper over them. Cover again and cook for a further 8 minutes.
- When cooked, lift the chicken pieces out with the cooked shallots, garlic and pan juices. Squeeze over the lemon juice, sprinkle with the remaining herbs and serve.

Moussaka

SERVES 6

INGREDIENTS:

3 large aubergines (sliced lengthways)
2 tablespoons olive oil
50g/2oz grated Parmesan cheese
½ teaspoon ground cinnamon
Salt and pepper

For the meat sauce:
1 large onion (chopped)
2 garlic cloves (chopped)
3 tablespoons olive oil
450g/1lb minced lamb
1 glass dry white wine
2 tablespoons tomato purée
450g/1lb fresh tomatoes (chopped)

1 teaspoon sugar
1½ teaspoons ground cinnamon
1 teaspoon dried oregano
3 tablespoons chopped fresh parsley

For the white sauce:
50g/2oz butter
50g/2oz flour
600ml/1pt milk
50g/2oz Parmesan cheese (grated)
Salt and pepper
1 egg
1 egg yolk

→

←
- Preheat the oven to 190°C/375°F/Gas mark 5
- To make the meat sauce, cook the onion and garlic gently in the olive oil until tender, without browning. Add the lamb and stir until it loses its raw look. Now add all the remaining meat sauce ingredients except the parsley and season with salt and pepper. Simmer for 20 to 30 minutes until thick. Stir in the parsley.
- Next make the white sauce. Melt the butter and stir in the flour. Keep stirring for about 1 minute. Take the pan off the heat and add the milk gradually, stirring well. Return to a gentle heat and let it simmer for 10 to 15 minutes, stirring frequently, until it is fairly thick.
- Remove from the heat and stir in the cheese and salt and pepper. Just before using, beat the whole egg and yolk into the sauce.
- Sprinkle the slices of aubergine with salt and leave for at least 30 minutes.
- Wipe clean and lay them on oiled baking sheets. Brush generously with olive oil and bake in the oven for about 20 minutes until tender and patched with brown.
- Brush a rectangular baking dish lightly with oil. Lay half the aubergine slices on the base, overlapping if necessary, then spread half the meat sauce on top.
- Repeat these layers, then spoon over the white sauce, covering the meat entirely. Sprinkle the grated cheese and the cinnamon over the top. Bake at 180°C/350°F/Gas mark 4 for 50 to 60 minutes until nicely browned. Let it settle for 5 minutes before serving.

Jerk pork

SERVES 4

INGREDIENTS:

4 red peppers (deseeded)	*3 bay leaves (crushed)*
3 spring onions	*2 teaspoons brown sugar*
3 garlic cloves	*1.kg/3lb pork shoulder (thickly sliced)*

- In a blender or food processor, blend all the ingredients except the pork to create a smooth paste seasoning. Cut slits in the pork and generously rub in the seasoning, ensuring that all the meat is covered. Leave to marinate for 8 to 12 hours.
- Preheat the oven to 180°C/350°F/Gas mark 4.
- Place the meat in a steamer and cook for 30 minutes. Transfer the steamed pork to a roasting tin and cook in the oven for 1$\frac{1}{2}$ hours or until well cooked and blackened. Serve with rice.

Penne with creamy tomato sauce

SERVES 4

INGREDIENTS:

350g/12oz tricolour penne
1 onion (roughly chopped)
3 tablespoons olive oil
225g/8oz lightly smoked rashers of
back bacon (diced)
1 teaspoon dried oregano
400g/14oz tinned chopped tomatoes
500g/1lb 2oz creamed tomatoes

4 tablespoons double cream
Salt and pepper
25g/1oz sun-dried tomatoes in oil
(roughly chopped)
25g/1oz black olives (stoned and
halved)
6 basil leaves (roughly chopped)

- Cook the pasta in a pan of boiling, salted water for 10 to 12 minutes or as per packet instructions.
- Gently fry the onion in the oil for 5 minutes, until soft. Add the bacon and cook quickly for 2 to 3 minutes. Stir in the oregano and chopped tomatoes and cook for 5 minutes, or until the sauce has thickened.
- Drain the pasta and transfer to a warm serving dish.
- Add the creamed tomatoes to the pan and heat through for 2 to 3 minutes. Stir in the cream and seasoning and pour the mixture over the pasta. Toss together and scatter over the sun-dried tomatoes, olives and basil over the top.

Mustard chicken

SERVES 4

INGREDIENTS:

50g/2oz butter
1 onion (finely chopped)
450g/1lb chicken breasts (skinned and
thinly sliced)
1 tablespoon cornflour
1 garlic clove (crushed)

150ml/¼pt chicken stock
1 teaspoon chilli paste
2 teaspoons ground coriander
1 tablespoon wholegrain mustard
Salt and pepper
1 tablespoon sesame seeds

- Heat the butter in a saucepan, add the onion and fry for about 5 minutes until

→

←
soft but not brown.
- Mix together the chicken pieces and cornflour and add to the pan with the garlic. Cook quickly, stirring occasionally, until golden brown.
- Stir in the stock, chilli paste, coriander, mustard and seasoning. Bring just to the boil, stirring, and simmer gently for about 10 minutes.
- Stir in the sesame seeds and serve with pasta or potatoes.

Soused herrings

SERVES 6

INGREDIENTS:

6 herrings (filleted)
1 carrot (thinly sliced)
1 onion (sliced into thin rings)

For the marinade:
300ml/½pt white wine vinegar
225g/8oz onion (sliced into thin rings)

1 carrot (sliced)
8 parsley sprigs
3 bay leaves
Sprig of tarragon
½ tablespoon salt
12 black peppercorns

- To make the marinade, put all the marinade ingredients in a pan and bring to the boil. Lower the heat and simmer gently for 20 to 30 minutes. Remove from the heat and allow to cool completely.
- Arrange the herring fillets skin-side down in a flameproof roasting pan, pour the marinade over them and slowly bring to the boil on the hob. Immediately remove from the heat and allow to cool.
- To finish the dish, blanch the carrot in boiling salted water for 2 to 3 minutes, then refresh in cold water and drain.
- Arrange the cooled herring fillets on a serving plate and spoon some of the marinade over them. Scatter the carrot slices over the fish and arrange rings of onion on top.

Spaghetti marinara

SERVES 6

INGREDIENTS:

20 black mussels
200g/7oz raw peeled medium prawns
50ml/2fl oz white wine
50ml/2fl oz fish stock
1 garlic clove (crushed)
350g/12oz spaghetti
25g/1oz butter
100g/4oz calamari rings
100g/4oz skinless cod fillets (cubed)
200g/7oz canned clams (drained)

For the tomato sauce:
2 tablespoons olive oil
1 onion (finely chopped)
1 carrot (sliced)
2 garlic cloves (crushed)
400g/14oz canned crushed tomatoes
125ml/4fl oz white wine
1 teaspoon sugar

- For the tomato sauce, heat the olive oil in a pan, add the onion and carrot and stir over a medium heat for 10 minutes, or until the vegetables are lightly browned.
- Add the garlic, tomatoes, white wine and sugar. Bring to the boil, reduce the heat and gently simmer for 30 minutes, stirring occasionally.
- Scrub the mussels with a stiff brush and pull out all the hairy beards. Discard any broken mussels, or open ones that do not close when tapped on the work surface. Rinse well.
- Peel the prawns and gently pull out the dark vein.
- Heat the wine together with the stock and garlic in a large pan. Add the mussels.
- Cover the pan and shake it over a high heat for 4 to 5 minutes. After 3 minutes, start removing any opened mussels and set them aside. After 5 minutes, discard any unopened mussels and reserve the liquid.
- Cook the spaghetti in a large pan of boiling salted water until al dente. Drain and keep warm.
- Melt the butter in a frying pan, add the calamari rings, fish and prawns in batches and stir-fry for 2 minutes, or until just cooked through. Remove from the heat and add the reserved liquid, mussels, calamari, fish, prawns and clams to the tomato sauce and stir gently until heated through. Gently combine the sauce with the pasta and serve at once.

Fragrant saffron chicken

SERVES 10

INGREDIENTS:

2 chickens (about 1.6kg/3½lb each)
1 carrot (sliced)
2 celery sticks (sliced)
6 black peppercorns
2 bay leaves
50g/2oz butter
225g/8oz onion (finely chopped)
1 teaspoon saffron strands

Grated zest of 1 lemon
4 dried apricots
300ml/½pt dry white wine
3 teaspoons clear honey
1 teaspoon mild curry paste
300ml/½pt mayonnaise
300ml/½pt double cream
Salt and pepper

- Place the chicken in large saucepans. Cover with cold water and add the carrot, celery, peppercorns and 1 bay leaf. Bring slowly to the boil, cover and simmer very gently for about 1 hour. Pierce the thigh joints with a skewer to test if cooked – the juices should run clear. Leave the chickens to cool in their liquid.
- Drain the chickens. Remove and discard the skin, take off all the flesh and discard the bones. Cut the flesh into bite sized pieces.
- Melt the butter in a medium saucepan and sauté the onion until soft. Grind the saffron strands to a powder with a pestle and mortar. Stir into the onions with the apricots, lemon zest, white wine, honey, curry paste and 1 bay leaf. Bring to the boil. Simmer uncovered until well reduced and the consistency of chutney. This should take about 10 minutes.
- Cool and purée in a blender or food processor, then sieve.
- Fold the cold saffron mixture into the mayonnaise. Whip the cream until it just holds its shape. Fold it in and season.
- Mix together the chicken and mayonnaise mixture, and serve on a bed of rice.

Potted shrimps

SERVES 4

INGREDIENTS:

300g/11oz butter
¼ teaspoon nutmeg

1 teaspoon cayenne pepper
500g/1lb 2oz peeled shrimps

- Melt the butter in a pan over a low heat. The milk solids will separate. Pour the clarified butter carefully through a muslin-lined sieve into a bowl, leaving the solids in the pan.

- Grate the nutmeg into the butter and season with cayenne pepper. Add the shrimps and turn to coat evenly.
- Leave in the hot butter for 2 minutes then pack into ramekins in 75g/3oz portions. Press down gently to ensure the surfaces of the shrimp are covered with butter. Chill before serving with rice.

Singapore noodles

SERVES 4

INGREDIENTS:

2 chickens (about 1.6kg/3½lb each)	4 dried apricots
1 carrot (sliced)	Grated zest of 1 lemon
2 celery sticks (sliced)	300ml/½pt dry white wine
6 black peppercorns	3 tablespoons clear honey
2 bay leaves	1 teaspoon mild curry paste
50g/2oz butter	300ml/½pt mayonnaise
225g/8oz onion (finely chopped)	300ml/½pt double cream
1 teaspoon saffron strands	Salt and pepper

- Soak the vermicelli in boiling water for about 5 minutes, or until soft. Drain well and cut into short lengths.
- Peel the prawns and pull out the dark veins. Heat 1 tablespoon oil in a wok over a high heat and add the garlic, pork and prawns in batches. Stir-fry for 2 minutes, or until the mixture is just cooked. Remove from the wok and set aside.
- Reduce the heat to medium. Add the remaining oil and stir-fry the onions and curry powder for 2 to 3 minutes. Add the beans, carrot, sugar and salt, sprinkle with a little water and stir-fry for 2 minutes.
- Toss the vermicelli and soy sauce through the mixture. Add the beansprouts, prawn and pork mixture to the wok. Toss well and serve.

Chinese chicken with cashew nuts

SERVES 4

INGREDIENTS:

4 boneless chicken breasts (skinned and sliced into strips)
3 garlic cloves (crushed)
4 tablespoons soy sauce
2 tablespoons cornflour

225g/8oz dried egg noodles
3 tablespoons sunflower oil
1 tablespoon sesame oil
100g/4oz roasted cashew nuts
6 spring onions (cut into 5cm/2in pieces)

- Place the chicken in a bowl with the garlic, soy sauce and cornflour and mix until the chicken is well coated. Cover and chill for about 30 minutes.
- Meanwhile, bring a pan of water to the boil and add the egg noodles. Turn off the heat and leave to stand for 5 minutes. Drain well and reserve.
- Heat the oils in a large frying pan or wok and add the chilled chicken and marinade juices. Stir-fry on a high heat for about 3 to 4 minutes, or until golden brown.
- Add the cashew nuts and spring onions to the pan or wok and stir-fry for 2 to 3 minutes.
- Add the drained noodles and stir-fry for a further 2 minutes. Toss the noodles well and serve immediately.

Seafood pilaki

SERVES 4

INGREDIENTS:

2 tablespoons olive oil
2 garlic cloves (crushed)
1 large onion (chopped)
2 celery sticks (chopped)
3 large carrots (sliced)
Finely grated zest and juice of 1 lemon
400g/14oz canned chopped tomatoes

700g/1½lb monkfish fillet (trimmed and cut into chunks)
450g/1lb cleaned squid (cut into rings)
900g/2lb mussels (cleaned)
½ tablespoon chopped fresh parsley
Salt and pepper

- Heat the oil in a large heavy-based pan. Add the garlic, onion, celery, carrots and lemon zest and cook for about 5 minutes, stirring all the time.
- Add the lemon juice and the tomatoes with their juice, cover and cook over a low heat for about 25 minutes, or until the vegetables are very tender, stirring occasionally.
- Add the fish and squid and a little water. Cover and cook for 3 to 5 minutes or until the fish is just tender. Arrange the mussels on the top, cover the pan and cook for about 5 minutes, stirring occasionally. The mussels should have opened; discard any that remain shut. Stir in parsley and season to taste with salt and pepper. Serve hot or cold.

Pan-fried scallops

SERVES 2

INGREDIENTS:

6 large scallops
2 tablespoons olive oil
12.5g/½ oz butter

For the salsa:
2 large ripe plum tomatoes

1 small ripe mango (peeled, stoned and diced)
1 large shallot (finely chopped)
Juice of 1 lime
¼ teaspoon Tabasco sauce
Salt and pepper

- First make the salsa. Place the tomatoes in a bowl of just-boiled water, then skin and dice them. Put the tomatoes, mango and shallot in a bowl and add the lime juice, Tabasco and salt and pepper to taste. Stir well to mix, then cover and chill in the refrigerator until ready to serve.
- Pat the scallops dry with kitchen paper. Heat the oil in a non-stick frying pan, add the butter and stir until foaming. Add the scallops to the pan and cook for 3 to 4 minutes, turning them once until lightly golden on both sides and tender to the touch.
- To serve, spoon the salsa on to 2 plates. Sit the scallops on top and serve immediately.

Vegetable curry

SERVES 4-6

INGREDIENTS:

2 tablespoons vegetable oil
1 onion (thinly sliced)
2 carrots (diced)
1 baking potato (diced)
1 tablespoon mild curry powder

Pinch of chilli powder
1 courgette (diced)
2 large tomatoes (diced)
225ml/8fl oz cold water
Salt and pepper

- Heat the oil in a flameproof casserole dish until hot, then add the onion, carrots, potato, curry powder and chilli powder. Stir-fry over a low heat for 5 minutes.
- Add the courgette, tomatoes, cold water and salt and pepper to taste. Bring to the boil, stirring, then cover and simmer over a low heat for 20 minutes, or until the vegetables are tender. Stir and check several times during cooking and add more water if the vegetables are dry. Serve hot with rice.

Courgette quiche

SERVES 4

INGREDIENTS:

175g/6oz plain flour
Salt and pepper
100g/4oz butter
100g/4oz Cheddar cheese (grated)
1 egg yolk (beaten)
350g/12oz courgettes (cut into

2.5cm/1in chunks)
3 eggs
150ml/¼pt double cream
2 teaspoons chopped fresh basil
Finely grated zest of 1 lime
A little egg white

- Make the pastry by sifting the flour into a bowl with a pinch of salt. Add the butter in pieces and rub in thoroughly with fingertips until the mixture resembles fine breadcrumbs.
- Stir in the cheese, then the egg yolk. Gather the mixture together with your fingers to make a smooth ball of dough. Wrap the dough in clingfilm and chill in the refrigerator for about 30 minutes.
- Preheat the oven to 200°C/400°F/Gas mark 6.
- Plunge the courgette pieces into boiling salted water, bring back to the boil, then simmer for 3 minutes. Drain and set aside.
- Put the eggs in a jug and beat lightly together with the cream. Stir in the basil

and lime zest and sprinkle with salt and pepper. Set aside.

- Roll out the chilled dough on a floured surface and use to line a loose-bottomed 23cm/9in flan tin. Refrigerate for 15 minutes.
- Prick the base of the dough with a fork, then line with aluminium foil. Stand the tin on a preheated baking sheet and bake in the oven for 10 minutes.
- Remove the foil and brush the inside of the pastry case with the egg white to seal. Return to the oven for 5 minutes.
- Stand the courgette chunks upright in the pastry case, and then slowly pour in the egg and cream mixture. Return to the oven for 20 minutes. Serve hot or cold.

Spicy Japanese noodles

SERVES 4

INGREDIENTS:

500g/1lb 2oz fresh Japanese noodles
1 tablespoon sesame oil
1 tablespoon sesame seeds
1 tablespoon sunflower oil
1 red onion (sliced)

100g/4oz mangetout
175g/6oz carrots (thinly sliced)
350g/12oz white cabbage (shredded)
3 tablespoons sweet chilli sauce
2 spring onions (sliced)

- Bring a large saucepan of water to the boil. Add the Japanese noodles to the pan and cook for 2 to 3 minutes. Drain the noodles thoroughly. Toss the noodles with the sesame oil and sesame seeds.
- Heat the sunflower oil in a large preheated wok. Add the onion slices, mangetout, carrot slices and shredded cabbage to the wok and stir-fry for about 5 minutes.
- Add the sweet chilli sauce to the wok and cook, stirring occasionally, for a further 2 minutes.
- Add the sesame noodles to the wok, toss thoroughly to combine and heat for a further 2 to 3 minutes.
- Transfer the Japanese noodles and spicy vegetables to warm individual serving bowls, scatter over the spring onions to garnish and serve immediately.

Waldorf salad

SERVES 4

INGREDIENTS:

450g/1lb eating apples (cored and diced)
2 tablespoons lemon juice
1 teaspoon sugar

150ml/¼pt mayonnaise
½ head celery (sliced)
50g/2oz walnuts (chopped)
1 lettuce

- Toss the diced apples in the lemon juice, sugar and 1 tablespoon of the mayonnaise and leave to stand for about 30 minutes.
- Just before serving, add the sliced celery, chopped walnuts and the remaining mayonnaise, and toss together. Serve in a bowl lined with lettuce leaves.

Potato salad with mustard dressing

SERVES 4-6

INGREDIENTS:

900g/2lb new potatoes
100g/4oz natural yogurt
3 tablespoons mayonnaise

1 tablespoon coarsegrain mustard
Salt and pepper
1 small bunch fresh chives

- Put the potatoes in a saucepan of salted boiling water, bring back to the boil and cook for 20 to 25 minutes until just tender. Drain the potatoes and plunge into a bowl of iced water for 5 minutes to stop them cooking. Drain well and leave to cool.
- Mix the yogurt, mayonnaise and mustard together in a large bowl and season with salt and pepper. Add the potatoes. Using scissors, snip most of the chives over the potatoes. Fold the potatoes in the dressing until evenly coated. Garnish with the remaining chives.

Vegetarian pizza

SERVES 4

INGREDIENTS:

1 large pizza base
200ml/7fl oz tomato purée
4 spinach leaves (stalks removed)
1 tomato (sliced)
1 celery stick (thinly sliced)
½ green pepper (thinly sliced)
1 baby courgette (sliced)
25g/1oz asparagus tips
25g/1oz sweetcorn

25g/1oz peas
4 spring onions (trimmed and chopped)
1 tablespoon mixed dried herbs
50g/2oz mozzarella cheese (grated)
2 tablespoons grated Parmesan
1 artichoke heart
Olive oil for drizzling
Salt and pepper

- Preheat the oven to 200°C/400°F/Gas mark 6.
- Place the pizza base on a large, greased baking tray. Spread the tomato purée over the base, almost to the edge.
- Arrange the spinach leaves on the sauce, followed by the tomato slices. Top with the remaining vegetables and the herbs.
- Mix together the cheeses and sprinkle over the top. Place the artichoke heart in the centre. Drizzle the pizza with a little olive oil and season.
- Bake in the oven for 18 to 20 minutes or until the edges are crisp and golden brown. Serve immediately.

Three green salad

SERVES 4

INGREDIENTS:

1 head of broccoli (cut into florets)
100g/4oz mangetouts (top and tailed)
100g/4oz fine green beans (topped and tailed)
4 spring onions (halved)
Salt and pepper

For the dressing:
2.5cm/1in piece of fresh root ginger (peeled and grated)
1 garlic clove (crushed)
75ml/3fl oz sunflower oil
3 tablespoons rice vinegar

- For the dressing, place the ginger and garlic in a bowl and mix together with the back of a spoon to form a paste. Whisk in the oil and vinegar.
- Cook the broccoli in a saucepan of boiling water for 4 minutes. In a separate

→

pan of boiling salted water, cook the mangetouts and beans for 2 minutes.
- Drain the vegetables well and turn into a bowl.
- Add the spring onions to the vegetables and pour the dressing over the top.
- Add salt and pepper to taste and toss gently to mix. Serve with rice.

Stuffed peppers

SERVES 4

INGREDIENTS:

3 green peppers
3 red peppers
2 yellow peppers
5 tablespoons olive oil
2 onions (chopped)
4 garlic cloves (crushed)
350g/12oz tomatoes (seeded and chopped)

1 tablespoon tomato purée
1 teaspoon sugar
Salt and pepper
3 tablespoons chopped fresh coriander
225g/8oz risotto rice
½ teaspoon ground cinnamon
150ml/¼pt water

- Cut a slice off the top of each pepper and reserve. Remove the cores, seeds and membranes and discard. Wash the peppers and pat dry.
- Heat 4 tablespoons of the oil in a large frying pan, add the peppers and fry gently for 10 minutes, turning them frequently so that they soften and colour on all sides. Remove from the pan with a slotted spoon and drain on kitchen paper.
- To make the stuffing, drain off all but 2 tablespoons of oil from the pan, then add the onion and garlic and fry very gently for about 15 minutes. Add the tomatoes and fry gently to soften, stirring constantly. Increase the heat and cook rapidly to drive off the liquid – the mixture should be thick and pulpy.
- Lower the heat, add the tomato purée, sugar and salt and pepper to taste and simmer gently for 5 minutes. Then remove the pan from the heat and stir in the chopped fresh coriander and the risotto rice. Spoon the stuffing into the peppers, dividing it equally between them.
- Stand the peppers close together in a heavy-based casserole dish. Sprinkle with the cinnamon, then the remaining 1 tablespoon oil. Put the reserved 'lids' on top.
- Pour the water into the base of the pan, then bring to the boil. Lower the heat, cover with a plate or saucer that just fits inside the rim of the dish, then place weights on top.
- Simmer gently for 1 hour, then remove from the heat and leave to cool. Chill in the refrigerator overnight, with the weights still on top. Serve chilled with garlic bread and a salad.

Potato hash

SERVES 4

INGREDIENTS:

25g/1oz butter
1 red onion (sliced)
1 carrot (diced)
25g/1oz French beans (trimmed and halved)
3 large potatoes (diced)

2 tablespoons plain flour
600ml/1pt vegetable stock
225g/8oz tofu (diced)
Salt and pepper

- Melt the butter in a frying pan. Add the onion, carrot, French beans and potatoes and fry gently, stirring, for 5 to 7 minutes or until the vegetables begin to brown.
- Add the flour to the frying pan and cook for 1 minute, stirring constantly.
- Gradually pour in the stock. Reduce the heat and leave the mixture to simmer for 15 minutes or until the potatoes are tender.
- Add the diced tofu to the mixture and cook for a further 5 minutes, and season to taste with salt and pepper. Serve hot from the pan.

Honey-roasted pumpkin

SERVES 4

INGREDIENTS:

700g/1½lb pumpkin
2 sweet potatoes
2 tablespoons olive oil

1 tablespoon clear honey
2 tablespoons Cajun spice
Salt and pepper

- Preheat the oven to 180°C/350°F/Gas mark 4.
- Cut the pumpkin into wedges and remove the peel, seeds and fibres. Peel the sweet potatoes and cut them into similar-sized pieces.
- Put the pumpkin and sweet potatoes in a large non-stick roasting tin and drizzle the oil and honey over them. Sprinkle with the spice and season generously with salt and pepper.
- Roast in the oven for 1 hour or until golden and tender, turning and basting occasionally. Serve hot.

Nut roast

SERVES 6

INGREDIENTS:

2 tablespoons olive oil
1 large onion (diced)
2 garlic cloves (crushed)
275g/10oz mushroom caps (wiped with damp kitchen paper and finely chopped)
200g/7oz raw cashew nuts

200g/7oz Brazil nuts
100g/4oz Cheddar cheese (grated)
25g/1oz Parmesan cheese (grated)
1 egg (lightly beaten)
2 tablespoons chopped fresh chives
75g/3oz fresh wholemeal breadcrumbs

- Grease a 14 x 21cm/5½ x 8½ in loaf tin and line the base with baking paper.
- Heat the oil in a frying pan and add the onion, garlic and mushrooms. Fry until soft, then cool.
- Process the nuts in a blender or food processor until finely chopped.
- Preheat the oven to 180°C/350°F/Gas mark 4.
- Combine the cooled mushrooms, chopped nuts, Cheddar, Parmesan, egg, chives and breadcrumbs in a bowl. Mix well and season to taste. Press into the loaf tin and bake for 45 minutes, or until firm. Leave for 5 minutes, then turn out and cut into slices. Serve with potatoes.

Mushroom vol-au-vent

SERVES 4

INGREDIENTS:

500g/1lb 2oz puff pastry
1 egg (beaten, for glazing)

For the filling:
30g/1oz butter

700g/1½lb mixed mushrooms
100ml/3½fl oz tablespoons white wine
4 tablespoons double cream
2 tablespoons chopped fresh chervil
Salt and pepper

- Preheat the oven to 220°C/425°F/Gas mark 7.
- Roll out the pastry to a 20cm/8in square on a lightly floured surface. Using a sharp knife, mark a square 2cm/1in from the pastry edge, cutting halfway through the pastry. Score the top in a diagonal pattern. Knock up the edges with a kitchen knife and put on a baking tray. Brush the top with beaten egg.
- Bake in the oven for 35 minutes.

- Cut out the central square. Discard the soft pastry inside the case, leaving the base intact. Return to the oven, with the central square, for 10 minutes.
- Make the filling by melting the butter in a frying pan and stir-frying the mushrooms over a high heat for 3 minutes. Add the wine and cook, stirring occasionally, for 10 minutes, until the mushrooms have softened. Stir in the cream and chervil and season to taste with salt and pepper.
- Pile the filling into the pastry case. Top with the pastry square and serve.

Greek salad

SERVES 6

INGREDIENTS:

2 large tomatoes (each cut into 8 wedges)
1 green pepper (sliced)
½ medium cucumber (sliced)
50g/2oz black olives (stoned)
225g/8oz feta cheese (diced)

8 tablespoons extra-virgin olive oil
3 tablespoons lemon juice
Salt and pepper
Large pinch of dried oregano
Pitta bread, to serve

- Arrange the tomatoes, pepper, cucumber and olives in a salad bowl. Add the cheese and pour the oil and lemon juice over the top. Season well. Toss well and sprinkle with oregano. Serve with warm pitta bread.

Chargrilled peppers & sweet potatoes

SERVES 4-6

INGREDIENTS:

2 red peppers
2 yellow peppers
2 green peppers
1 sweet potato
2 tablespoons oil

For the dressing:
1 teaspoon cumin seeds
2 teaspoons clear honey
2 tablespoons balsamic vinegar
1 tablespoon walnut oil
1 tablespoon olive oil
Salt and pepper

→

- Halve the peppers lengthways and discard the stalks, cores and seeds. Cut each half lengthways into 4 pieces. Peel the sweet potato and slice it into rings about 8mm/¼in thick.
- To make the dressing, in a small frying pan, dry-fry the cumin seeds over a low heat for a few minutes, taking care not to burn them. Place them in a bowl with the honey, vinegar and oils and whisk together. Season with salt and pepper.
- Heat a ridged cast iron griddle pan until very hot. Place the sweet potato slices on the pan and lightly brush each piece with olive oil. Cook for about 10 minutes, turning the pieces over once, then remove them from the pan and keep warm.
- Add half the pepper pieces, brush with olive oil and cook for about 8 minutes, turning them over several times. Remove and add to the sweet potatoes, then repeat with the remaining peppers.
- To serve, place the vegetables on a large shallow dish and drizzle the dressing over them. Serve warm with rice.

Tomatoes au gratin

SERVES 6

INGREDIENTS:

900g/2lb tomatoes
50g/2oz butter (softened)
3 garlic cloves (chopped)
1 teaspoon sugar
4 teaspoons chopped fresh basil

Salt and pepper
300ml/½pt double cream
50g/2oz dried breadcrumbs
25g/1oz Parmesan cheese (grated)

- Preheat the oven to 180°C/350°F/Gas mark 4.
- Place the tomatoes in a bowl of just-boiled water and leave them for 30 seconds. Skin and then slice thinly.
- Brush the inside of an ovenproof dish liberally with some of the butter.
- Arrange a layer of tomato slices in the bottom of the dish then sprinkle with a little of the garlic, sugar and basil, then salt and pepper to taste. Pour over a thin layer of cream. Repeat these layers until all the ingredients are used up.
- Mix the breadcrumbs and Parmesan together, then sprinkle over the top of the tomatoes and cream. Dot with the remaining butter.
- Bake in the oven for 20 to 30 minutes or until the topping is golden brown. Serve hot.

Couscous vegetable loaf

SERVES 6–8

INGREDIENTS:

1.2 litres/2pt vegetable stock
450g/1lb couscous
25g/1oz butter
3 tablespoons olive oil
2 garlic cloves (crushed)
1 onion (finely chopped)
1 tablespoon ground coriander
1 teaspoon ground cinnamon
1 teaspoon garam marsala
225g/8oz cherry tomatoes (quartered)
1 courgette (finely chopped)

150g/5oz canned sweetcorn (drained)
8 large basil leaves
150g/5oz sun-dried peppers in oil
50g/2oz fresh basil (chopped)

For the dressing:
75ml/3fl oz orange juice
1 tablespoon lemon juice
3 tablespoons chopped fresh parsley
1 teaspoon honey
1 teaspoon ground cumin

- Bring the stock to the boil in a saucepan. Place the couscous and butter in a large bowl, cover with the stock and set aside for 10 minutes.
- Heat 1 tablespoon oil in a large frying pan and cook the garlic and onion over a low heat for 5 minutes, or until the onion is soft. Add the spices and cook for 1 minute, or until fragrant. Remove from the pan.
- Add the remaining oil to the pan and fry the tomatoes, courgette and corn over a high heat in batches until soft.
- Line a 3 litre/5pt loaf tin with clingfilm, allowing it to overhang the sides. Place the basil leaves along the base. Drain the peppers, reserving 2 tablespoons oil, then roughly chop. Add the garlic, fried vegetables, capsicums and chopped basil to the couscous and mix. Press into the tin and fold the clingfilm over to cover. • Weigh down and refrigerate overnight.
  For the dressing, place all the ingredients in a jar with a lid and shake well.
- Turn out the loaf and serve with dressing and potatoes.

Spanish omelette

SERVES 4

INGREDIENTS:

2 large potatoes (quartered)
Salt and pepper
6 eggs

2 tablespoons olive oil
1 Spanish onion (chopped)

→

←

- Boil the potatoes in a saucepan of salted water for 15 to 20 minutes or until just tender. Drain and leave until cool enough to handle, then cut into slices.
- Beat the eggs in a bowl with salt and pepper to taste.
- Heat the oil in a deep non-stick frying pan, add the onion and diced potatoes and fry over a low heat for 10 to 15 minutes, stirring frequently, until soft and golden. Preheat the grill.
- Add the eggs to the pan and cook undisturbed for 5 minutes, or until the eggs are just beginning to set in the centre. Slide the frying pan under the hot grill and cook for a few minutes until the top is golden brown. Serve hot or cold.

Pasticcio

SERVES 4-6

INGREDIENTS:

1 red pepper (chopped)
1 yellow pepper (chopped)
1 aubergine (chopped)
1 large courgette (chopped)
2 garlic cloves (crushed)
1 teaspoon dried mixed herbs
2 tablespoons olive oil
Salt and pepper
225g/8oz short pasta
200ml/7fl oz vegetable stock
300g/11oz mozzarella cheese (diced)

For the tomato sauce:
30g/1oz sun-dried tomatoes (chopped)
400g/14oz canned chopped tomatoes
½ teaspoon sugar
500g/1lb 2oz ripe plum tomatoes
(seeded and chopped)
2 teaspoons balsamic vinegar

- Preheat the oven to 200°C/400°F/Gas mark 6.
- For the tomato sauce, place the sun-dried tomatoes in a saucepan with the canned tomatoes and sugar. Bring to simmering point and simmer for 5 minutes.
- Add the diced plum tomatoes and cook gently for 10 minutes, stirring occasionally.
- Remove the pan from the heat and stir in the balsamic vinegar. Set aside.
- Place the peppers, aubergine and courgette chunks in a large non-stick roasting tin and mix in the garlic, dried herbs, oil and salt and pepper to taste. Roast in the oven for 30 to 40 minutes, stirring occasionally.
- Cook the pasta in boiling salted water until al dente. Drain well. In a separate pan, heat the tomato sauce with the stock.
- Place the vegetables and pasta in a large baking dish and mix well. Pour the tomato sauce over them and mix in, then put the Mozzarella cubes on top. Bake for 15 to 20 minutes or until melted and golden. Leave to stand for 5 to 10minutes before serving.

Gado gado

SERVES 4

INGREDIENTS:

100g/4oz white cabbage (shredded)
100g/4oz French beans (each cut into 3)
100g/4oz carrots (cut into matchsticks)
100g/4oz cauliflower florets
100g/4oz beansprouts

For the dressing:
100ml/4fl oz vegetable oil
100g/4oz unsalted peanuts
2 garlic cloves (crushed)
1 small onion (finely chopped)
½ teaspoon chilli powder
½ teaspoon brown sugar
Salt
450ml/¾pt water
Juice of ½ lemon

- Cook the vegetables separately in a saucepan of salted boiling water for 4 to 5 minutes. Drain well and chill.
- To make the dressing, heat the oil in a frying pan and fry the peanuts, tossing frequently, for 3 to 4 minutes. Remove from the pan with a slotted spoon and drain on kitchen paper. Process the peanuts in a blender or food processor or crush with a rolling pin until a fine mixture is formed.
- Pour all but 1 tablespoon of the oil from the pan and fry the garlic and onion for 1 minute. Add the chilli powder, sugar, a pinch of salt and the water and bring to the boil.
- Stir in the peanuts. Reduce the heat and simmer for 4 to 5 minutes, until the sauce thickens. Add the lemon juice and set aside to cool.
- Arrange the vegetables in a serving dish and place the peanut dressing in a small bowl in the centre.

Spinach & ricotta pie

SERVES 4

INGREDIENTS:

225g/8oz spinach
25g/1oz pine kernels
100g/4oz ricotta cheese
2 large eggs (beaten)

50g/2oz ground almonds
40g/1½oz Parmesan cheese (grated)
250g/9oz puff pastry
1 small egg (beaten, to glaze)

→

←

- Preheat the oven to 220°C/425°F/Gas mark 7.
- Rinse the spinach, place in a large pan and cook with just the water clinging to the leaves for 4 to 5 minutes until wilted. Drain thoroughly. When the spinach is cool enough to handle, squeeze out the excess liquid.
- Place the pine kernels on a baking tray and lightly toast under a medium grill for 2 to 3 minutes, or until golden brown.
- Place the ricotta, spinach and eggs in a bowl and mix together. Add the pine kernels, beat well, then stir in the ground almonds and Parmesan cheese.
- Roll out the puff pastry and make 2 squares, 20cm/8in wide. Trim the edges, reserving the pastry trimmings.
- Place 1 pastry square on a baking tray. Spoon over the spinach mixture to within 1cm/½in of the edge of the pastry. Brush the edges with beaten egg and place the second square over the top.
- Using a round-bladed knife, press the pastry edges together by tapping along the sealed edge. Use the pastry trimmings to decorate the pie.
- Bake in the oven for 10 minutes. Reduce the oven temperature to 190°C/375°F/Gas mark 5 and bake for a further 25 to 30 minutes. Serve hot.

Sweet & sour tofu

SERVES 4

INGREDIENTS:

2 tablespoons vegetable oil
2 garlic cloves (crushed)
2 celery sticks (sliced)
1 carrot (cut into matchsticks)
1 green pepper (diced)
75g/3oz mangetout (halved)
8 baby corn cobs
150g/5oz beansprouts
450g/1lb tofu (cubed)

For the sauce:
2 tablespoons brown sugar
2 tablespoons wine vinegar
225ml/8fl oz vegetable stock
1 teaspoon tomato purée
1 tablespoon cornflour

- Heat the vegetable oil in a preheated wok until it is almost smoking. Reduce the heat slightly, then add the garlic, celery, carrot, pepper, mangetout and baby corn cobs and stir-fry for 3 to 4 minutes.
- Add the beansprouts and tofu to the wok and cook for 2 minutes, stirring well.
- To make the sauce, combine the sugar, wine vinegar, stock, tomato purée and cornflour, stirring well to mix. Stir into the wok, bring to the boil and cook, stirring, until the sauce thickens and clears. Continue for cook for 1 minute.
- Serve with rice or noodles.

Tagliatelle with lemon sauce

SERVES 4

INGREDIENTS:

50g/2oz butter
350ml/12fl oz double cream
Grated zest of 4 large lemons
50ml/2fl oz brandy

Salt
White pepper
500g/1lb 2oz fresh tagliatelle
4 tablespoons grated Parmesan cheese

- Melt the butter in a wide frying pan over a medium-low heat. Add the cream, half the lemon zest and the brandy. Increase the heat to medium and cook for 3 to 5 minutes, or until the cream has come to a simmer. Sprinkle in the remaining lemon zest and season to taste. Remove from the heat.
- Bring a large saucepan of salted water to the boil. Add the fresh tagliatelle.
- Return to the boil and then cook for 15 seconds. Drain the tagliatelle and add to the frying pan with the sauce. Toss everything together and serve with 1 tablespoon of Parmesan sprinkled over each serving.

Satay noodles

SERVES 4

INGREDIENTS:

275g/10oz wide rice noodles
3 tablespoons groundnut oil
2 garlic cloves (crushed)
2 shallots (sliced)
225g/8oz green beans (sliced)

100g/4oz cherry tomatoes (halved)
1 teaspoon chilli flakes
4 tablespoons crunchy peanut butter
150ml/¼pt coconut milk
1 tablespoon tomato purée

- Place the noodles in a large bowl and pour over enough boiling water to cover.
- Leave to stand for 10 minutes, or as per instructions on the packet.
- Heat the groundnut oil in a large preheated wok or heavy-based frying pan. Add crushed garlic and sliced shallots to the wok or frying pan and stir-fry for 1 minute.
- Drain the noodles thoroughly. Add the green beans and drained noodles to the wok and stir-fry for about 5 minutes. Add the cherry tomatoes and mix well.
- Mix together the chilli flakes, peanut butter, coconut milk and tomato purée.
- Pour the chilli mixture over the noodles, toss well until all the ingredients are thoroughly combined and heat through.
- Transfer the satay noodles to warm serving dishes and serve immediately.

Mushroom pizza

SERVES 4

INGREDIENTS:

For the dough:
15g/¹⁄₂oz dried yeast
1 teaspoon sugar
250ml/9fl oz hot water
350g/12oz plain flour
1 teaspoon salt
1 tablespoon olive oil

For the topping:
400g/14oz canned chopped tomatoes
2 garlic cloves (crushed)
1 teaspoon dried basil
1 tablespoon olive oil
Salt and pepper
2 tablespoons tomato purée
200g/7oz mushrooms (chopped)
175g/6oz Mozzarella cheese (grated)

- Place the yeast and sugar in a measuring jug and mix with 4 tablespoons of the water. Leave in a warm place for 15 minutes, or until frothy.
- Mix the flour with the salt in a large bowl, and make a well in the centre. Add the oil, the yeast mixture and the remaining water. Using a wooden spoon, mix to form a dough. Turn the dough out on to a floured surface and knead for 4 to 5 minutes or until smooth. Return the dough to the bowl, cover with an oiled sheet of cling film and leave to rise for 30 minutes, or until doubled in size.
- Preheat the oven to 200°C/400°F/Gas mark 6.
- Remove the dough from the bowl and knead for 2 minutes. Using a rolling pin, roll out the dough to form an oval or circle shape and place on an oiled baking tray, pushing out the edges until even. The dough should be no more than 8mm/¹⁄₄in thick because it will rise during cooking.
- To make the topping, place the tomatoes, garlic, dried basil, olive oil and salt and pepper in a large pan and simmer for 20 minutes or until the sauce has thickened. Stir in the tomato purée and leave to cool slightly.
- Spread the sauce over the base of the pizza, top with the mushrooms and scatter the Mozzarella over it. Bake in the oven for 25 minutes and serve hot.

Beetroot fettuccine

SERVES 4

INGREDIENTS:

450g/1lb beetroot pasta
50g/2oz butter
400g/14oz courgettes (shredded)
1 small onion (grated)

225ml/8fl oz double cream
3 tablespoons grated Parmesan cheese
Pinch of grated nutmeg
Salt and pepper

- Using a sharp knife, cut the pasta into fettuccine noodles, 8mm/¼in wide.
- Melt the butter in a deep, large frying pan. Add the shredded courgettes and onion. Stir and sauté for about 4 minutes, until the onion is wilted. Cover the pan and sauté for a further 3 minutes until soft. Stir in the cream and allow it to come to a gentle simmer.
- Remove the pan from the heat and stir in the Parmesan, nutmeg, salt and pepper to taste.
- Bring a large saucepan of salted water to the boil and add the fresh fettuccine.
- Return to the boil and then cook for 15 seconds. Drain and add to the frying pan with the sauce. Toss everything together and serve immediately.

Tabbouleh

SERVES 4-6

INGREDIENTS:

225g/8oz cracked wheat (washed and drained)
4 medium-sized tomatoes (diced)
25g/1oz fresh mint (finely chopped)
1 onion (finely sliced)
50g/2oz fresh flat-leaf parsley (coarsely chopped)

25g/1oz fresh coriander (coarsely chopped)
Grated zest and juice of 1 lemon
2 tablespoons extra-virgin olive oil
Salt and pepper
2 mint sprigs to garnish

- Mix together the wheat, tomatoes, mint, onion, parsley and coriander into a salad bowl. Add the lemon and olive oil, together with seasoning to taste.
- Serve at room temperature, garnished with the mint sprigs. Serve with warm pitta bread.

Fusilli with tomato & mozzarella

SERVES 4

INGREDIENTS:

*1kg/2½lb vine-ripened tomatoes
(chopped)
100g/4oz Mozzarella cheese (diced)
125ml/4fl oz extra-virgin olive oil
2 garlic cloves (chopped)
20 large basil leaves (torn into pieces)*

*5 anchovy fillets (cut into small pieces)
¼ teaspoon chopped fresh oregano
½ teaspoon salt
Freshly ground black pepper
450g/1lb fusilli*

- Place the chopped tomatoes in a serving bowl. Add all the remaining sauce ingredients to the tomatoes. Season with the salt and pepper to taste and mix well. Leave to marinate for 1 to 3 hours at room temperature to enable the flavours to mingle and develop.
- Bring a large saucepan of salted water to the boil. Cook the fusilli until al dente, stirring frequently to prevent sticking. Drain and add to the bowl with the sauce, tossing everything together. Serve immediately.

Vegetable jalousie

SERVES 4

INGREDIENTS:

*500g/1lb 2oz puff pastry
1 egg (beaten)*

For the filling:
*25g/1oz butter
1 leek (chopped finely)
2 garlic cloves (crushed)
1 red pepper (sliced)
1 yellow pepper (sliced)*

*50g/2oz mushrooms (wiped with damp
kitchen paper and sliced)
75g/3oz small asparagus spears
2 tablespoons plain flour
100ml/3½fl oz vegetable stock
100ml/3½fl oz milk
4 tablespoons dry white wine
1 tablespoon chopped fresh oregano
Salt and pepper*

- Preheat the oven to 200°C/400°F/Gas mark 6.
- Melt the butter in a frying pan and sauté the leek and garlic, stirring frequently,

for 2 minutes. Add the remaining vegetables and cook for 3 to 4 minutes.

- Add the flour and fry for 1 minute. Remove the pan from the heat and stir in the vegetable stock, milk and white wine. Return the pan to the heat and bring to the boil, stirring, until thickened. Stir in the oregano and season with salt and pepper to taste.
- Roll out half of the pastry on a lightly floured surface to form a rectangle measuring 38 x 15cm/15 x 6in. Roll out the other half of the pastry to the same shape, but a little larger all round. Put the smaller rectangle on a baking tray lined with dampened baking parchment.
- Spoon the filling evenly on top of the smaller rectangle, leaving a 1cm/1/2in margin around the edges.
- Using a sharp knife, cut parallel diagonal slits across the larger rectangle to within 2cm/1in on each of the long edges.
- Brush the edges of the smaller rectangle with beaten egg and place the larger rectangle on top, pressing the edges.
- Brush the whole jalousie with egg to glaze and bake in the oven for about 30 to 35 minutes, until risen and golden. Serve immediately.

Spiced fruity couscous

SERVES 4-6

INGREDIENTS:

2 teaspoons cumin seeds
500ml/18fl oz vegetable stock
200g/7oz couscous
75g/3oz ready-to-eat prunes

75g/3oz ready-to-eat dried apricots
2 tablespoons extra-virgin olive oil
2 tablespoons chopped fresh coriander
Salt and pepper

- Dry-fry the cumin seeds over a low heat in a non-stick frying pan for a few minutes, stirring constantly. Crush the seeds finely with a pestle in a mortar and set aside.
- Bring the stock to the boil in a large saucepan, add the couscous and stir well.
- Turn off the heat, cover the pan and leave to stand for 10 minutes.
- Fork the couscous through. Using scissors, snip the dried fruit into the couscous, then add the cumin seeds, oil, half the coriander and salt and pepper to taste. Fork through until evenly mixed. Turn into a serving bowl and sprinkle with the remaining coriander. Serve hot or at room temperature.

Ravioli

SERVES 4

INGREDIENTS:

450g/1lb fresh egg pasta
1 egg white
Salt

For the filling:
700g/1½lb fresh spinach
700g/1½lb ricotta (drained)

2 egg yolks
¼ teaspoon freshly grated nutmeg
½ teaspoon salt
¼ teaspoon pepper
50g/2oz Parmesan cheese (grated)
1 tablespoon chopped fresh parsley

- To make the filling, place the spinach in a deep lidded pan with no water except the drops still clinging to the leaves after washing. Steam the spinach for 5 to 10 minutes, until tender, tossing occasionally. Drain off the water. Wring out as much water as you can. Chop the spinach and set aside.
- Combine all the ingredients for the filling in a bowl, blending well with a wooden spoon. Cover and refrigerate.
- Divide the pasta dough into 6 portions. Working with one portion at a time, roll the dough as thinly as possible into 10cm/4in wide strips. Work with two strips at a time, keeping the others covered with a damp cloth. Work quickly to prevent the dough drying out.
- Place a teaspoon of filling at 5cm/2in intervals in rows along one of the pasta strips. Dip a pastry brush in the egg white and paint around each spoonful of filling.
- Place the second rolled-out sheet of pasta over the filled sheet. Press down firmly around each mound of filling to seal it, forcing out any trapped air. Use a knife to cut the ravioli into squares. Place the squares on a tray and leave to dry for 2 hours.
- Bring a pan of water to the boil, add salt and cook the ravioli in batches for 3 to 5 minutes. When cooked, transfer to a serving dish. Can be served with tomato sauce, or buttered.

Falafels

SERVES 4-6

INGREDIENTS:

800g/1lb 14oz canned chickpeas
¼ onion
2 garlic cloves
15g/½oz flat-leaf parsley leaves
15g/½oz fresh coriander leaves
1 teaspoon ground cumin
1 tablespoon lemon juice
½ beaten egg

2 tablespoons olive oil

For the dressing:
1 small handful of fresh mint
1 garlic clove
200g/7oz Greek yogurt
Salt and pepper

- Drain and rinse the chickpeas, then blend them in a blender or food processor with the remaining ingredients except the egg and oil. Turn the mixture into a bowl and beat in the egg, then cover and chill in the refrigerator for 30 to 60 minutes, or longer if more convenient.
- Preheat the oven to 180°C/350°F/Gas mark 4.
- With wet hands, shape the mixture into 20 equal-size balls. Place the falafels on an oiled baking sheet and flatten them slightly, then brush them with more oil.
- Bake for 20 minutes, turning them over halfway.
- To make the dressing, blend the mint, garlic and yogurt in the blender or food processor, turn into a bowl and add salt and pepper to taste.
- To serve, place the falafels on a serving platter and spoon the dressing over them. Serve hot.

Fresh herb risotto

SERVES 4-6

INGREDIENTS:

1 tablespoon olive oil
1 onion (chopped)
2 garlic cloves (chopped)
225g/8oz risotto rice
125ml/4fl oz dry white wine

700ml/1¼pt hot vegetable stock
Salt and pepper
3 tablespoons chopped dried mixed herbs
Grated zest of 1 lemon

→

- Heat the oil in a medium-sized saucepan and gently fry the onion and garlic until soft. Add the rice and stir over a low to medium heat for 1 to 2 minutes, then pour in the wine and let it sizzle.
- Pour in a third of the stock and stir well. Season to taste, then simmer until the stock is absorbed, stirring frequently. Add the remaining stock in two stages and continue to simmer and stir for about 15 to 20 minutes, or until all the liquid has been absorbed and the rice is tender.
- Remove from the heat and stir in 2 tablespoons of the fresh herbs and the lemon zest. Season well and garnish with the remaining herbs.

Kidney bean Kiev

SERVES 4

INGREDIENTS:

For the garlic butter:
100g/4oz butter
3 garlic cloves (crushed)
1 tablespoon chopped fresh parsley

For the bean patties:
700g/1½lb canned red kidney beans
150g/5oz fresh white breadcrumbs

25g/1oz butter
1 leek (chopped)
1 celery stick (chopped)
1 tablespoon chopped fresh parsley
Salt and pepper
1 egg (beaten)
Vegetable oil for shallow frying

- To make the garlic butter, put the butter, garlic and parsley in a bowl and blend together with a wooden spoon. Place the garlic butter on to a sheet of baking parchment, roll into a cigar shape and wrap in the baking parchment.
- Chill in the refrigerator until required.
- Using a potato masher, mash the red kidney beans in a mixing bowl and stir in 75g/3oz of the breadcrumbs until thoroughly blended.
- Melt the butter in a heavy-based frying pan. Add the leek and celery and sauté over a low heat, stirring constantly, for 3 to 4 minutes.
- Add the bean mixture to the pan, together with the parsley and a pinch of salt.
- Mix thoroughly. Remove the pan from the heat and set aside to cool slightly.
- Divide the kidney bean mixture into 4 equal portions and shape them into ovals.
- Slice the garlic butter into 4 pieces and place a slice in the centre of each bean patty. With your hands, mould the bean mixture around the garlic butter to encase it completely.
- Dip each bean patty into the beaten egg to coat and then roll in the remaining breadcrumbs.
- Heat a little oil in a frying pan and fry the patties, turning once, for 7 to 10 minutes, or until golden brown. Serve immediately.

Roasted vegetable lasagne

SERVES 4-6

INGREDIENTS:

4 medium red onions (sliced
into wedges)
3 red peppers (chopped)
3 yellow peppers (chopped)
4 medium courgettes (chopped)
4 garlic cloves (chopped)
100ml/3½fl oz olive oil
Salt and pepper
450g/1lb cherry tomatoes
800g/1¾lb canned artichokes (drained
and quartered)
100ml/3½fl oz tomato purée
75g/3oz pitted black and green olives

350g/12oz Mozzarella cheese (grated)
14–16 sheets lasagne

For the sauce:
1.8 litres/3pt full-fat milk
1 bay leaf
Pinch of ground nutmeg
6 peppercorns (crushed)
100g/4oz butter
100g/4oz plain flour
75g/3oz Pecorino cheese (grated)
3 tablespoons chopped fresh basil

- Preheat the oven to 220°C/425°F/Gas mark 7.
- Divide the onions, peppers and courgettes between two large roasting tins, sprinkle the garlic over them, drizzle each with half of the oil, season well with salt and pepper and toss together. Cook for 30 minutes on 2 shelves, stirring from time to time.
- To make the sauce, put the milk in a pan with the bay leaf, nutmeg and peppercorns and bring to the boil. Turn off the heat, leave to infuse for 15 minutes, then strain.
- Melt the butter in a separate pan, stir in the flour until smooth and cook for 1 minute. Gradually add the strained milk, whisking until smooth. Bring to the boil, stirring, and cook for 2 minutes until thickened. Stir in the Pecorino cheese and basil. Cover with a wet disc of greaseproof paper and put to one side.
- Remove the roasting tins from the oven, then toss the cherry tomatoes and artichokes through the vegetables. Switch the position of the tins in the oven and cook for a further 20 minutes, until the vegetables are slightly charred at the edges.
- Remove from the oven and, into each, stir half of the tomato purée and half the olives. Reduce the oven temperature to 200°C/400°F/Gas mark 6.
- Layer the vegetables, Mozzarella, lasagne and sauce into 2 deep ovenproof dishes, finishing with the sauce and Mozzarella. Bake for 35 to 40 minutes or until bubbling and golden at the edges.

Spinach & ricotta shells

SERVES 4

INGREDIENTS:

20 giant conchiglie (shell pasta)
1 tablespoon extra-virgin olive oil
1 onion (finely chopped)
450g/1lb spinach (chopped)

700g/1½lb ricotta cheese
25g/1oz Parmesan cheese (grated)
225g/8oz tomato pasta sauce

- Cook the conchiglie in a pan of rapidly boiling salted water until al dente (about 8 to 10 minutes), then drain thoroughly.
- Heat the oil in a pan, add the onion and stir over a medium heat for 3 minutes, or until lightly browned. Add the spinach and stir over a low heat until wilted. Add the ricotta cheese and stir until combined.
- Spoon the mixture into the pasta shells and sprinkle with Parmesan. Put the shells on a cold, lightly oiled grill tray. Cook under a medium-high heat for 3 minutes, or until lightly browned and heated through.
- Put the tomato pasta sauce in a small pan and stir over a high heat for 1 minute, or until heated through. Spoon the sauce on to a serving platter and top with the shells.

Bubble & squeak

SERVES 4

INGREDIENTS:

450g/1lb potatoes (diced)
225g/8oz Savoy cabbage (shredded)
5 tablespoons vegetable oil
2 leeks (chopped)

1 garlic cloves (crushed)
225g/8oz smoked tofu (cubed)
Salt and pepper

- Cook the diced potatoes in a saucepan of lightly salted boiling water for 10 minutes, until tender. Drain and mash the potatoes.
- In a separate saucepan, blanch the cabbage in boiling water for 5 minutes. Drain well and add to the potato.
- Heat the oil in a heavy-based frying pan. Add the leeks, garlic and tofu and fry gently for 2 to 3 minutes. Stir into the potato and cabbage mixture.
- Carefully turn the whole mixture over and continue to cook over a moderate heat for a further 5 to 7 minutes, until crispy underneath. Serve immediately.

Chole

SERVES 4-6

INGREDIENTS:

275g/10oz channa dal
1.2 litres/2pt cold water
3 tablespoons vegetable oil
2 medium onions (finely chopped)
1 tablespoon ground coriander
1 tablespoon ground cumin
2 teaspoons chilli powder

450g/1lb potatoes (cut into small cubes)
4 tomatoes (chopped)
1 tablespoon garam masala
450ml/³/₄pt cold water
1 teaspoon salt
Pepper

- Pick over the chana dal removing any stones or other debris. Put the channa dal in a large bowl, pour over the cold water and leave to soak for at least 8 hours, or preferably overnight.
- Place the channa dal and soaking liquid in a saucepan and bring to the boil.
- Skim off the scum, half cover the saucepan with a lid and simmer for 20 minutes or until soft and almost dry. Remove from the heat. Drain and leave to cool.
- Heat 2 tablespoons of the oil in a heavy, flameproof casserole dish over a medium heat, add the onions and cook gently, stirring frequently, for about 10 minutes until softened. Add the remaining oil and when hot, add the coriander, cumin and chilli powder. Stir for 2 to 3 minutes. Add the channa dal and stir well to mix.
- Add the potatoes, tomatoes and garam masala. Pour in the cold water and bring to the boil, stirring constantly. Add the salt, and pepper to taste, then lower the heat, cover and simmer for 30 minutes or until the potato is very soft. Stir occasionally during the cooking time and add more water if necessary.
- Transfer to a warmed serving dish. Serve immediately.

Black bean & vegetables

SERVES 4

INGREDIENTS:

4 tablespoons sesame oil
8 spring onions (thinly sliced)
2 garlic cloves (crushed)
225g/8oz button mushrooms (sliced)
1 red pepper (cut into thin strips)

1 green pepper (cut into thin strips)
2 large carrots (cut into matchsticks)
4 tablespoons black bean sauce
100ml/3¹/₂fl oz warm water
225g/8oz beansprouts

→

← • Heat the oil in a large preheated wok until very hot. Add the spring onions and garlic and stir-fry for 30 seconds. Add the mushrooms, peppers and carrots. Stir-fry for 5 to 6 minutes over a high heat until the vegetables are just beginning to soften.
• Mix the black bean sauce with the water. Add to the wok and cook for 3 to 4 minutes. Stir in the beansprouts and cook for 1 minute more, until all the vegetables are coated in the sauce. Serve with rice.

Green bean &
tomato tagliatelle

SERVES 4

INGREDIENTS:

350g/12oz green beans
1 garlic clove (peeled)
150ml/¼pt double cream
6 plum tomatoes (chopped)

3 tablespoons chopped fresh
basil leaves
350g/12oz egg tagliatelle
50g/2oz Parmesan cheese (grated)

• Cook green beans in boiling salted water for 8 minutes or until tender, then drain.
• Place the garlic in a pan with the cream and bring to the boil. Remove the garlic and add the tomato, green beans and basil. Stir to combine.
• Cook the tagliatelle in a large saucepan of boiling salted water for about 8 minutes or until al dente. Drain, and add to the tomato and beans. Serve with Parmesan cheese.

Indian green bean stir-fry

SERVES 4

INGREDIENTS:

4 tablespoons vegetable oil
1 teaspoon mustard seeds
10 curry leaves
1 teaspoon urad dal
2 dried red chillies
100g/4oz onions (finely chopped)

3 green chillies (deseeded and
halved lengthways)
1 teaspoon ground turmeric
200g/7oz green beans (finely chopped)
4 tablespoons water
50g/2oz freshly grated coconut
Salt

- Heat the oil in a large frying pan or wok. Add the mustard seeds and, as they begin to pop, add the curry leaves, urad dal and dried chillies. Cook, stirring, until the urad dal turns golden.
- Add the onions and stir-fry for 5 minutes or until the onions are soft. Add the green chillies and turmeric and cook for another 2 minutes.
- Stir in the beans and water. Lower the heat to minimum, cover the pan and cook for 10 minutes, stirring occasionally.
- Add the coconut and some salt to taste. Raise the heat to medium and stir-fry the mixture for 5 minutes. Remove from the heat and serve.

Chakchouka

SERVES 4-6

INGREDIENTS:

1 large aubergine (finely diced)
Salt and pepper
4 tablespoons olive oil
1 large onion (finely chopped)
2 garlic cloves (crushed)
1 red pepper (diced)

4 medium courgettes (diced)
450g/1lb ripe tomatoes (chopped)
300ml/½pt water
2 tablespoons tomato purée
2 teaspoons chilli powder
Pinch of sugar

- Place the aubergine in a colander, sprinkle liberally with salt and cover with a plate or saucer. Place a heavy weight on top of the plate or saucer, then leave for 30 minutes.
- Rinse the aubergine under cold running water, then drain thoroughly. Heat the oil in a large flameproof casserole dish, add the aubergine and onion and cook gently, stirring frequently, until softened.
- Add the garlic, pepper, courgettes and tomatoes. Stir well to mix, then pour in the water and bring to the boil, stirring. Lower the heat, then add the tomato purée, chilli powder, sugar and salt and pepper to taste. Cover and simmer gently for 30 minutes, stirring occasionally and adding more water if the chakchouka becomes dry. Taste and adjust the seasoning before serving.

Macaroni cheese

SERVES 4-6

INGREDIENTS:

Salt
225g/8oz macaroni
100g/4oz butter
2 spring onions (finely sliced)
2 tablespoons plain flour
225ml/8fl oz evaporated milk

225g/8fl oz single cream
2 tablespoons mayonnaise
275g/10oz Cheddar cheese (grated)
2 eggs (lightly beaten)
100g/4oz Parmesan cheese (grated)

- Fill a large saucepan with water, add 1 teaspoon of salt and bring it to the boil.
- Carefully pour the macaroni into the boiling water and cook for about 10 minutes (or as per cooking instructions) until al dente. Do not overcook the macaroni. Remove from the heat, drain and set aside.
- Preheat the oven to 180°C/350°F/Gas mark 4. Grease a large casserole dish.
- In a heavy-based frying pan, melt the butter and sauté the spring onions over a medium heat until soft. Add the flour and stir to mix well. Continue to sauté for about 3 minutes, then blend in first the evaporated milk, then the cream, and then the mayonnaise. Finally add the Cheddar cheese.
- Stir the beaten eggs through the macaroni until evenly combined.
- Mix the macaroni with the cheese sauce and pour into the casserole dish. Sprinkle the top with the Parmesan cheese and bake in the oven for about 20 to 30 minutes or until the top has browned and the macaroni is piping hot. Turn off the heat and allow the macaroni cheese to cool a little. Serve warm.

Veggie burgers

SERVES 2

INGREDIENTS:

100g/4oz green beans
100g/4oz cracked wheat
225ml/8fl oz boiling water
1 small courgette
1 small carrot (peeled)
½ Granny Smith apple (peeled)
100g/4oz canned chickpeas (rinsed and drained)

1 tablespoon minced onion
1 tablespoon peanut butter
1½ tablespoons vegetable oil
½ teaspoon curry powder
½ teaspoon chilli powder
Salt and pepper
100g/4oz breadcrumbs

- Cook green beans in boiling water until tender. Drain and chop finely.
- Cook the cracked wheat in the boiling water for 1 minute. Remove from the heat and cover.
- Grate the courgette, carrot and apple. Place in a tea towel and squeeze out excess moisture. Combine with the green beans in a mixing bowl.
- In a blender or food processor blend the chickpeas, onion, peanut butter, vegetable oil, curry powder and chilli powder until smooth. Season with salt and pepper. Add to the grated vegetables.
- Drain the cracked wheat through a strainer, pressing with the back of a spoon to extract excess liquid. Add to the bowl. Add the breadcrumbs and refrigerate for 1 hour. With wet hands, shape into 4 burgers.
- Cook under a medium grill for 3 minutes on each side.

Ratatouille

SERVES 4

INGREDIENTS:

2 large aubergines (coarsely chopped)
4 courgettes (coarsely chopped)
Salt and pepper
150ml/¼pt olive oil
2 onions (sliced)
2 garlic cloves (chopped)
1 large red pepper (coarsely chopped)

2 large yellow peppers (coarsely chopped)
Fresh rosemary sprig
Fresh thyme sprig
1 teaspoon coriander seeds (crushed)
3 plum tomatoes (chopped)
8 fresh basil leaves (torn)

- Sprinkle the aubergines and courgettes with salt, and then place them in a colander with a plate and a weight on top to extract the bitter juices. Leave them to stand for about 30 minutes.
- Heat the olive oil in a large pan. Add the onions, fry gently for about 6 to 7 minutes, until just softened, then add the garlic and cook for another 2 minutes.
- Rinse the aubergines and courgettes and pat dry with kitchen paper.
- Add to the pan with the peppers, increase the heat and sauté until the peppers are just turning brown. Add the herbs and coriander seeds, then cover the pan and cook gently for about 40 minutes. Add the tomatoes and season well. Cook gently for 10 minutes, until the vegetables are soft but not too mushy.
- Remove the herb sprigs. Stir in the basil leaves and taste for seasoning.

Vegetable biryani

SERVES 4

INGREDIENTS:

4 tablespoons vegetable oil
2 onions (sliced)
2 garlic cloves (crushed)
2cm/1in piece of root ginger (peeled and sliced)
1 teaspoon ground turmeric
½ teaspoon chilli powder
1 teaspoon ground coriander
2 teaspoons ground cumin
100g/4oz red lentils (drained)

3 tomatoes (chopped)
1 aubergine (cut into cubes)
1.8 litres/3pt vegetable stock
1 red pepper (diced)
350ml/12oz basmati rice
100g/4oz French beans (halved)
225g/8oz cauliflower florets
225g/8oz mushrooms (quartered)
50g/2oz unsalted cashew nuts

- Heat the oil in a saucepan, add the onions and fry gently for 2 minutes. Stir in the garlic, ginger and spices and fry gently, stirring frequently, for 1 minute.
- Add the lentils, tomatoes, aubergine and 600ml/1pt stock, mix well, then cover and simmer gently for 20 minutes.
- Add the pepper and cook for a further 10 minutes, or until the lentils are tender and all the liquid has been absorbed.
- Rinse the rice under cold running water. Drain and place in another pan with the remaining stock. Bring to the boil, add the French beans, cauliflower and mushrooms, then cover and cook gently for 15 minutes, or until the rice and vegetables are tender. Remove from the heat and set aside, covered, for 10 minutes.
- Add the lentil mixture and the cashews to the cooked rice and mix lightly together. Serve hot.

Vegetable paella

SERVES 4

INGREDIENTS:

3 tablespoons olive oil
2 small fennel bulbs (halved lengthways)
225g/8oz cherry tomatoes (halved)
2 teaspoons coriander seeds (crushed)
Salt and pepper

900ml/1½pt vegetable stock
100g/4oz wild rice
200g/7oz long-grain white rice
2 tablespoons chopped fresh coriander
Juice of ½ lemon

- Preheat the oven to 200°C/400°F/Gas mark 6. Brush a roasting tin with oil.
- Place the fennel and tomatoes in the roasting tin and sprinkle the coriander seeds, salt and pepper over them. Roast the vegetables, turning them once or twice, for about 40 minutes or until tender.
- Bring the stock to the boil in a large saucepan. Add the wild rice and simmer for 30 minutes. Then add the white rice and continue to cook for 15 to 20 minutes or until both types of rice are tender. Drain through a sieve.
- Turn the rice and roasted vegetables into a large bowl and toss to mix. Add the chopped coriander and the lemon juice. Serve hot.

Vegetable toad-in-the-hole

SERVES 4

INGREDIENTS:

For the batter:
100g/4oz plain flour
Pinch of salt
2 eggs (beaten)
200ml/7fl oz milk
2 tablespoons wholegrain mustard
2 tablespoons vegetable oil

For the filling:
25g/1oz butter

2 garlic cloves (crushed)
1 onion (cut into 8)
75g/3oz baby carrots (halved lengthways)
50g/2oz French beans
50g/2oz canned sweetcorn (drained)
2 tomatoes (seeded and cut into chunks)
1 teaspoon wholegrain mustard
1 tablespoon dried mixed herbs
Salt and pepper

- Preheat the oven to 200°C/400°F/Gas mark 6.
- To make the batter, sift the flour and salt into a bowl. Beat in the eggs and milk to make a batter. Stir in the mustard and leave to stand.
- Pour the oil into a shallow ovenproof dish and heat in the oven for 10 minutes.
- To make the filling, melt the butter in a frying pan and sauté the garlic and onion, stirring constantly, for 2 minutes. Cook the carrots and beans in a saucepan of boiling water for 7 minutes, or until tender. Drain well.
- Add the sweetcorn and tomatoes to the frying pan with the mustard and herbs.
- Season well and add the carrots and beans.
- Remove the dish from the oven and pour in the batter. Spoon the vegetables into the centre, return to the oven and cook for 30 to 35 minutes, until the batter had risen and set. Serve immediately.

Tofu stir-fry

SERVES 4

INGREDIENTS:

3 tablespoons vegetable oil
225g/8oz firm tofu (cut into strips)
2 garlic cloves (crushed)
3 spring onions (chopped)
2 green chillies (finely chopped)
175g/6oz French beans
175g/6oz baby sweetcorn (halved)

100g/4oz beansprouts
100g/4oz hard white cabbage
(shredded)
3 tablespoons smooth peanut butter
1½ tablespoons soy sauce
300ml/½pt coconut milk

- Heat 2 tablespoons of the oil in a large wok. When the oil is hot, add the tofu, stir-fry for 3 minutes and remove. Set aside. Wipe out the wok with kitchen paper.
- Add the remaining oil. When it is hot, add the garlic, spring onions and chillies and stir-fry for 1 minute. Add the French beans, sweetcorn, beansprouts and white cabbage and stir-fry for a further 2 minutes. Then add the peanut butter and soy sauce to the wok. Stir well to coat the vegetables. Add the tofu to the vegetables in the wok.
- Pour the coconut milk over the vegetables, simmer for 3 minutes and serve immediately with rice or noodles.

Parsee pilau rice

SERVES 4-6

INGREDIENTS:

2 tablespoons ghee
6 cardamom pods (bruised)
5 whole cloves
7.5cm/3in piece of cinnamon stick
(broken in half)
¼ teaspoon lightly crushed black
peppercorns

¼ teaspoon saffron threads
350g/12oz basmati rice
¾ teaspoon salt
600ml/1pt water
25g/1oz sultanas
25g/1oz roasted cashew nuts
25g/1oz pistachio nuts

- Heat the ghee in a wide, heavy-based saucepan. Stir in the cardamom pods, cloves, cinnamon stick and peppercorns, and fry over a gentle heat, stirring constantly, for 2 minutes until fragrant. Add the saffron threads and rice to the

pan and fry, stirring constantly, for a further 1 minute.
- Add the salt and water. Stir well to mix. Bring to the boil, then reduce the heat, cover the pan and cook the rice gently for 15 minutes without removing the lid.
- Remove the pan from the heat and lightly loosen the rice grains with a fork (all the water should have been absorbed). Stir the sultanas into the rice, cover the pan with a clean, dry tea towel and allow the rice to cook in its own heat for a further 5 minutes.
- Just before serving, stir the two types of nuts into the rice. Serve hot.

Potato, apple & bean salad

SERVES 4

INGREDIENTS:

225g/8oz new potatoes (quartered)
225g/8oz mixed canned beans
1 red dessert apple (diced and tossed
in 1 tablespoon lemon juice)
1 small yellow pepper (diced)
1 shallot (sliced)
½ head fennel (sliced)
Crisp lettuce leaves

For the dressing:
1 tablespoon red wine vinegar
2 tablespoons olive oil
½ tablespoon American mustard
1 garlic cloves (crushed)
2 teaspoons chopped fresh thyme

- Cook the potatoes in a saucepan of boiling water for 15 minutes until tender.
- Drain and transfer to a mixing bowl.
- Add the potatoes to the mixed beans with the apple and yellow pepper, and the shallots and fennel. Mix well, taking care not to break up the cooked potatoes.
- In a bowl, whisk all the dressing ingredients together. Pour the dressing over the salad.
- Line a plate or salad bowl with the lettuce leaves and spoon the salad in the centre. Serve immediately.

Chinese salad nests

SERVES 4

INGREDIENTS:

For the potato nests:
450g/1lb potatoes (grated)
100g/4oz cornflour
Vegetable oil for frying

For the salad:
100g/4oz pineapple (cubed)
1 green pepper (cut into strips)
1 carrot (cut into strips)

50g/2oz mangetout (thickly sliced)
25g/1oz beansprouts
2 spring onions (sliced)
For the dressing:
1 tablespoon clear honey
1 teaspoon soy sauce
1 garlic clove (crushed)
1 teaspoon lemon juice

- To make the nests, rinse the potatoes several times in cold water. Drain well on kitchen paper so they are completely dry to prevent spitting when they are cooked in the fat. Place the potatoes in a mixing bowl. Add the cornflour, mixing well to coat the potatoes.
- Half fill a wok with vegetable oil and heat until smoking. Line a sieve with the potato mixture and press another sieve of the same size on top.
- Lower the sieves into the oil and cook for 2 minutes until the potato nest is golden brown and crisp. Remove from the wok, allowing the excess oil to drain off. Place the nest on a serving dish.
- Repeat 3 more times to use up all of the mixture and make a total of 4 nests.
- Leave to cool.
- Mix the salad ingredients together then spoon into the potato nests.
- Mix the dressing ingredients together in a bowl. Pour the dressing over the salad, and serve immediately.

Desserts

Send your dinner guests home with some fond memories and find your inspiration in this selection of after-dinner treats, both hot and cold. In spring and summer prepare desserts such as Raspberry sorbet, Brandy Trifle or Angel cake. For the colder months there is comfort in the shape of Rhubarb crumble, Apple pie or Rice pudding.

Shortbread

SERVES 4–8

INGREDIENTS:

100g/4oz unsalted butter
50g/2oz caster sugar

100g/4oz plain flour
50g/2oz rice flour

- Preheat the oven to 160°C/325°F/Gas mark 3. Place a 15cm/6in plain flan ring on a baking sheet.
- Beat together the butter and sugar until light and fluffy. Stir in both flours, then knead lightly until smooth.
- Press the dough evenly into the flan ring, then lift the ring away. Crimp the edges of the dough with your thumb and finger. Prick the surface of the short bread with a fork and mark into 6 or 8 wedges.
- Bake for 40 minutes, until pale biscuit coloured and just firm to the touch. Leave the shortbread to cool for a few minutes, then carefully transfer to a wire rack to cool completely.

Tiramisu

SERVES 6

INGREDIENTS:

500ml/18fl oz strong black coffee (cooled)
50ml/2fl oz Marsala wine
2 eggs (separated)
50g/2oz caster sugar

225g/8oz Mascarpone
225ml/8fl oz double cream
16 large sponge finger biscuits
2 tablespoons dark cocoa powder

- Combine the coffee and Marsala in a bowl and set aside. Beat the egg yolks and sugar in a bowl with an electric beater for 3 minutes, or until thick and pale. Add the Mascarpone and mix. Transfer to a large bowl. Beat the cream in a sep arate bowl, with an electric beater, until soft peaks form, then fold into the Mascarpone mixture.
- Place the egg whites in a small, clean, dry bowl and beat, with an electric beater, until soft peaks form. Fold quickly and lightly into the cream mixture.
- Dip half the biscuits into the coffee mixture, drain off any excess and arrange in a large glass serving dish. Spread half the cream mixture over the biscuits.
- Dip the remaining biscuits into the remaining coffee mixture and repeat layering. Smooth the surface, dust liberally with the cocoa powder. Refrigerate overnight.

Summer pudding

SERVES 6

INGREDIENTS:

1 loaf of crusty white bread (sliced)
700g/1 1/2lb fresh redcurrants
75g/3oz granulated sugar

6 tablespoons water
450g/1lb mixed berries
Juice of 1/2 lemon

- Trim the crusts from the bread slices. Cut a round of bread to fit in the bottom of a 1.5 litre/2 1/2pt pudding basin. Line the basin with bread slices, overlapping them slightly. Reserve enough bread slices to cover the top of the basin.
- Mix the redcurrants with 50g/2oz of the sugar and the water in a saucepan. Heat gently, crushing the berries lightly to help the juices flow. When the sugar has dissolved, remove from the heat.
- Tip the redcurrant mixture into a blender or food processor and blend until quite smooth. Press through a fine-mesh nylon strainer set in a bowl. Discard the fruit pulp left in the strainer.
- Put the mixed berries in a bowl with the remaining sugar and the lemon juice. Stir well.
- One at a time, remove the cut bread pieces from the basin and dip them in the redcurrant purée. Replace to line the basin evenly.
- Spoon the berries into the lined basin, pressing them down evenly. Top with the reserved bread slices, which have been dipped in the redcurrant purée.
- Cover the basin with clingfilm. Set a small plate, just big enough to fit inside the rim of the basin, on top of the pudding. Weigh it down and chill it in the refrigerator for 24 hours.

Sponge cake

SERVES 6–8

INGREDIENTS:

75g/3oz plain flour
150g/5oz self-raising flour
6 eggs
200g/7oz caster sugar

2 tablespoons boiling water
150g/5oz strawberry jam
225ml/8fl oz double cream
Icing sugar to dust

- Preheat the oven to 180°C/350°F/Gas mark 4. Lightly grease two 23cm/9in sandwich tins or round cake tins and line the bases with baking parchment.

→

← Dust the tins with a little flour, shaking off any excess.

- Sift the flours together onto a sheet of greaseproof paper. Beat the eggs in a large bowl with an electric beater for 7 minutes, or until thick and pale. Gradually add the sugar to the eggs, beating well after each addition. Using a large metal spoon, quickly and gently fold in the sifted flour and the boiling water.
- Spread the mixture evenly into the tins and bake for 25 minutes, or until the sponges are lightly golden. Leave the sponges in their tins for 5 minutes before turning out on to a wire rack to cool.
- Spread jam over one of the sponges. Beat the cream in a small bowl until stiff, then spoon into a piping bag and pipe rosettes over the jam. Place the other sponge on top and dust with icing sugar.

Florentines

SERVES 5–10

INGREDIENTS:

25g/1oz butter
50g/2oz caster sugar
25g/1oz plain flour (sifted)
50g/2oz almonds (chopped)
50g/2oz mixed peel (chopped)

25g/1oz raisins
25g/1oz glacé cherries (chopped)
Grated zest of 1 lemon
125g/41/2oz dark chocolate (melted)

- Preheat the oven to 180°C/350°F/Gas mark 4. Line 2 large baking trays with baking parchment.
- Heat the butter and caster sugar in a small saucepan until the butter has just melted and the sugar dissolved. Remove the pan from the heat.
- Stir in the flour and mix well. Stir in the almonds, mixed peel, raisins, cherries and lemon zest. Place teaspoonfuls of the mixture well apart on the baking trays.
- Bake in the oven for 10 minutes or until lightly golden.
- As soon as the Florentines are removed from the oven, press the edges into neat shapes while still on the baking trays, using a biscuit cutter. Leave to cool on the baking trays until firm, then carefully transfer to a wire rack to cool completely.
- Spread the melted chocolate over one side of each Florentine. Leave chocolate side up until set.

Mixed fruit jelly

SERVES 5–10

INGREDIENTS:

225g/8oz dried apricots
300ml/¹/₂pt unsweetened orange juice
2 tablespoons lemon juice

3 teaspoons clear honey
1 tablespoon powdered gelatine
4 tablespoons boiling water

- Place the apricots in a saucepan and pour in the orange juice. Bring to the boil, cover and simmer for 15 to 20 minutes until plump and soft.
- Transfer the mixture to a blender or food processor and blend until smooth. Stir in the lemon juice and add the honey. Pour the mixture into a measuring jug and make up to 600ml/1pt with cold water.
- Dissolve the gelatine in the boiling water and stir into the apricot mixture. Pour the mixture into a mould and leave in the refrigerator to set.

Chocolate chip cookies

SERVES 8–10

INGREDIENTS:

100g/4oz butter
100g/4oz brown sugar
100g/4oz granulated sugar
1 egg
³/₄ teaspoon vanilla essence

350g/12oz plain flour
1 tablespoon baking powder
¹/₂ teaspoon salt
100g/4oz peanuts (chopped)
100g/4oz chocolate chips

- Preheat the oven to 190°C/375°F/Gas mark 5.
- Cream the butter and both sugars in a bowl until smooth and light. Beat in the egg and vanilla essence. Sieve the flour, baking powder and salt and stir into the mixture, blending well. Stir in the nuts and chocolate chips.
- Drop teaspoons of mixture on to greased trays, about 2.5cm/1in apart. Bake for 8 to 10 minutes, or until lightly browned.

Carrot cake

SERVES 6–8

INGREDIENTS:

100g/4oz self-raising flour
100g/4oz plain flour
2 teaspoons ground cinnamon
½ teaspoon ground nutmeg
1 teaspoon bicarbonate of soda
225ml/8fl oz vegetable oil
175g/6oz brown sugar
4 eggs
175g/6oz golden syrup

400g/14oz grated carrot
50g/2oz chopped pecan nuts

For the lemon icing:
175g/6oz cream cheese (softened)
50g/2oz butter (softened)
175g/6oz icing sugar
1 teaspoon vanilla essence
2 teaspoons lemon juice

- Preheat the oven to 160°C/325°F/Gas mark 3. Lightly grease a 23cm/9in round cake tin and line the base and side with baking parchment.
- Sift the flours, spices and bicarbonate of soda into a large bowl and make a well in the centre. Whisk together the oil, sugar, eggs and golden syrup in a jug until combined. Add this mixture to the well in the flour and gradually stir into the dry ingredients with a metal spoon until smooth. Stir in the carrot and nuts, then spoon into the tin and smooth the surface. Bake for 1½ hours.
- Leave the cake in the tin for at least 15 minutes before turning out on to a wire rack to cool completely.
- For the lemon icing, beat the cream cheese and butter with an electric beater until smooth. Gradually add the icing sugar alternately with the vanilla and lemon juice, beating until light and creamy. Spread the icing over the cooled cake using a flat-bladed knife.

Raspberry sorbet

SERVES 6–8

INGREDIENTS:

450g/1lb raspberries
400ml/14fl oz water

175g/6oz sugar
50ml/2fl oz lemon juice

- Liquidize the raspberries in a blender or food processor and strain.
- Boil 300ml/½pt water and the sugar for 5 minutes in a pan. Remove from the heat and allow to cool. Add the lemon juice and the rest of the water and the raspberries. Freeze.

Ginger cake

SERVES 6–8

INGREDIENTS:

100g/4oz butter
175g/6oz black treacle
175g/6oz golden syrup
175g/6oz plain flour
100g/4oz self-raising flour
1 teaspoon bicarbonate of soda

3 teaspoons ground ginger
1 teaspoon mixed spice
½ teaspoon ground cinnamon
150g/5oz brown sugar
225ml/8fl oz milk
2 eggs (lightly beaten)

- Preheat the oven to 180°C/350°F/Gas mark 4. Lightly grease a deep 20cm/8in square cake tin and line the base with baking parchment.
- Combine the butter, treacle and golden syrup in a saucepan and stir over a low heat until the butter has melted. Remove from the heat.
- Sift the flours, bicarbonate of soda and spices into a large bowl, add the sugar and stir until well combined. Make a well in the centre. Add the butter mixture to the well, then pour in the combined milk and eggs. Stir with a wooden spoon until the mixture is smooth and well combined. Pour into the tin and smooth the surface. Bake for 45 to 60 minutes.
- Leave the cake in the tin for 20 minutes before turning out on to a wire rack to cool.

Strawberry shortcake

SERVES 4

INGREDIENTS:

450g/1lb strawberries (sliced)
¼ teaspoon honey
2 teaspoons orange juice
50g/2oz caster sugar
450g/1lb flour
4 tablespoons baking powder

½ teaspoon salt
Grated zest of 1 orange
50g/2oz butter
50g/2oz solid shortening
100g/4oz sour cream
600ml/1pt whipping cream

- Preheat the oven to 200°C/400°F/Gas mark 6.
- Combine the strawberries, honey and orange juice in a mixing bowl and leave to stand at room temperature for 1 hour.
- Sift all the dry ingredients together into a medium bowl. Add the orange zest, butter and shortening and work into the flour mixture thoroughly.

→

←

- Lightly mix in the sour cream with a fork to form a soft dough. Roll the dough out onto a lightly floured board until 2.5cm/1in thick and cut into 4 circles.
- Place on ungreased baking parchment and bake for about 20 minutes, until golden.
- To serve, top the shortcake with the berry mixture. Whip the cream into soft peaks and serve with the shortcake.

Chocolate mousse

SERVES 6

INGREDIENTS:

2 tablespoons cocoa
50ml/2fl oz hot water
1 teaspoon gelatine
275g/10oz silken tofu

1 tablespoon brandy
2 egg whites
50g/2oz caster sugar

- Stir the cocoa with the hot water until dissolved. Sprinkle the gelatine in an even layer onto 1 tablespoon water in a small bowl and leave to go spongy. Bring a small pan of water to the boil, remove from the heat and place the bowl in the pan. The water should come halfway up the side of the bowl. Stir the gelatine until dissolved.
- Drain the tofu and place in a blender or food processor. Add the cocoa mixture and brandy and blend until smooth, scraping down the sides. Transfer to a bowl and stir in the gelatine mixture.
- Whisk the eggs whites in a clean dry bowl until soft peaks form. Gradually add the sugar, beating well between each addition, until stiff and glossy peaks form.
- Fold into the chocolate mixture and spoon into a dish. Refrigerate until set.

Lemon syllabub

SERVES 6

INGREDIENTS:

100g/4oz caster sugar
Juice and zest of 2 lemons

3 tablespoons brandy
600ml/1pt double cream

- Whisk together the caster sugar, lemon juice and zest and the brandy.
- In another bowl, whisk the double cream until thick, then slowly whisk in the lemon mixture. Pour into wine glasses and refrigerate overnight.

Fairy cakes

SERVES 4–6

INGREDIENTS:

100g/4oz butter (softened)
150g/5oz caster sugar
175g/6oz self-raising flour
125ml/4fl oz milk
2 teaspoons vanilla essence

2 eggs
125ml/4fl oz cream (whipped to
soft peaks)
100g/4oz strawberry jam

- Preheat the oven to 180°C/350°F/Gas mark 4.
- Line a 12-hole shallow patty tin with baking paper cases. Put the butter, sugar, flour, milk, vanilla and eggs in a bowl and beat with an electric beater on a low speed for 2 minutes, or until well mixed. Increase the speed and beat for 2 minutes, or until smooth and pale.
- Divide the mixture evenly among the cases and bake for 20 minutes, or until cooked and golden. Transfer to a wire rack to cool completely.
- Place a half tablespoon of cream and a teaspoon of jam on top of each cake.

Brandy trifle

SERVES 6

INGREDIENTS:

20cm/8in sponge cake
150g/5oz apricot jam
125ml/4fl oz brandy
50ml/2fl oz water
75g/3oz apricot jelly crystals
600ml/1pt boiling water

2 bananas (sliced)
450ml/³⁄₄pt prepared custard
225ml/8fl oz double cream (whipped)
50g/2oz toasted almonds (chopped)
Pulp of 2 passion fruit

- Cut the sponge into small cubes and put in a large serving bowl. Combine the jam, brandy and water and sprinkle over the sponge.
- Add the jelly crystals to the water and stir until dissolved. Pour into a tin and refrigerate until set.
- Cut the jelly into cubes over the sponge and top with the sliced bananas and custard. Decorate with whipped cream, almonds and passion fruit. Keep in the refrigerator until required.

Christmas cake

SERVES 6–8

INGREDIENTS:

175g/6oz candied peel (chopped)
175g/glacé cherries (quartered)
450g/1lb sultanas
450g/1lb currants
350g/12oz raisins
125g/4oz almonds (blanched and chopped)
300g/11oz flour
300g/11oz butter

300g/11oz brown sugar
Grated zest of 1 orange
Grated zest of 1 lemon
1 tablespoon black treacle
6 eggs (beaten)
½ teaspoon salt
½ teaspoon mixed spice
½ teaspoon grated nutmeg
5 tablespoons brandy

- Preheat the oven to 170°C/325°F/Gas mark 3.
- In a large bowl, coat the candied peel, cherries, sultanas, currants, raisins and almonds with a tablespoon of the flour.
- In a separate bowl, cream the butter and sugar until light and fluffy, then beat in the grated orange and lemon zest and the black treacle. Beating with a wooden spoon, gradually add the beaten eggs, with a sprinkling of flour to stop the mixture from curdling. Then stir in the remaining flour, sifted with the salt and spices, and enough of the brandy to make a batter that will drop easily when shaken from the spoon. Stir in the fruit and nuts.
- Turn the batter into a 12cm/5in deep cake tin, well greased and lined with greaseproof paper.
- Bake in the oven for 20 minutes, then reduce the heat to 140°C/275°F/Gas mark 1 and bake for a further 4½ hours. Let the cake cool for 1 hour before turning it out.

Rum & raisin ice-cream

SERVES 8

INGREDIENTS:

250g/9oz raisins
100ml/3½fl oz dark rum
4 large egg yolks

3 tablespoons golden syrup
1 tablespoon treacle
600ml/1pt double cream (whipped)

- Put the raisins in a pan, add the rum and bring to the boil. Remove from the

heat and leave the mixture to soak.
- Put the egg yolks, syrup and treacle in a small bowl. Whisk with an electric mixer for 2 to 3 minutes until it has a mousse-like consistency. Pour into the cream and whisk for 3 to 4 minutes until thick.
- Pour the mixture into a large roasting tin and freeze for 1 hour, or until it begins to harden around the edges.
- Add the soaked fruit and any remaining liquid to the ice-cream and mix well.
- Put back in the freezer for 45 minutes. Spoon into a sealable container and freeze for at least 2½ hours.

Blancmange

SERVES 6

INGREDIENTS:

100g/4oz blanched almonds
100ml/3½fl oz cold water
250ml/9fl oz milk

125g/4oz caster sugar
3 teaspoons gelatine
300ml/½pt double cream

- Grease 6 x 125ml/4fl oz fluted moulds or ramekins. Process the almonds and half of the water in a blender or food processor until finely chopped and paste-like.
- With the blender still rotating, gradually add the milk. Pour into a small pan, add the sugar and stir over a low heat until the sugar had completely dissolved.
- Allow to cool.
- Strain the mixture through a strainer lined with muslin. Twist the muslin tightly to extract as much of the liquid as possible.
- Place the rest of the water in a small heatproof bowl, sprinkle the gelatine in an even layer over the surface and leave to go spongy. Do not stir.
- Bring a small pan filled with about 4cm/1½in water to the boil, remove from the heat and place the bowl into the pan. The water should come halfway up the side of the bowl. Stir the gelatine until clear and dissolved, then stir it through the almond milk. Allow to cool completely.
- Whip the cream into firm peaks, then fold the almond mixture through. Pour into the moulds and refrigerate for 6 to 8 hours, or until set.

Coconut cake

SERVES 6–8

INGREDIENTS:

2 x packets 450g/1lb chocolate
cake mix
225g/8oz desiccated coconut

2 eggs
125ml/4fl oz sour cream
125ml/4fl oz milk

- Preheat the oven to 180°C/350°F/Gas mark 4.
- Beat together the cake mix, coconut, eggs, sour cream and milk for 3 to 4 minutes, or until smooth. Pour into a greased loaf tin.
- Bake in the oven for 45 to 50 minutes. Turn on to a wire rack to cool.

Chocolate profiteroles

SERVES 8–10

INGREDIENTS:

60g/2½oz plain flour
Pinch of salt
50g/2oz butter
150ml/¼pt water
2 eggs (beaten)
450ml/¾pt whipping cream

For the chocolate sauce:
125g/4oz plain chocolate
50ml/2fl oz water

- Preheat the oven to 220°C/425°F/Gas mark 7. Grease two baking sheets.
- Sift the flour and salt on to a sheet of parchment. Put the butter and water into a pan and heat gently until the butter has melted. Bring to the boil and then tip in the flour all at once. Remove from the heat. Beat until the mixture forms a ball and leaves the sides of the pan. Cool slightly.
- Gradually add the beaten eggs, beating well after each addition, until a smooth thick paste is formed. Spoon into a large piping bag with a 1cm/½in plain nozzle and pipe 24 walnut-sized balls on to the baking sheets. Bake at the top of the oven for 20 to 25 minutes.
- Make a slit in each one for the steam to escape, then return to the oven for 5 minutes. Cool on a wire rack. Place all but 50ml/2fl oz of the whipping cream in a bowl, whip until just thick, then spoon into a large piping bag fitted with a plain nozzle. Cut each profiterole in half, fill with cream and reassemble.

- To make the chocolate sauce, place the chocolate in a pan with the water and the reserved cream. Heat gently over a very low heat until the chocolate has melted.
- Pile all the profiteroles in a pyramid on a serving dish and pour the hot sauce over.

Chocolate fluff

SERVES 2

INGREDIENTS:

3 egg whites
3 tablespoons caster sugar
½ teaspoon vanilla essence

150ml/¼pt cream
2 tablespoons melted plain chocolate
Chopped nuts to serve

- Beat the egg whites until they are stiff, then gradually stir in the sugar and vanilla essence.
- Whip the cream until firm and fold into the egg whites. Gradually fold in the chocolate. Put into individual glasses and serve sprinkled with chopped nuts.

Gingerbread

SERVES 8–10

INGREDIENTS:

2 tablespoons milk
½ teaspoon bicarbonate of soda
25g/1oz sultanas
50g/2oz stem ginger (chopped)
100g/4oz butter
100g/4oz brown sugar

2 eggs
225ml/8fl oz treacle
25g/1oz raisins
225g/8oz plain flour
1 teaspoon ground ginger

- Preheat the oven to 160°C/325°F/Gas mark 3.
- Warm the milk gently with the bicarbonate of soda and take off the heat. Add the sultanas and ginger.
- Cream the butter, add the sugar and beat until light and fluffy.
- Add in the eggs, one at a time. Stir in the treacle and raisins, then add the flour and ground ginger. Mix well. Pour into a large loaf tin which has been lined with baking parchment.
- Bake for 1½ hours, then turn out and cool on a wire rack.

Banana split

SERVES 4

INGREDIENTS:

200g/7oz dark chocolate
175ml/6fl oz cream
25g/1oz butter

4 bananas
12 scoops vanilla ice-cream
Chopped nuts to serve

- Put the chocolate, cream and butter in a pan and stir over a low heat until smooth. Cool slightly.
- Split the bananas in half lengthways and arrange in 4 glass dishes. Place 3 scoops of ice-cream in each dish, and pour the chocolate sauce over the top.
- Sprinkle with chopped nuts.

Crème caramel

SERVES 8

INGREDIENTS:

Melted butter
175g/6oz sugar
50ml/2fl oz water
750ml/1¼pt milk

75g/3oz caster sugar
4 eggs
1 teaspoon vanilla essence

- Preheat the oven to 160°C/325°F/Gas mark 3. Brush 8 x 125ml/4fl oz ramekins or moulds with melted butter.
- Place the sugar and water in a pan. Stir over a low heat until the sugar dissolves. Bring to the boil, reduce the heat and simmer until the mixture turns golden and starts to caramelize. Remove from the heat immediately and pour enough hot caramel into each ramekin to cover the base.
- To make the custard, heat the milk in a pan over a low heat until almost boiling.
- Remove from the heat. Whisk together the sugar, eggs and vanilla essence for 2 minutes, then stir in the warm milk. Strain the mixture into a jug and pour into the ramekins.
- Place the ramekins in a baking dish and pour in enough boiling water to come halfway up the sides of the ramekins. Bake for 30 minutes, or until the custard is set. Allow to cool and refrigerate for at least 2 hours.

Marzipan

SERVES 4–8

INGREDIENTS:

225g/8oz ground almonds
100g/4oz caster sugar
100g/4oz icing sugar (sifted)

1 teaspoon lemon juice
1 egg (beaten)

- Mix together the ground almonds and sugars in a bowl. Add the lemon juice and the egg to bind the mixture.
- Knead the mixture lightly until smooth. Cut into bite-sized chunks and serve.

Tarte tatin

SERVES 6

INGREDIENTS:

For the pastry:
225g/8oz plain flour
150g/5oz butter
½ teaspoon salt
50g/2oz icing sugar
1 large egg
Vanilla essence

For the caramel:
125g/4oz butter
200g/7oz caster sugar
1.4kg/3lb dessert apples (peeled, cored and quartered)
Juice of ½ lemon

- To make the pastry, sift the flour on to a surface, make a hollow in the centre and add the butter with the salt. Work the butter and salt together until smooth and pliable. Add the icing sugar to the butter mixture and mix in, then add the egg and vanilla essence and mix in until the mixture resembles scrambled eggs. Cut the flour into the butter mixture with a palette knife. Knead lightly until smooth, then wrap and chill for 1 hour or until firm.
- To make the caramel, melt the butter in a 28cm/11in tarte tatin mould and add the sugar. Pack the apples tightly in the mould and cook over a medium heat for 20 to 25 minutes until well caramelized. Add the lemon juice and allow the apples to cool.
- Preheat the oven to 220°C/425°F/Gas mark 7.
- Roll the pastry out so that it is 2.5cm/1in larger all round than the top of the mould or pan. Lay on top of the cooked apples. Prick the pastry with the tip of a sharp knife. Bake for 25 to 30 minutes until the pastry is brown all over.
- Leave to cool for 10 minutes. Turn out on to a plate and serve with cream.

Crème Anglaise trifle

SERVES 4

INGREDIENTS:

450ml/³/₄pt full-fat milk
1 vanilla pod (split lengthways)
1 large egg
2 egg yolks
4 tablespoon caster sugar

200ml/7fl oz double cream
200ml/7fl oz sweet sherry
8 trifle sponges
450g/1lb cherries (stoned), plus extra to decorate

- Put the milk in a pan with the vanilla pod and bring slowly to the boil. Remove from the heat, then cover and leave to infuse for 20 minutes.
- Whisk the egg, yolks and caster sugar together and add the milk. Return to a clean pan and cook gently without boiling until the custard thickens. Strain into a bowl and cool for 1 hour, then chill for 3 hours.
- Lightly whip the cream until just stiff, then whisk in the chilled custard. Pour 1 tablespoon of sherry into the bottom of 4 tall glasses. Make layers with the sponges, custard, stoned cherries and sherry, finishing with the custard.
- Decorate with cherries.

Black Forest cake

SERVES 6–8

INGREDIENTS:

200g/7oz butter (softened)
175g/6oz caster sugar
3 eggs (lightly beaten)
1 teaspoon vanilla essence
200g/7oz self-raising flour
50g/2oz plain flour
75g/3oz cocoa powder
1 tablespoon instant coffee powder
½ teaspoon bicarbonate of soda
125ml/4fl oz buttermilk

75ml/3fl oz milk
275ml/10fl oz whipping cream (whipped)
400g/14oz canned stoned cherries (drained)

For the chocolate topping:
275g/10oz dark chocolate (chopped)
350g/12oz butter (softened)

- Preheat the oven to 180°C/350°F/Gas mark 4. Grease a 23cm/9in round cake tin and line the base and side with baking parchment.
- Cream the butter and sugar in a small bowl with electric beaters until light and

fluffy. Add the egg gradually, beating thoroughly after each addition. Add the vanilla essence and beat until well combined.

- Transfer the mixture to a large bowl. Using a metal spoon, fold in the sifted flours, cocoa, coffee and soda alternately with the combined buttermilk and milk. Stir until the mixture is just combined and almost smooth.
- Pour the mixture into the tin and smooth the surface. Bake for 40 to 50 minutes.
- Leave the cake in the tin for 20 minutes before turning out on to a wire rack to cool.
- For the chocolate topping, bring a saucepan of water to the boil and remove from the heat. Place the chocolate in a heatproof bowl and sit the bowl over the pan, making sure the bowl is not touching the water. Allow to stand, stirring occasionally, until the chocolate is melted. Beat the butter in a small bowl until light and creamy. Add the chocolate, beating for 1 minute, or until the mixture is glossy and smooth.
- Turn the cake upside down and cut into 3 layers horizontally. Place the first layer on a serving plate. Spread evenly with half the whipped cream, then top with half the cherries. Continue layering with the remaining cake, cream and cherries, ending with the cake on top. Spread the chocolate topping over the top and side, using a flat-bladed knife.

Mascarpone ice-cream

SERVES 6–8

INGREDIENTS:

5 tablespoons full fat milk
Pinch of freshly grated nutmeg
2 large egg yolks
1 teaspoon cornflour

75g/3oz caster sugar
250g/9oz Mascarpone cheese
200g/7oz fromage frais

- Place the milk and nutmeg in a saucepan and bring to a gentle simmer.
- In a bowl, whisk together the egg yolks, cornflour and caster sugar until light and creamy.
- Whisk the warmed milk into the egg mixture and return to the pan. Bring back to a gentle simmer, whisking continuously.
- Remove from the heat, cover the mixture and allow to cool.
- When cool, whisk in the Mascarpone and fromage frais, ensuring they are thoroughly mixed.
- Put into a suitable container and place in the freezer for 2 hours. Remove and beat well, then return to freezer until completely frozen.

Chocolate muffins

SERVES 6–8

INGREDIENTS:

275g/10oz self-raising flour
50g/2oz cocoa powder
½ teaspoon bicarbonate of soda
175g/6oz caster sugar

350ml/12fl oz buttermilk
2 eggs
150g/5oz butter (melted and cooled)

- Preheat the oven to 200°C/400°F/Gas mark 6. Lightly grease 12 muffin pans.
- Sift the flour, cocoa powder and bicarbonate of soda into a bowl and add the sugar. Make a well in the centre.
- In a jug, whisk the buttermilk and eggs together and pour into the well. Add the butter and fold gently with a metal spoon until just combined.
- Fill each pan about three-quarters full. Bake for 20 to 25 minutes, or until the muffins are risen. Allow to cool for a 2 minutes and transfer to a wire rack to cool.

Crunchy pears in cinnamon & honey wine

SERVES 4–6

INGREDIENTS:

4 tablespoons white wine
4 tablespoons honey
1 teaspoon ground cinnamon
50g/2oz butter

100g/4oz wholemeal breadcrumbs
50g/2oz demerara sugar
4 ripe dessert pears

- Preheat the oven to 190°C/375°F/Gas mark 5.
- In a jug, mix together the wine, honey and half of the cinnamon. Set aside.
- Melt the butter in a small pan, add the breadcrumbs, sugar and remaining cinnamon and stir together until evenly mixed. Set aside.
- Peel and halve the pears. Remove the cores. Arrange the pear halves, cut side down, in a greased ovenproof dish and pour over the white wine mixture.
- Sprinkle the pears evenly with the breadcrumb mixture and bake in the oven for 40 minutes.
- Allow to cool and refrigerate until required.

Chocolate pretzels

SERVES 10

INGREDIENTS:

100g/4oz butter
100g/4oz caster sugar
1 egg
225g/8oz plain flour
2 tablespoons cocoa powder

To finish:
15g/¹/₂oz butter
100g/4oz dark chocolate
Icing sugar for dusting

- Lightly grease a baking tray. Beat together the butter and sugar in a mixing bowl until light and fluffy. Beat in the egg.
- Sift together the flour and cocoa powder and gradually beat in to form a soft dough Use your fingers to incorporate the last of the flour and bring the dough together. Chill for 15 minutes.
- Preheat the oven to 190°C/375°F/Gas mark 5.
- Break small pieces from the dough and roll into thin sausage shapes about 10cm/4in long and 8mm/¹/₄in thick. Twist into pretzel shapes by making a circle, then twisting the ends through each other. Place the pretzels on the prepared baking tray, allowing room to expand.
- Bake in the oven for 8 to 12 minutes. Leave to cool slightly on the baking tray, then transfer to a wire rack to cool completely.
- Melt the butter and chocolate in a bowl set over a pan of gently simmering water, stirring to combine. Dip half of each pretzel in the chocolate and allow any excess to drip back into the bowl. Place on a sheet of baking parchment and leave to set. When set, dust the plain side of each pretzel with icing sugar.

Easter biscuits

SERVES 4–8

INGREDIENTS:

125g/4oz butter
75g/3oz caster sugar
1 egg (separated)
200g/7oz plain flour
Pinch of salt
¹/₂ teaspoon mixed spice

¹/₂ teaspoon ground cinnamon
50g/2oz currants
25g/1oz chopped mixed peel
2 tablespoons milk
Caster sugar for sprinkling

→

← • Preheat the oven to 200°C/400°F/Gas mark 6.
- Cream together the butter and sugar and beat in the egg yolk.
- Sift together the flour, salt and spices. Fold into the creamed mixture with the currants and peel. Add the milk to give a soft dough.
- Knead lightly on a floured surface and roll out to 8mm/¼in thick. Cut out, using a 6cm/2½in fluted cutter, and place on greased baking trays.
- Bake in the oven for 10 minutes, then brush with egg white and sprinkle with caster sugar. Return to the oven for a further 10 to 15 minutes.
- Remove from oven and place on a cooling rack.

Frozen egg nog

SERVES 4

INGREDIENTS:

2 egg yolks
3 tablespoons caster sugar
2 tablespoons dark rum

1 tablespoon brandy
300ml/½pt double cream

- Place the egg yolks, rum and brandy in a pan over hot water and whisk until the mixture is thick and creamy. Remove from the heat and continue whisking until the mixture has cooled slightly. Transfer to a freezer-proof container.
- Whip the cream until it stands in soft peaks, and then fold carefully into the egg mixture.
- Freeze for a minimum of 4 hours.

Refrigerator biscuits

SERVES 10–12

INGREDIENTS:

175g/6oz butter (softened)
175g/6oz brown sugar
1 teaspoon vanilla essence

1 egg
250g/9oz plain flour
1 teaspoon baking powder

- Cream the butter and sugar in a small bowl with electric beaters until light and fluffy. Add the vanilla essence and egg and beat until well combined. Transfer to a large bowl and add the sifted flour and baking powder. Using a knife, mix to a soft dough. Gather together, then divide the mixture into 2 portions.

- Place one portion of the dough on a sheet of baking parchment and press lightly until the dough is 30cm/12in long and 4cm/1½in thick. Fold the parchment around the dough and roll into a log shape. Twist the edges of the parchment to seal. Repeat the process with the other portion. Refrigerate for 20 minutes or until firm.
- Preheat the oven to 180°C/350°F/Gas mark 4. Line 2 baking trays with baking parchment.
- Remove the baking parchment, then cut the logs into slices about 1cm/½in thick.
- Place on the prepared trays, leaving 3cm/1¼in between each slice. Bake for 10 to 15 minutes, or until golden. Cool on the trays for 3 minutes before transferring to a wire rack to cool completely.

Coconut tart

SERVES 8

INGREDIENTS:

For the pastry:
200g/7oz plain flour (sifted)
2 tablespoons icing sugar
Pinch of salt
75g/3oz butter (diced)
1 egg (beaten)

For the filling:
75g/3oz butter (softened)
75g/3oz caster sugar
250g/9oz coconut yogurt
2 eggs (beaten)
225g/8oz creamed coconut (grated)
2 tablespoons plain flour (sifted)

- To make the pastry, put the flour, icing sugar and the salt in a blender or food processor, add the butter and process until the mixture resembles breadcrumbs. Add the egg and blend to form a dough. Bring together on a lightly floured surface, wrap in clingfilm and chill for 30 minutes.
- Preheat the oven to 200°C/400°F/Gas mark 6 and put a baking sheet in the oven to heat.
- Dust the work surface with flour, roll out the pastry and use to line a 20cm/8in loose-bottomed sandwich tin. Prick the base all over with a fork. Line the pasty case with greaseproof paper, fill with baking beans and bake blind for 15 minutes.
- Carefully remove the baking beans and paper and bake for a further 5 minutes until the pastry is dry.
- To make the filling, put the butter, sugar, yogurt and eggs in a large bowl and combine with an electric hand mixer. Mix in the coconut and flour.
- Spoon into the pastry case, level the surface and bake for 30 minutes or until set and golden. Allow to cool for 10 minutes, then remove from the tin and leave to cool on a wire rack.

Glazed nectarine tart

SERVES 6

INGREDIENTS:

175g/6oz puff pastry
25g/1oz butter (melted)

600g/1¼lb nectarines (quartered,
stoned and sliced)
2 tablespoons apricot jam

- Preheat the oven to 230°C/450°F/Gas mark 8.
- Roll out the pastry thinly to a 28cm/11in round. Put on a non-stick baking sheet and prick well all over with a fork. Bake for 8 to 10 minutes, or until well browned and cooked through.
- Brush some of the melted butter over the pastry and arrange the fruit slices on top, right to the edges of the pastry. Drizzle with the remaining butter and grill for 5 minutes or until the fruit is just tinged with colour. Cool slightly.
- Warm the apricot jam with a little water and brush over the fruit to glaze.

Irish sherry trifle

SERVES 8–10

INGREDIENTS:

450g/1lb trifle sponges
225g/8oz raspberry jam
5 eggs
1¼ tablespoons caster sugar

¾ teaspoon vanilla essence
750ml/1¼pt full-fat milk
175ml/6fl oz sweet sherry

- Sandwich the trifle sponges together in pairs with raspberry jam.
- Whisk the eggs with the sugar and vanilla essence. Heat the milk and add it to the egg, whisking all the time. Put into a heavy saucepan and stir over a gentle heat until the custard coats the back of a spoon. Do not let it boil.
- Cut the sponge sandwiches into 2.5cm/1in slices, and use half of these to line the bottom of a 1.8 litre/3pt glass bowl, sprinkling generously with sherry. Pour in some custard and add the remaining sponge and the remainder of the sherry.
- Spread the rest of the custard over the top. Cover and leave overnight.
- Serve with whipped cream.

Chocolate cream pudding

SERVES 6

INGREDIENTS:

25g/1oz cornflour
75g/3oz unsweetened cocoa
125g/41/2oz demerera sugar

750ml/1¼pt milk
2 teaspoons vanilla essence

- Sift the cornflour with the cocoa and the sugar and place in a saucepan.
- Gradually stir in the milk over a low heat until free of lumps. Add the vanilla when slightly cooled, then pour into a serving dish and refrigerate until required.

Lemon cheesecake

SERVES 6

INGREDIENTS:

225g/8oz plain chocolate digestive biscuits
50g/2oz butter
3 lemons
350g/12oz cream cheese

150g/5oz caster sugar (plus 2 tablespoons extra)
2 tablespoons sultanas
3 eggs (separated)
2 tablespoons plain flour

- Preheat oven to 160°C/325°F/Gas mark 3.
- Put the biscuits into a blender or food processor with the butter and blend to a crumb. Place in a 23cm/9in non-stick cake tin and press down into an even layer.
- Grate the zest from 2 lemons and reserve. Juice all three.
- Beat the cheese with an electric whisk until smooth, then beat in the 150g/5oz caster sugar. Continue to beat until fluffy. Fold in the sultanas. Beat the egg yolks into the cheese, along with the flour, lemon zest and juice.
- With a clean whisk, beat the egg whites until peaks start to form. Add the remaining 2 tablespoons of sugar and continue to whisk until stiff. Fold into the cheese and spoon over the biscuit base.
- Stand the tin in a water bath and bake for 1 hour, when the cheese should be set and golden. Remove, allow to cool and refrigerate for at least 4 hours.

Danish pastries

SERVES 4–6

INGREDIENTS:

6g/¼oz dried yeast
125ml/4fl oz warm milk
1 teaspoon + 50g/2oz caster sugar
225g/8oz plain flour

½ teaspoon salt
1 egg (lightly beaten)
1 teaspoon vanilla essence
225g/8oz butter
400g/14oz canned apricot halves
(drained)
1 egg (lightly beaten)
50g/2oz flaked almonds

For the glaze:
75g/3oz apricot jam
1 tablespoon water

For the pastry cream:
2 tablespoons caster sugar
2 egg yolks
2 teaspoons plain flour
2 teaspoons cornflour
125ml/4fl oz hot milk

- Stir the yeast, milk and 1 teaspoon sugar together in a small bowl until dissolved.
- Leave in a warm place for 10 minutes, or until bubbles appear on the surface.
- The mixture should be frothy and slightly increased in volume.
- Sift the flour and salt into a large bowl and stir in the remaining sugar. Make a well in the centre and add the yeast mixture, egg and vanilla essence. Mix to a firm dough. Turn out on to a floured surface and knead for 10 minutes to form a smooth, elastic dough.
- Place the dough in a lightly greased bowl, cover and set aside in a warm place for 1 hour, or until doubled in size.
- Meanwhile, roll the butter between 2 sheets of baking parchment to a 15 x 20cm/6 x 8in rectangle and then refrigerate until required.
- Punch down the dough and knead for 1 minute. Roll out to a rectangle measuring 25 x 30cm/10 x 12in. Place the butter in the centre of the dough and fold up the bottom and top of the dough over the butter to join in the centre. Seal the edges with a rolling pin.
- Give the dough a quarter turn clockwise then roll out to a 20 x 45cm/8 x 18in rectangle. Fold over the top third of the pastry, then the bottom third and then give another quarter turn clockwise. Cover and refrigerate for 30 minutes. Repeat the rolling, folding, turning and chilling 4 more times. Wrap in clingfilm and chill for at least another 2 hours before using.
- For the pastry cream, place the sugar, egg yolks and flours in a saucepan and whisk to combine. Pour in the hot milk and whisk until smooth. Bring to the boil over a moderate heat, stirring all the time, until the mixture boils and thickens.
- Cover and set aside.

- Preheat the oven to 200°C/400°F/Gas mark 6 and line 2 baking trays with baking paper. On a lightly floured surface, roll the dough into a rectangle or square 3mm/⅛in thick. Cut the dough into 10cm/4in squares and place on the baking trays.
- Spoon a tablespoon of pastry cream into the centre of each square and top with 2 apricot halves. Brush one corner with the beaten egg and draw up that corner and the diagonally opposite one to touch in the middle between the apricots. Press firmly in the centre. Leave in a warm place to prove for 30 minutes. Brush each pastry with the egg and sprinkle with the flaked almonds. Bake for 15 to 20 minutes, or until golden. Cool on wire racks.
- Melt the apricot jam with the water and then strain. Brush the tops of the apricots with the glaze and serve.

Port & orange jellies

SERVES 8

INGREDIENTS:

450ml/¾pt ruby port
6 tablespoons powdered gelatine
125g/4½oz granulated sugar

600ml/1pt cold water
8 oranges (segmented)

- Splash cold water into 8 x 150ml/¼pt fluted moulds and chill.
- Pour the port into a bowl and sprinkle the gelatine into it. Put to one side.
- Put the sugar in a large pan with the water. Heat gently to dissolve, then bring to the boil and simmer until the liquid has reduced by half.
- Stir in the soaked gelatine until completely dissolved.
- Put the orange segments in the flutes of the mould so they stand up, pressed against the sides of the mould. Pour in enough liquid to come halfway up the sides. Chill to set then pour in the rest of the liquid and chill again.

Wild strawberry creams

SERVES 4

INGREDIENTS:

4 tablespoons grenadine
4 eggs
50g/2oz caster sugar

½ teaspoon vanilla essence
400ml/14oz milk
75g/3oz fraises des bois (hulled)

→

←
- Preheat the oven to 150°C/300°F/Gas mark 2.
- Pour 1 tablespoon grenadine into each of 4 x 200ml/7fl oz moulds.
- Beat the eggs and sugar into a bowl with the vanilla essence. Scald the milk in a saucepan and slowly stir in the egg mixture. Strain into a jug, then pour into the moulds. The grenadine will mix into the milk, but then sink to the bottom.
- Divide the fraises des bois between the moulds. They will float.
- Place the moulds gently in a bain-marie of hot water and bake in the oven until just set, about 30 to 40 minutes. Leave to cool and then cover and chill in the refrigerator for at least 4 hours.
- Sprinkle with grenadine and sugar to taste, cover and chill in the refrigerator until serving time.

Mississippi mud pie

SERVES 8

INGREDIENTS:

225g/8oz plain flour (plus extra for dusting)
2 tablespoons cocoa powder
150g/5oz butter
2 tablespoons caster sugar
2 tablespoons cold water
450ml/3/4pt double cream (whipped)

For the filling:
175g/6oz butter
350g/12oz muscovado sugar
4 eggs (beaten lightly)
4 tablespoons cocoa powder (sifted)
150g/5oz dark chocolate (melted)
300ml/1/2pt single cream
1 teaspoon cocoa powder (dissolved in hot water)

- To make the pastry, sift the flour and cocoa powder into a mixing bowl. Rub in the butter until the mixture resembles fine breadcrumbs. Stir in the sugar and enough cold water to mix to a soft dough. Chill for 15 minutes.
- Preheat the oven to 190°C/375°F/Gas mark 5.
- Roll out the pastry dough on a lightly floured surface and use to line a 23cm/9in loose-bottomed flan tin. Line with aluminium foil and baking beans. Bake blind in the oven for 15 minutes. Remove the beans and foil and cook for a further 10 minutes, until crisp.
- To make the filling, beat the butter and sugar in a bowl and gradually beat in the eggs with the cocoa powder. Beat in the melted chocolate with the single cream and the dissolved cocoa powder.
- Pour the mixture into the cooked pastry case and bake at 170°C/325°F/Gas mark 3 for 45 minutes or until the filling is set.
- Leave to cool completely then transfer to a serving plate. Cover with the whipped cream and leave to chill.

Mango & lime mousse

SERVES 6

INGREDIENTS:

Juice and grated zest of 2 limes
8g/¹/₃oz gelatine
3 eggs
2 egg yolks

50g/2oz caster sugar
300ml/10fl oz mango purée
100ml/4fl oz double cream (lightly whipped)

- Put the lime juice into a small heatproof bowl, then sprinkle in the gelatine and leave to soak for 10 minutes.
- In a large bowl, whisk together the whole eggs, egg yolks and sugar for about 4 to 5 minutes, until thick and mousse-like. Gently fold the mango purée, whipped cream and the zest of the limes into the mousse mixture.
- Put the heatproof bowl over a pan of boiling water to dissolve the gelatine and lime juice mixture. Then lightly fold into the mango mixture, making sure everything is evenly combined.
- Pour the mousse into glasses, put in the freezer for 20 minutes, then transfer to the refrigerator for at least 1 hour.

Apricot delight

SERVES 8

INGREDIENTS:

850g/1³/₄lb canned apricots
4 tablespoons fructose
1 tablespoon lemon juice

1¹/₂ tablespoons powdered gelatine
450ml/³/₄pt custard (see page 221)
150ml/¹/₄pt natural yogurt (strained)

- Line the base of a 1.2 litre/2pt cake tin with non-stick baking parchment.
- Drain the apricots, reserving the juice. Put the apricots in a blender or food processor. Add the fructose and 4 tablespoons of the apricot juice. Blend to a smooth purée.
- Measure 2 tablespoons apricot juice into a small bowl. Add the lemon juice, then sprinkle over 2 teaspoons of the gelatine. Leave for 5 minutes, until spongy.
- Stir the gelatine into half the apricot purée and pour into the tin. Chill in the refrigerator for 1¹/₂ hours, or until firm.
- Sprinkle the remaining gelatine over 4 tablespoons of the apricot juice. Soak and dissolve as before. Mix the remaining apricot purée with the custard, yogurt and

→

← gelatine. Pour onto the layer of set fruit purée and chill in the fridge for 3 hours.

Cinnamon sugar buns

SERVES 4–8

INGREDIENTS:

300g/11oz pizza base mix
200ml/7fl oz hot water
50g/2oz butter (melted)
125g/4oz brown sugar

1 1/2 teaspoons ground cinnamon
75g/3oz flaked almonds
2 tablespoons golden syrup (warmed)

- Preheat the oven to 190°C/375°F/Gas mark 5.
- Put the pizza base mix into a bowl, add the hot water and mix to form a dough.
- Knead on a lightly floured surface for 5 minutes, until smooth and elastic.
- Roll out the dough on a lightly floured surface to form a rectangle measuring 35 x 23cm/14 x 9in. Brush all over with some of the melted butter, reserving a little for later. Mix the sugar with half the cinnamon and two-thirds of the nuts.
- Sprinkle over the dough.
- Starting from a long side, roll up like a Swiss roll. Dampen the edge with water and press down firmly to seal the roll. Cut the roll into 8 equal slices. Put the slices flat and push down with the palm of your hand to form neat pinwheels.
- Generously butter a 23cm/9in round sandwich tin and coat with the cinnamon. Arrange slices of the roll in the tin. Brush all over with the remaining butter and sprinkle with the remaining cinnamon sugar and flaked almonds.
- Cover with a lightly oiled polythene bag and leave to prove in a warm place until doubled in size. Bake in the oven for 25 minutes. Drizzle with the warmed golden syrup while still hot.
- Stand on a wire rack to cool. Can be eaten warm or cool.

Exotic fruit pavlovas

SERVES 4–6

INGREDIENTS:

6 egg whites
375g/13oz caster sugar
1½ teaspoons white wine vinegar
2 pinches of cream of tartar

For the topping:
150g/5oz ripe pineapple
1 large mango

2 peaches
200g/7oz Greek yogurt
2 teaspoons clear honey
1 teaspoon vanilla essence
1 banana
Juice of ½ lemon
2 passion fruit

- Preheat the oven to 150°C/300°F/Gas mark 2 and line a large baking sheet with non-stick baking parchment.
- Whisk the egg whites with an electric mixer until stiff, then gradually add the sugar and continue whisking until the meringue is shiny. Whisk in the vinegar and cream of tartar with the last of the sugar.
- Mound the meringue into 12 large egg shapes on the parchment. Bake for 45 to 60 minutes until crisp on the outside but still soft inside. Transfer the pavlovas to a wire rack and leave to cool.
- To make the topping, peel and stone the pineapple, mango and peaches as necessary and cut the flesh into slices or small cubes. Place the fruit in a bowl and stir gently to combine.
- In a separate bowl, mix together the yogurt, honey and vanilla essence. Peel and chop the banana and toss in a little lemon juice. Fold into the yogurt.
- To serve, spoon the yogurt mixture over the pavlovas, then the exotic fruit mixture. Halve the passion fruit and scrape the seeds over the top.

Chocolate éclairs

SERVES 4–8

INGREDIENTS:

125g/4oz butter
250ml/9fl oz water
125g/4oz plain flour (sifted)
4 eggs (lightly beaten)

300ml/½pt cream (whipped)
150g/5oz dark chocolate (broken into small pieces)

→

←

- Preheat the oven to 210°C/425°F/Gas mark 7. Grease 2 baking trays.
- Combine the butter and water in a large heavy-based saucepan. Stir over medium heat until the butter melts. Increase the heat, bring to the boil and then remove from the heat.
- Add the flour to the saucepan all at once and quickly beat into the water with a wooden spoon. Return to the heat and continue beating until the mixture leaves the side of the pan and forms a ball. Transfer to a large bowl and cool slightly.
- Beat the mixture to release any remaining heat. Gradually add the egg, about 3 teaspoons at a time. Beat well after each addition until all the egg has been added and the mixture is glossy.
- Spoon the mixture into a piping bag fitted with a 1.5cm/⅝in plain nozzle.
- Sprinkle the baking trays lightly with water. Pipe 15cm/6in lengths onto the trays, leaving room for them to expand. Bake for 10 to 15 minutes. Reduce the heat to 180°C/350°F/Gas mark 4. Bake for another 15 minutes, or until golden and firm. Cool on a wire rack.
- Split each éclair, removing any uncooked dough, and fill with whipped cream.
- Put the chocolate in a heatproof bowl. Bring a saucepan of water to the boil and remove the pan from the heat. Sit the bowl over the pan, making sure the bowl is not touching the water. Allow to stand, stirring occasionally, until the chocolate has melted. Spread over the tops of the éclairs. Cool and serve.

Coeurs à la crème

SERVES 4–6

INGREDIENTS:

225g/8oz cottage cheese
25g/1oz caster sugar
300ml/½pt double cream

1 teaspoon lemon juice
2 egg whites (stiffly whisked)
150ml/¼pt single cream, to serve

- Press the cottage cheese through a nylon sieve into a bowl. Add sugar and mix well.
- Whip the cream until stiff, then add the lemon juice. Mix into the cheese and sugar mixture.
- Fold the stiffly whisked egg whites into the cheese mixture.
- Spoon the mixture into 4 or 6 individual moulds. Refrigerate overnight. Serve with single cream and/or fresh fruit.

Iced strawberry meringues

SERVES 6

INGREDIENTS:

225g/8oz strawberries (hulled)
25g/1oz caster sugar
2 tablespoons water
300ml/½pt double cream

18 medium meringue shells (about
150g/5oz total weight)
2 tablespoons brandy

- Place the strawberries in a small saucepan with the caster sugar and water. Cover the pan and heat gently for about 5 minutes until mushy, then cool slightly.
- Purée the pan ingredients in a blender or food processor and rub through a nylon sieve to remove any pips. Allow the purée to cool for about 1 hour.
- Lightly whip the cream in a large mixing bowl. Break each meringue shell into 3 or 4 pieces, then fold these pieces through the double cream together with the brandy and the cold fruit purée.
- Spoon the mixture into individual ramekins. Open freeze for 6 to 8 hours or overnight until firm, then wrap with aluminium foil and return to the freezer until required.
- Transfer to the refrigerator 20 to 30 minutes before serving.

Turkish delight

SERVES 6–8

INGREDIENTS:

450g/1lb granulated sugar
900ml/1½pt water
¼ teaspoon tartaric acid
200g/7oz icing sugar (sifted)
75g/3oz cornflour
50g/2oz clear honey

A few drops of rose water
Red food colouring

To coat:
175g/6oz icing sugar
1½ teaspoons bicarbonate of soda
¾ teaspoon citric acid

- Place the granulated sugar in a saucepan with the water and heat gently, stirring continuously until the sugar has dissolved.
- Bring to the boil. Add the tartaric acid and remove from the heat.
- Place the icing sugar and cornflour in a saucepan and gradually blend in the remaining water. Bring to the boil, stirring well until thick and syrupy.

→

←

- Lower the heat and gradually beat in the sugar syrup. Bring to the boil, and boil steadily for 30 minutes until very pale golden and transparent.
- Beat in the honey and rose water, add a little colouring and pour into an oiled 18cm/7in square tin. Leave to set.
- Sift together the coating ingredients, cut the Turkish delight into squares and toss in the coating.

Kesari

SERVES 5

INGREDIENTS:

5 cardamom pods
200g/7oz ghee (plus extra for greasing)
1 tablespoon cashew nuts (broken)
1 tablespoon raisins

400ml/14fl oz milk
150g/5oz white sugar
2–3 pinches saffron threads
200g/7oz semolina

- Using a pestle and mortar, crush the whole cardamom pods to a fine powder. Set aside.
- Heat 1 tablespoon of the ghee in a frying pan over a medium heat. Add the cashew nuts and raisins and cook, stirring, until the cashews brown and the raisins swell. Remove from the heat, drain on kitchen paper and set aside.
- Heat the milk, sugar and saffron in a heavy-based saucepan until the sugar dissolves. When the milk comes to the boil, remove it from the heat and set aside.
- In a large, heavy pan, melt 100g/3½oz of the ghee over a medium heat. Add the semolina, lower the heat and cook, stirring constantly, until brown.
- Slowly add the flavoured milk to the semolina, stirring quickly. Mix in the remaining ghee, then the cashew nuts, raisins and cardamom. Stir until the mixture forms a thick paste.
- Transfer the mixture to a shallow tray and spread out. Leave to cool, then chill the mixture for about 4 hours or until set. To serve, cut into squares.

Honey fruit cake

SERVES 6–8

INGREDIENTS:

175g/6oz butter, softened
175g/6oz clear honey
Grated zest of 1 lemon
3 eggs (lightly beaten)
225g/8oz plain flour
2 teaspoons baking powder
1 teaspoon mixed spice

125g/4oz raisins
125g/4oz sultanas
125g/4oz chopped dried dates
50g/2oz ready-to-eat dried apricots
(finely chopped)
25g/1oz ground almonds

- Preheat the oven to 160°C/325°F/Gas mark 3.
- Cream together the butter, honey and lemon zest until light and fluffy.
- Gradually add the eggs, then fold in the flour, baking powder and mixed spice.
- Stir in the fruit and ground almonds. Mix together.
- Spoon into a greased and lined 20cm/8in round deep tin. Make slight hollow in the centre.
- Bake in the oven for 2 hours.
- Leave to cool in the tin for 10 minutes, then turn onto a wire rack until completely cool.

Amaretti

SERVES 4–6

INGREDIENTS:

300g/11oz blanched almonds
300g/11oz caster sugar

5 egg whites

- Preheat the oven to 180°C/350°F/Gas mark 4.
- Put the almonds in a mortar and add 100g/4oz of the sugar little by little, pounding constantly.
- Beat the egg whites until stiff. Fold in the remaining sugar and add the almonds.
- Cut ribbons of greaseproof paper 5cm/2in wide and put on a baking tray. Spoon teaspoonfuls of the mixture on, about 2cm/3/4in apart.
- Sprinkle with sugar and bake for 20 minutes.

Raspberry meringue gâteau

SERVES 6

INGREDIENTS:

Butter for greasing
4 egg whites
225g/8oz caster sugar
Few drops of vanilla essence
1 teaspoon distilled malt vinegar
125g/4¹/₂oz roasted hazelnuts (ground)

450g/1lb raspberries
4 tablespoons icing sugar (sifted)
1 tablespoon orange liqueur
300ml/¹/₂pt double cream
Icing sugar, for dusting

- Preheat the oven to 180°C/350°F/Gas 4. Grease two 20cm/8in sandwich tins and line the bases with rounds of greaseproof paper.
- Whisk the egg whites in a large bowl until they hold stiff peaks, then gradually whisk in the caster sugar, 1 tablespoon at a time, whisking well after each addition.
- Continue whisking the meringue mixture for a minute or two until very stiff, then fold in the vanilla essence, vinegar and ground hazelnuts.
- Divide the meringue mixture between the prepared sandwich tins and spread it level. Bake for 50 to 60 minutes, until the meringue rounds are crisp. Remove the meringues from the tins and leave them to cool on a wire rack.
- Meanwhile, make the raspberry sauce. Purée 225g/8oz of the raspberries with the icing sugar and orange liqueur in a blender or food processor, then press the purée through a fine nylon sieve to remove any pips. Chill the sauce until ready to serve.
- Whip the cream until it forms soft peaks, then gently fold in the remaining raspberries. Sandwich the meringue rounds together with the raspberry cream.
- Dust the top of the gâteau with icing sugar and serve with the sauce.

Truffles

SERVES 4–8

INGREDIENTS:

175g/6oz dark chocolate
2 tablespoons Amaretto
40g/1¹/₂oz butter

50g/2oz icing sugar
50g/2oz ground almonds
50g/2oz grated milk chocolate

- Melt the dark chocolate with the Amaretto in a heatproof bowl set over a saucepan of hot water, stirring until well combined. Add the butter and stir until it has melted. Stir in the icing sugar and the ground almonds.

- Leave the mixture in a cool place until firm enough to roll into 24 balls.
- Place the grated chocolate on a plate and roll the truffles in the chocolate to coat them.
- Place the truffles in paper cases and chill.

Strawberry & melon cup

SERVES 6–8

INGREDIENTS:

300g/11oz ogen melon (peeled and quartered)
350g/12oz strawberries (hulled and sliced)

1.2 litres/2pt chilled lemonade
450ml/³/₄pt Pimms

- Put the melon into a blender or food processor and blend until smooth, then sieve.
- Pour into a jug, add the strawberries and top up with chilled lemonade and
- Pimms. Add plenty of ice-cubes and serve.

Banana lassi

SERVES 4

INGREDIENTS:

250g/9oz plain yogurt
200g/7oz banana (peeled and cut into chunks)

125ml/4fl oz milk
4 teaspoons granulated sugar

- Place all the ingredients in a blender or food processor and blend for 2 minutes.
- Pour the lassi into individual glasses and serve, or cover and store in the refrigerator for up to 24 hours.

Mixed berry sorbet

SERVES 6

INGREDIENTS:

225g/8oz strawberries (hulled)
225g/8oz redcurrants (stalks removed)
150ml/¹/₄pt water (plus 2 tablespoons extra)

100g/4oz caster sugar
150ml/¹/₄pt sparkling white wine
2 egg whites

- Place the strawberries and redcurrants in a saucepan with 2 tablespoons water.
- Cook for about 10 minutes, until soft. Push through a sieve to make a purée.
- Dissolve the sugar in 150ml/¹/₄pt water over a low heat and simmer for 10 minutes. Leave to cool for 1 hour.
- Stir the wine and fruit purée into the cooled syrup. Pour into a shallow freezer container and leave for 3 hours.
- Transfer the frozen mixture to a chilled basin and break up with a fork. Whisk the egg whites until stiff and fold into the mixture.
- Return to the freezer for 3 hours.
- Transfer to the refrigerator 30 minutes before serving to soften.

Coffee house gâteau

SERVES 8

INGREDIENTS:

For the sponge:
75g/3oz caster sugar
3 eggs
100g/4oz plain flour

For the crème au beurre:
150g/5oz caster sugar
100ml/3¹/₂fl oz water
3 egg yolks

250g/9oz butter
1¹/₂ tablespoon coffee granules
(dissolved in 1 tablespoon boiling water)

For the praline:
50g/2oz unblanched almonds
50g/2oz caster sugar
Butter for greasing

- Preheat the oven to 190°C/375°F/Gas mark 5. Grease a 33 x 23cm/13 x 9in Swiss roll tin and line the base and sides with greaseproof paper.
- To make the sponge, put the sugar and eggs in a bowl, place over a pan of hot water and whisk with an electric whisk until very pale and creamy. Remove the

210

mixture from the heat and whisk until cool.
- Sift the flour, a little at a time, over the mixture and fold in lightly using a metal spoon. Turn the mixture into the prepared tin and level the surface.
- Bake in the oven for 10 to 12 minutes, until well risen and golden brown. Turn the sponge out onto greaseproof paper, remove the lining paper and leave to cool.
- To make the crème au beurre, put the sugar and water into a small heavy saucepan and dissolve over a low heat. Once dissolved, boil steadily for 2 to 3 minutes.
- Beat the egg yolks in a bowl and pour over the hot syrup in a thin, steady stream, whisking all the time. Continue whisking until the mixture is thick and cool. In another bowl, cream the butter until soft, then gradually beat in the egg syrup, a little at a time, until thoroughly combined. Beat in the cold coffee mixture.
- To make the praline, put the almonds and sugar in a non-stick frying pan. Heat very gently until the sugar melts and turns brown.
- Butter a baking tray. Pour the almond caramel on to the tray. Leave to cool and set.
- Roughly crush the praline in a blender or food processor.
- Cut the sponge horizontally into 3 equal layers. Spread half the crème au beurre over 2 layers of sponge, then sandwich all 3 together. Spread the remaining crème au beurre over the top and sides of the gâteau. Cover the sides of the gâteau with crushed praline.

Fruit salad

SERVES 6

INGREDIENTS:

40g/1½oz granulated sugar
150ml/¼pt water
1 cinnamon stick
4 cardamom pods (crushed)
1 clove
Juice of 1 orange

Juice of 1 lime
½ honeydew melon
¼ watermelon
2 guavas
3 nectarines
18 strawberries

- To prepare the syrup, put the sugar, water, cinnamon, cardamom pods and clove into a pan and bring to the boil, stirring to dissolve the sugar. Simmer for 2 minutes, then remove from heat.
- Add the orange and lime juices to the syrup and leave to cool and infuse while preparing the fruits.
- Peel and remove the seeds from the melons and cut the flesh into neat slices.
- Cut the guavas in half, scoop out the seeds, then peel and slice the flesh neatly.
- Cut the nectarines into slices and hull and slice the strawberries.
- Arrange the slices of slices of fruit attractively on 6 serving plates. Strain the prepared cooled syrup over the sliced fruits.

Chocolate fudge

SERVES 5

INGREDIENTS:

500g/18oz dark chocolate
75g/3oz butter

400g/14oz condensed milk
½ teaspoon vanilla essence

- Lightly grease a 20cm/8in square cake tin.
- Break the chocolate into pieces and place in a large saucepan with the butter and condensed milk. Heat gently, stirring, until the chocolate and butter melt and the mixture is smooth. Do not allow to boil.
- Remove from the heat. Beat in the vanilla essence, then beat the mixture for a few minutes until thickened. Pour into the prepared tin and level the top. Chill the mixture in the refrigerator until firm.
- Tip the fudge out onto a chopping board and cut into squares to serve.

Hazelnut pavlova

SERVES 6

INGREDIENTS:

4 egg whites
225g/8oz caster sugar
1 teaspoon distilled malt vinegar

300ml/½pt double cream
50g/2oz toasted hazelnuts (chopped)

- Preheat the oven to 130°C/250°F/Gas mark ½.
- Mix together the egg whites, sugar and vinegar in a clean grease-free heatproof bowl and place over a pan of gently simmering water. Beat with an electric whisk for 10 minutes or until very stiff and shiny.
- Line a baking sheet with non-stick baking parchment and spread the meringue mixture into a rectangle. Bake for 40 minutes then leave to cool.
- Whip the cream until it just holds its shape and spread over the cold pavlova.
- Sprinkle with the nuts and chill for 2 to 3 hours or overnight. Cut into thick slices to serve.

Angel cake

SERVES 6–8

INGREDIENTS:

125g/4oz self-raising flour
375g/13oz caster sugar
12 egg whites
1½ teaspoons cream of tartar

¼ teaspoon salt
½ teaspoon vanilla essence
¼teaspoon almond essence
Icing sugar to dust

- Preheat the oven to 180°C/350°F/Gas mark 4. Have an ungreased angel food tin ready. Sift the flour and 175g/6oz sugar together 4 times.
- Using an electric beater, beat the egg whites with the cream of tartar and salt until stiff peaks form. Beat in the remaining sugar, 1 tablespoon at a time. Fold in the vanilla and almond essences. Sift a quarter of the flour and sugar mixture onto the egg white and, using a spatula, gradually fold in. Repeat with the remaining flour and sugar.
- Spoon the mixture into the angel food tin and bake for 35 to 40 minutes, or until puffed and golden. Turn upside down on a wire back and leave in the tin until cool. Gently shake to remove the cake. Dust cake with icing sugar.

Orange ice-cream

SERVES 4

INGREDIENTS:

8 oranges
1 lemon
200g/7oz caster sugar

500ml/18fl oz double cream
4 tablespoons Grand Marnier

- Finely grate the zest of the oranges and the lemon, and put in a bowl. Add the juices of 2 oranges and leave to steep while preparing the other ingredients.
- Squeeze the juice of the remaining oranges, combine with the sugar and cook to reduce to a thick syrup.
- Whip the cream to soft peaks. Stir the reserved juice and zest into the syrup. Add the juice of the lemon and stir into the cream, which will immediately thicken. Add the Grand Marnier.
- Freeze in a shallow container, stirring every 30 minutes for 4 hours. Leave overnight to freeze.

Chocolate banana sundae

SERVES 4

INGREDIENTS:

For the chocolate sauce:
50g/2oz dark chocolate
4 tablespoons golden syrup
1 tablespoon butter
1 tablespoon brandy

For the sundae:
4 bananas
150ml/¼pt double cream
12 scoops vanilla ice-cream
75g/3oz chopped almonds (toasted)
4 fan wafer biscuits

- To make the chocolate sauce, break the chocolate into small pieces and place in a heatproof bowl with the syrup and butter. Heat over a pan of hot water until melted, stirring until well combined. Remove the bowl from the heat and stir in the brandy.
- Peel and slice the bananas and whip the cream until just holding its shape. Place a scoop of ice-cream in the bottom of each of 4 tall sundae glasses. Top with slices of banana, some chocolate sauce, a spoonful of cream and the nuts.
- Repeat the layers, finishing with a good dollop of cream. Sprinkle with nuts and serve with fan wafer biscuits.

Marzipan cherries

SERVES 5

INGREDIENTS:

12 glacé cherries
2 tablespoons rum

250g/9oz marzipan
125g/4oz dark chocolate

- Line a baking tray with a sheet of baking parchment.
- Cut the cherries in half and place them in a small bowl. Add the rum and stir well to coat. Leave the cherries to soak for at least 1 hour, stirring occasionally.
- Divide the marzipan into 24 pieces and roll each piece into a ball. Press half a cherry into the top of each marzipan ball.
- Break the chocolate into pieces, place in a heatproof bowl and over a pan of hot water. Stir until all the chocolate has melted.
- Dip each sweet into the melted chocolate using a cocktail stick, allowing the excess to drip back into the bowl. Place the coated cherries on the baking paper and chill until set.

Creamy fruit baskets

SERVES 6

INGREDIENTS:

3 oranges
500g/18oz Mascarpone cheese
5 tablespoons crème fraîche
2 tablespoons clear honey (warmed)

6 half-coated chocolate waffle or
brandy snap baskets
100g/4oz strawberries

- Finely grate and reserve 1 tablespoon of orange zest. Then peel all the oranges, removing as much of the white pith as possible, and divide into segments.
- Place the Mascarpone cheese in a bowl with the orange zest and beat until smooth. Add half of the crème fraîche with the honey to taste and stir, adding more of the crème fraîche to give a fairly stiff dropping consistency. Cover and refrigerate.
- After at least half an hour, fill the baskets with the mixture and top with the orange segments and sliced strawberries. Decorate with orange zest.

Nougat

SERVES 4–6

INGREDIENTS:

75g/3oz clear honey
50g/2oz granulated sugar
150ml/¼pt water
50g/2oz liquid glucose

3 egg whites
225g/8oz mixed chopped glacé
cherries, angelica and almonds
2 sheets rice paper

- Place the honey in a small bowl over a pan of hot water and leave to melt.
- Place the sugar and water in a saucepan and heat gently, stirring continuously until the sugar has dissolved. Add the glucose, bring to the boil, and boil steadily.
- Pour the honey into the sugar syrup and continue boiling.
- Whisk the egg whites in a large bowl until very stiff and gradually whisk in the hot syrup. Place the bowl over a pan of hot water and whisk until the mixture is very thick and firm.
- Remove the bowl from the pan, stir in the fruit and nuts and turn into an 18cm/7in square tin lined with rice paper.
- Cover the nougat with more rice paper, place a thick piece of card over the top, and weigh down overnight.
- Turn out and cut into bite size squares.

→

Spotted dick

SERVES 4

INGREDIENTS:

175g/6oz plain flour
1 teaspoons baking powder
100g/4oz sugar
1½ teaspoons ground ginger
150g/5oz fresh breadcrumbs
50g/2oz sultanas

100g/4oz currants
100g/4oz suet (grated)
2 teaspoons finely grated lemon zest
2 eggs (lightly beaten)
175ml/6fl oz milk

- Sift the flour, baking powder, sugar and ginger into a large bowl. Add the breadcrumbs, sultanas, currants, suet and lemon zest. Mix with a wooden spoon.
- Combine the egg and milk, add to the dry ingredients and mix well. Add a little more milk if necessary, then set aside for 5 minutes.
- Lay a sheet of baking paper on a work surface and form the mixture into a roll shape about 20cm/8in long. Roll up the pudding in the paper and fold up the ends – but do not wrap too tightly. Wrap in a tea towel, put it in the top of a steamer, cover and steam for 1½ hours. Do not let the pudding boil dry – replenish with boiling water as the pudding cooks.
- Serve with custard or cream.

Apple pie

SERVES 6

INGREDIENTS:

6 large Granny Smith apples
2 tablespoons caster sugar
1 teaspoon finely grated lemon zest
Pinch of ground cloves
2 tablespoons water

For the filling:
225g/8oz plain flour

25g/1oz self-raising flour
150g/5oz butter (chilled and cubed)
2 tablespoons caster sugar
4–5 tablespoons iced water
2 tablespoons marmalade
1 egg (lightly beaten)
1 tablespoon sugar

- Lightly grease a 23cm/9in pie plate. Peel, core and cut the apples into wedges.
- Place in a saucepan with the sugar, lemon zest, cloves and water. Cover and cook over a low heat for 8 minutes, or until the apples are just tender, shaking

the pan occasionally. Drain and cool completely.
- Sift the flours into a bowl and rub in the butter, using your fingertips, until the mixture resembles fine breadcrumbs. Stir in the sugar, then make a well in the centre. Add almost all the water and mix with a flat-bladed knife, using a cutting action, until the mixture comes together. Gather together and lift out onto a lightly floured surface. Press into a ball and divide into 2, making one half a little bigger.
- Cover with clingfilm and refrigerate for 20 minutes.
- Preheat the oven to 200°C/400°F/Gas mark 6.
- Roll out the larger piece of pastry between 2 sheets of baking paper and line the base and side of the pie plate. Using a small sharp knife, trim away any excess pastry. Brush the marmalade over the base and spoon the apple into the shell. Roll out the other pastry between the baking paper until large enough to cover the pie.
- Brush water around the rim and place the pastry on the top. Pinch the edges to seal and cut a couple of steam slits in the top.
- Bake for 20 minutes, then reduce the oven temperature to 180°C/350°F/Gas mark 4 and bake for another 15 to 20 minutes, until golden.

Swiss roll

SERVES 4–6

INGREDIENTS:

75g/3oz self-raising flour
3 eggs (lightly beaten)

175g/6oz caster sugar
150g/5oz strawberry jam

- Preheat the oven to 190°C/375°F/Gas mark 5.
- Lightly grease a shallow Swiss roll tin and line the base with baking paper, extending over the two long sides. Sift the flour on to the baking paper.
- Beat the eggs with an electric beater in a small bowl for 5 minutes, or until thick and pale. Add 100g/4oz of the sugar gradually, beating constantly until the mixture is pale and glossy.
- Transfer to a large bowl. Using a metal spoon, fold in the flour quickly and lightly. Spread into the tin and smooth the surface. Bake for 10 to 12 minutes, or until lightly golden and springy to touch. Meanwhile, place a clean tea towel on a work surface, cover with baking paper and lightly sprinkle with the remaining caster sugar. When the cake is cooked, turn it out immediately on to the sugar.
- Using the tea towel as a guide, carefully roll the cake up from the short side, rolling the paper inside the roll. Stand the rolled cake on a wire rack for 3 minutes, then carefully unroll, spread with jam and re-roll. Trim the ends with a knife to neaten.

Dark chocolate cake

SERVES 6–8

INGREDIENTS:

*200g/7oz plain chocolate (broken
into pieces)*
100g/4oz butter
3 eggs (separated)
100g/4oz brown sugar
50ml/2fl oz brandy
½ teaspoon vanilla essence
75g/3oz plain flour
50g/2oz ground almonds

For the icing:
*175g/6oz plain chocolate (broken into
pieces)*
25g/1oz butter
175g/6oz icing sugar (sifted)
3 tablespoons warm water
*300ml/½pt double cream (swiftly
whipped)*

- Preheat the oven to 180°C/350°F/Gas mark 4.
- Grease and flour a deep 20cm/8in round cake tin and line the base with greaseproof paper.
- To make the cake, put the chocolate and butter into a heatproof bowl and set over a pan of hot water until melted.
- Meanwhile, put the egg yolks and sugar in a large heatproof bowl, place over a pan of hot water and whisk with an electric whisk until very pale and creamy.
- Remove from the heat and whisk until cool. Add the brandy and vanilla essence and whisk in the melted chocolate and butter mixture.
- Add the sifted flour and the ground almonds and fold in gently, using a metal spoon. Whisk the egg whites until stiff then very lightly fold into the mixture, a little at a time.
- Pour the mixture into the cake tin and bake in the oven for 45 to 50 minutes or until firm to the touch. Cool in the tin for 10 minutes, then turn out and cool completely on a wire rack.
- To make the icing, melt the chocolate and butter in a heatproof bowl set over a pan of hot water. Remove from the heat and gradually stir in the icing sugar and warm water to make a thick icing. Keep warm over the pan of hot water until ready to use.
- Cut the cake in half and spread a third of the icing over one half of the cake, then top with a third of the whipped cream. Put the remaining cake on top. Spoon the rest of the icing over the top and completely coat the top and sides of the cake.
- Leave to set.

Bread & butter pudding

SERVES 6

INGREDIENTS:

50g/2oz butter (softened)
6 slices white bread
25g/1oz currants
25g/1oz sultanas
3 eggs

550ml/18fl oz milk
50g/2oz light muscovado sugar
Pinch of ground mixed spices
Single cream for drizzling

- Lightly grease a 1.2 litres/2pt ovenproof dish with a little of the butter. Use the rest to spread evenly over the bread then cut each slice in half diagonally.
- Arrange the slices in the dish, each one slightly overlapping the last, and sprinkle the currants and sultanas over the top.
- Beat together the eggs, milk, sugar and mixed spices in a bowl and pour over the bread. Leave to soak for 30 minutes. Preheat the oven to 180°C/350°F/Gas mark 4.
- Bake the pudding in the oven for 45 to 55 minutes or until golden brown but still slightly moist in the centre. Serve with a drizzle of single cream.

Apple strudel

SERVES 6–8

INGREDIENTS:

100g/4oz breadcrumbs
900g/2lb cooking apples
Juice of 3 lemons
225g/8oz cranberries
225g/8oz seedless raisins
2 teaspoons ground cinnamon

½ teaspoon freshly grated nutmeg
225g/8oz chopped walnuts
175g/6oz brown sugar
450g/1lb filo pastry sheets
175g/6oz butter

- Heat a dry frying pan over a medium heat, then pour in the breadcrumbs.
- Stirring all the time, lightly toast the crumbs for about 1 to 2 minutes. Remove from the heat and set aside to cool.
- Peel, core and dice the apples, put them in a large bowl and cover them with the lemon juice. Add the cranberries, raisins, cinnamon, nutmeg, walnuts and sugar.
- Mix well together.
- Preheat the oven to 180°C/350°F/Gas mark 4.

→

←

- Spread a moist tea towel on a work surface and place the sheets of pastry on it.
- Remove 1 sheet and place on a second moist tea towel. Quickly cover the remaining pastry with a third moist tea towel.
- Melt some butter in a pan and brush over the single pastry sheet. Then sprinkle with some of the breadcrumbs. Uncover the pastry sheets, lift off a second sheet of pastry and place this on top of the first. Cover the remaining sheets as before.
- Brush the second sheet of pastry with melted butter and sprinkle with breadcrumbs. Repeat this procedure with another 2 pastry sheets. On the fourth sheet spread half the apple and walnut filling. Using the tea towel underneath, slowly and carefully roll the sheets of pastry forwards to form a log, tucking the edges inwards as you go.
- Repeat the entire procedure until you have 2 pastry logs, keeping the first one moist while making the second.
- Lightly grease a baking tray and carefully place the strudel logs on it. Brush the tops of both logs with the remaining butter and bake in the oven for 30 to 40 minutes until brown and crisp. Remove from the oven and allow to cool slightly before serving.

Scones

SERVES 4–8

INGREDIENTS:

Butter for greasing
225g/8oz plain flour
1 tablespoon baking powder
50g/2oz butter (cubed)

1 egg (beaten)
5 tablespoons milk
Flour for rolling
1 egg (beaten, to glaze)

- Preheat the oven to 220°C/425°F/Gas mark 7. Lightly butter a baking sheet.
- In a bowl, sift together the flour and baking powder, then rapidly rub in the butter using the tips of your fingers. Make a well in the centre of the flour mixture, add the beaten egg and milk and mix to form a soft dough using a round-bladed knife or a metal spatula.
- Turn the dough onto a floured surface and knead very lightly until smooth. Roll out to a 2cm/1in thickness and cut into 10 or 12 rounds with a 5cm/2in plain or fluted cutter dipped in flour.
- Transfer to the baking sheet, brush with egg then bake for about 8 minutes, until risen and golden. Cool slightly on a wire rack, then serve.

Hot cross buns

SERVES 6–8

INGREDIENTS:

25g/1oz fresh yeast
75g/3oz caster sugar
300ml/½pt tepid milk
450g/1lb strong white flour
75g/3oz butter
¼ teaspoon cinnamon
¼ teaspoon nutmeg
1 teaspoon mixed spice

Pinch of salt
2 eggs
75g/3oz currants
50g/2oz sultanas
25g/1oz chopped orange peel
50g/2oz shortcrust pastry
Egg wash (milk, sugar and 1 egg yolk, to glaze)

- Dissolve the yeast with 1 tablespoon of the sugar in a little tepid milk.
- Put the flour in a bowl. Rub in the butter, add the cinnamon, nutmeg, mixed spice, salt and the remainder of the sugar. Mix well.
- Whisk the eggs and add the milk. Make a well in the centre of the flour. Add the yeast and most of the liquid and mix to a soft dough.
- Leave for 2 to 3 minutes, then knead until smooth. Add the currants, sultanas and chopped peel and continue to knead until the dough is shiny. Cover the bowl and let the dough rise in a warm place until it doubles in size. Knock back the dough by kneading for 3 to 4 minutes. Rest it for a few minutes, then shape into buns, approximately 25g/1oz each. Place them onto a baking sheet and brush the tops with the egg wash. Mark the tops with crosses made out of the shortcrust pastry.
- Preheat the oven to 220°C/425°F/Gas mark 7.
- Leave the buns to rise again to double their size, and brush again with the egg wash.
- Bake in the oven for 5 minutes, then reduce the heat to 200°C/400°F/Gas mark 6 and cook for a further 10 minutes, or until golden. Cool on a wire rack.

Classic custard

SERVES 4

INGREDIENTS:

3 eggs
350ml/12fl oz milk

50g/2oz caster sugar
1 teaspoon vanilla essence

→

←

- Whisk the eggs and milk in a heatproof bowl. Add the sugar gradually, whisking to dissolve completely. Stir in the vanilla essence.
- Place the bowl over a pan of boiling water and heat gently. Serve hot.

Cherry pie

SERVES 6–8

INGREDIENTS:

150g/5oz plain flour
25g/1oz icing sugar
100g/4oz butter (cubed)
50g/2oz ground almonds

3 tablespoons chilled water
700g/1½lb pitted morello cherries
1 egg (lightly beaten)
Caster sugar for sprinkling

- Sift the flour and icing sugar into a bowl. Add the butter and rub in with just your fingertips until the mixture is fine and crumbly. Stir in the ground almonds, then add almost all the water and stir into the flour mixture with a flat-bladed knife until the mixture forms a dough, adding the remaining water if necessary.
- Turn the dough on to a lightly floured surface and gather together into a ball.
- Roll out on a sheet of baking paper into a circle about 26cm/10½in in diameter.
- Flatten slightly, cover with clingfilm and refrigerate for 20 minutes.
- Spread the cherries into a 23cm/9in pie dish.
- Preheat the oven to 200°C/400°F/Gas mark 6.
- Cover the pie dish with the pastry and trim the overhanging edge. Brush the pastry top all over with beaten egg and sprinkle lightly with caster sugar. Place the pie dish on a baking tray and cook for 35 to 40 minutes or until golden brown.
- Serve warm with cream or ice-cream.

Brownies

SERVES 4–6

INGREDIENTS:

50g/2oz unsweetened pitted dates (chopped)
50g/2oz dried prunes (chopped)
100ml/3½fl oz unsweetened apple juice
4 eggs (beaten)
300g/11oz dark muscovado sugar

1 teaspoon vanilla essence
4 tablespoons drinking chocolate powder
2 tablespoons cocoa powder
175g/6oz plain flour
50g/2oz dark chocolate chips

- Preheat the oven to 180°C/350°F/Gas mark 4.
- Grease and line an 18 x 28cm/7 x 11in cake tin with baking parchment.
- Place the dates and prunes in a small saucepan and add the apple juice. Bring to the boil, cover and simmer for 10 minutes until soft. Beat to form a smooth paste, then set aside to cool.
- Place the cooled fruit in a mixing bowl and stir in the eggs, sugar and vanilla essence. Sift in the drinking chocolate powder, cocoa and flour, and fold in along with the chocolate chips.
- Spoon the mixture into the prepared tin and smooth over the top. Bake for 25 to 30 minutes until firm to the touch.
- Cut into 12 bars and allow to cool slightly before serving.

Mince pies

SERVES 4–6

INGREDIENTS:

150g/5oz butter (cut into pieces)
225g/8oz plain flour
50g/2oz ground almonds
25g/1oz caster sugar
A few drops of almond essence

Grated zest of 1 orange
1 egg yolk
1 tablespoon water
225g/8oz mincemeat
1 egg white (lightly beaten)

- Preheat the oven to 200°C/400°F/Gas mark 6. Rub the butter into the flour. Add the almonds, sugar, almond essence, orange zest, egg yolk and water and mix to form a firm dough.
- Knead briefly on a floured surface, then wrap and chill for 30 minutes. Roll out thinly and stamp out 12 rounds, about 7.5cm/3in. Use the pastry to line 12 bun tins. Spoon in the mincemeat to come two-thirds of the way up the bun tins.
- Use the remaining pastry to cut into seasonal shapes – such as holly leaves or
- Christmas trees – and place on top of the mincemeat. Bake for 20 minutes until crisp and golden brown. Serve with cream or brandy butter.

Warmed spiced pears

SERVES 4

INGREDIENTS:

225g/8oz granulated sugar
225ml/8fl oz cold water
225ml/8fl oz red wine
1 cinnamon stick
5 cloves

Pared zest of 1 orange
Pared zest of 1 lemon
8 pears
Juice of ½ lemon

- Put the sugar in a saucepan and add the water. Heat gently until the sugar has dissolved, then increase the heat and boil for 1 minute. Add the wine, spices and citrus zests and simmer for about 10 minutes.
- Peel the pears. With a small pointed vegetable peeler, remove the cores. Brush with lemon juice immediately, then lower them into the wine mixture. Cover with a circle of greaseproof paper and cook gently for about 30 to 35 minutes until tender. Remove from the heat and leave to cool until lukewarm.
- Lift the pears carefully out of the spiced wine and place in serving bowls. Strain the cooking liquid into a clean pan and boil rapidly until reduced by half. Pour over and around the pears and serve warm.

Christmas pudding

SERVES 8–10

INGREDIENTS:

650g/23oz sultanas, currants and raisins
300g/11oz mixed dried fruit (chopped)
50g/2oz mixed peel
120ml/4fl oz brown ale
2 tablespoons brandy
75ml/3fl oz orange juice
75ml/3fl oz lemon juice
1 teaspoon grated orange zest
1 teaspoon grated lemon zest

225g/8oz suet (grated)
225g/8oz brown sugar
3 eggs (lightly beaten)
200g/7oz white breadcrumbs
75g/3oz self-raising flour
1 teaspoon mixed spice
¼ teaspoon grated nutmeg
100g/4oz blanched almonds (roughly chopped)
Salt

- Put the sultanas, currants, raisins, mixed dried fruit, mixed peel, brown ale, brandy, orange and lemon juices and zests into a large bowl and stir together.

- Cover and leave overnight.
- Add the suet, brown sugar, eggs, breadcrumbs, flour, mixed spice, nutmeg, almonds and a pinch of salt to the bowl and mix well.
- Put a 2 litres/3pt pudding basin on a trivet or upturned saucer in a large saucepan with a lid and pour in enough water to come halfway up the side of the basin. Remove the basin and put the water on to boil.
- Brush the basin with melted butter and line the base with baking parchment. Fill with the pudding mixture. Place a sheet of aluminium foil on a bench, top with a piece of baking parchment the same size and brush the parchment with melted butter. Fold a pleat across the centre of the foil and paper. Place the paper and foil, foil-side up, over the basin and smooth it down the side. Tie a double length of string around the rim of the basin, then tie another double length of string to form a handle. Steam the pudding for 8 hours, replenishing with boiling water when necessary.

Baked Alaska

SERVES 6

INGREDIENTS:

1.2 litres/2pt round tub of vanilla ice-cream
1 Victoria sponge cake

4 egg whites
75g/3oz caster sugar
1 tablespoon raspberry jam

- Freeze the ice-cream in the coldest section of the freezer. Cut the sponge to match the top of the ice-cream tub, then freeze the sponge on a baking sheet overnight.
- Preheat the oven to 230°C/450°F/Gas mark 8.
- To make the meringue, whisk the eggs whites with an electric mixer to soft peaks, then increase the mixer speed and gradually add the sugar until the peaks are firm. Take care not to exceed this point or the meringue will separate.
- Spread the sponge with the jam. Turn out the ice-cream to sit on top of the jam.
- Smooth the meringue all over it with a palette knife, taking it right down to the edge to seal in the ice-cream entirely, with no gaps.
- Bake for 4 to 5 minutes, until the meringue is just beginning to colour. Remove from the oven and serve immediately.

Banana custard

SERVES 4

INGREDIENTS:

1 egg (lightly beaten)
2 tablespoons custard powder
2 tablespoons sugar

225ml/8fl oz milk
125ml/4fl oz double cream
2 bananas (sliced into discs)

- Combine the beaten egg, custard powder, sugar, milk and cream in a heatproof bowl and whisk until smooth.
- Place the bowl over a pan of water and stir constantly over a low heat for 5 minutes, or until the custard thickens slightly and coats the back of a wooden spoon.
- Remove the bowl from the heat and gently stir in the banana. Serve hot.

Fried bananas

SERVES 4

INGREDIENTS:

100g/4oz plain flour
1/2 teaspoon bicarbonate of soda
Salt
2 tablespoons sugar
1 egg

6 tablespoons water
2 tablespoons desiccated coconut
4 firm bananas
Vegetable oil for deep-frying
2 tablespoons clear honey

- Sift the flour, bicarbonate of soda and a pinch of salt into a bowl. Stir in the sugar. Whisk in the egg and just enough water to make a thin batter. Then whisk in the shredded coconut.
- Peel the bananas. Carefully cut each one in half lengthways, then cut in half widthways.
- Heat the oil in a preheated wok. Dip the bananas in the batter, then gently drop a few pieces at a time into the hot oil. Fry until golden brown.
- Remove the bananas from the oil and drain on kitchen paper. Serve immediately with honey.

Rice pudding

SERVES 4

INGREDIENTS:

50g/2oz pudding rice
50g/2oz granulated sugar
400g/14oz evaporated milk
300ml/½pt fresh milk

Pinch of freshly ground nutmeg
25g/1oz butter
Strawberry jam to serve

- Preheat the oven to 150°C/300°F/Gas mark 2. Lightly oil a large ovenproof dish.
- Sprinkle the rice and the sugar into the dish and mix.
- Bring the evaporated milk to the boil in a small pan, stirring occasionally. Stir the evaporated and fresh milk into the rice and mix well until the rice is coated thoroughly.
- Sprinkle over the nutmeg, cover with aluminium foil and bake in the oven for 30 minutes.
- Remove the pudding from the oven and stir well, breaking up any lumps. Cover with the same aluminium foil. Bake in the oven for a further 30 minutes.
- Remove from the oven and stir well again.
- Dot the pudding with butter and bake for a further 45 to 60 minutes, until the rice is tender and the skin browned.
- Divide the pudding into 4 individual serving bowls. Top with a large spoonful of jam and serve immediately.

Coffee cake

SERVES 4–6

INGREDIENTS:

175g/6oz margarine
175g/6oz caster sugar
3 eggs
175g/6oz self-raising flour (sifted)
50ml/2fl oz rum

225ml/8fl oz strong coffee
225ml/8fl oz double cream
2 drops vanilla essence
25g/1oz toasted flaked almonds

- Preheat the oven to 190°C/375°F/Gas mark 5.
- Cream the margarine and sugar until light and fluffy. Gradually beat in the eggs, and fold in the flour. Spoon into a greased cake tin. Bake for 40 to 45 minutes. Leave for 4 minutes then turn out on to a wire tray to cool slightly.

→

←

- Pour the rum into the coffee and sweeten to taste. Put the cake back in the tin and pour the coffee mixture over.
- Whip the cream and add the vanilla essence. Turn the cake onto a plate, spread with whipped cream and decorate with toasted almonds.

Peach cobbler

SERVES 4–6

INGREDIENTS:

4 large peaches (peeled and thickly sliced, with stones removed)
175ml/6fl oz maple syrup
1 teaspoon ground nutmeg
1 teaspoon ground cinnamon

½ teaspoon ground cloves
½ teaspoon ground ginger
225g/8oz plain flour
225ml/8fl oz milk
2 egg whites

- Preheat the oven to 190°C/375°F/Gas mark 5.
- Arrange the peaches in a glass dish measuring about 20cm/8in in diameter. Mix together the maple syrup with half of each of the ground nutmeg, cinnamon, cloves and ginger. Drizzle the mixture over the peaches, making sure each piece of fruit is well coated. Allow to stand for 10 to 15 minutes.
- In a mixing bowl, combine the flour, milk and egg whites and blend to mix.
- Pour carefully over the top of the fruit, then sprinkle with the other half of the spices.
- Bake, uncovered, in the oven for 45 to 50 minutes until the topping is cooked and beautifully browned. Serve hot with cream or ice-cream.

Griddle cakes

SERVES 4–8

INGREDIENTS:

125g/4oz plain flour
2 teaspoons baking powder
2 tablespoons caster sugar
2 eggs (separated)

1 tablespoon melted butter
125ml/4fl oz fresh milk
50g/2oz stoned, chopped fresh cherries
50g/2oz chopped dried apricots

- Sieve the flour, baking powder and sugar together. Beat the egg yolks, melted butter and milk together and then stir into the dry ingredients to form a smooth batter.

- Fold the cherries and apricots into the batter.
- Whisk the egg whites until stiff and dry, then fold carefully into the batter.
- Preheat the griddle on a medium high setting. Brush with melted butter place spoonfuls of the batter on the griddle and cook until golden brown.
- Serve with warmed honey or golden syrup.

Semolina

SERVES 4

INGREDIENTS:

6 tablespoons pure ghee
3 whole cloves
3 whole cardamoms
8 tablespoons coarse semolina
1/2 teaspoon saffron

50g/2oz sultanas
150g/5oz caster sugar
300ml/1/2pt water
300ml/1/2pt milk

- Place the ghee in a saucepan and melt over a medium heat. Add the cloves and the whole cardamoms to the melted ghee and reduce the heat, stirring to mix.
- Add the semolina to the mixture in the pan and stir-fry until it turns a slightly darker colour. Add the saffron, sultanas and the sugar to the semolina mixture, stirring to mix well.
- Pour in the water and milk and cook the mixture constantly until the semolina has softened. Add a little more water if required.
- Remove the pan from the heat and transfer the semolina to a warmed serving dish. Serve with cream, chopped nuts and desiccated coconut, if desired.

Treacle tart

SERVES 6

INGREDIENTS:

Shortcrust pastry case (23cm/9in, baked)
400g/14oz golden syrup
2 tablespoons treacle

150g/5oz slivered almonds
125g/41/2oz fresh breadcrumbs
2 eggs
Zest of 1/2 lemon

- Preheat the oven to 130°C/250°F/Gas mark 1/2. Place the pastry shell on a baking sheet.

→

- In a bowl, mix together the golden syrup, treacle, slivered almonds, breadcrumbs, eggs and lemon zest. Spoon the mixture into the pastry case and bake for about 1 hour.
- Serve warm with clotted cream or double cream.

Rhubarb & apple cobbler

SERVES 6

INGREDIENTS:

900g/2lb rhubarb (cut into 2cm/1in lengths)
450g/1lb cooking apples (peeled, cored, quartered and sliced)
6 tablespoons caster sugar
4 tablespoons plain flour
1 tablespoon cornflour
1/2 teaspoon ground ginger
1 tablespoon butter
Grated zest of 1 orange

For the dough:
150g/5oz plain flour
2 teaspoons baking powder
Pinch of salt
50g/2oz butter (softened)
3 tablespoons caster sugar
125ml/4fl oz buttermilk
2 tablespoons double cream
1 teaspoon demerara sugar

- Preheat the oven to 220°C/425°F/Gas mark 7.
- Mix together the rhubarb, apples, sugar, flour, cornflour, ginger, butter and orange zest. Place the mixture in a 25cm/10in shallow ovenproof dish and put to one side.
- To make the dough, sift the flour, baking powder and salt into a bowl. Rub in the softened butter until the mixture resembles fine breadcrumbs. Stir in the caster sugar and buttermilk. Spoon the dough on to the rhubarb in small mounds, making sure it does not completely cover the fruit. Mix the cream with the demerara sugar and drizzle on the top.
- Put the dish on a baking tray and bake for 10 minutes, then lower the heat to 190°C/375°F/Gas mark 5 and bake for a further 20 to 30 minutes, or until puffed and brown and the fruit is just soft. Remove from the oven and leave to stand for 10 minutes, then serve warm with cream.

Chocolate fudge pudding

SERVES 4

INGREDIENTS:

50g/2oz margarine (plus extra for greasing)
75g/3oz brown sugar
2 eggs (beaten)
350ml/12fl oz milk

50g/2oz chopped walnuts
50g/2oz plain flour
2 tablespoons cocoa powder (plus extra for dusting)
Icing sugar (to dust)

- Preheat the oven to 180°C/350°F/Gas mark 4. Lightly grease a 1.2 litres/2pt ovenproof dish.
- Cream together the margarine and sugar in a large mixing bowl until fluffy. Beat in the eggs.
- Gradually stir in the milk and add the walnuts, stirring to mix.
- Sift the flour and cocoa powder into the mixture and fold in gently, with a metal spoon, until well mixed.
- Spoon the mixture into the dish and cook in the oven for 35 to 40 minutes.
- Dust with icing sugar and cocoa powder and serve.

Pear & blackberry crumble

SERVES 6

INGREDIENTS:

450g/1lb blackberries
450g/1lb pears (peeled and halved lengthways)
Juice of 1 lemon
225g/8oz caster sugar

1 teaspoon mixed spice
100g/4oz butter
225g/8oz plain flour
75g/3oz ground almonds

- Preheat the oven to 200°C/400°F/Gas mark 6.
- Fill the sink with cold water. Put the blackberries in a colander and lower carefully into the water. Toss the fruit to wash thoroughly. Lift out the colander and leave the blackberries to drain.
- Halve the pears again and core, then slice each quarter into 2 or 3 pieces. Put the pieces in a bowl, add the lemon juice and toss well.
- Add 100g/4oz of the sugar to the sliced pears, along with the mixed spice, then add in the blackberries and toss thoroughly to coat.

→

←

- Grease a shallow dish with a little butter, then carefully tip the fruit into the dish in an even layer.
- Put the butter, flour, almonds and the remaining sugar in to a blender or food processor and pulse until the mixture begins to look like breadcrumbs. Tip in to a bowl and bring parts of it together with your hands to make lumps.
- Spoon the crumble topping evenly over the fruit, then bake for 35 to 45 minutes until the fruit is tender and the crumble is golden and bubbling. Serve with cream or ice-cream.

Doughnuts

SERVES 10

INGREDIENTS:

275g/10oz bread flour (plus more for dusting)
175g/6oz plain flour (plus extra for dusting)
1 teaspoon salt
8g/¼oz sachet easy-blend yeast
175ml/6fl oz warm milk

75g/3oz butter (softened and diced)
2 eggs (beaten)
75g/3oz caster sugar
Grated zest of 1 lemon
1 teaspoon ground cinnamon
Oil for greasing and deep-frying
Caster sugar for dusting

- Sift the flours into a bowl with the salt and yeast. Put the warm milk in a food mixer, and turn on at the lowest speed. Pour in the flour mix and add the softened butter a piece at a time. When fully incorporated, add the beaten eggs, one at a time. Then add the sugar, lemon zest and cinnamon, and run the machine for 10 minutes, turning it to full speed for the last 2 minutes.
- Turn the sticky dough out on to a heavily floured surface and finish kneading by hand, incorporating more of the dusting flour until you have a smooth, elastic ball.
- Brush this with a little oil, place in a lightly oiled bowl and cover with clingfilm.
- Leave to rise at room temperature for 2 hours, when it should have doubled in size.
- Knock down the dough by kneading it lightly, then divide it into 20 equal pieces, and roll them into balls. Make a hole in the centre by pushing your finger through, circling it to enlarge the hole to about 2cm/¾in in diameter. Put the rings on a floured tray, cover with a cloth and leave to rise for 40 to 50 minutes, when again they will have doubled in size.
- Heat oil for deep-frying. Fry the doughnuts in small batches for 1 to 2 minutes.
- Drain on kitchen paper. Put some caster sugar on a plate and turn the doughnuts in it to coat while they are still warm. Serve when cooled.

Baked apples & figs

SERVES 4

INGREDIENTS:

4 small dessert apples
4 large figs
50g/2oz marzipan
1 tablespoon whole blanched almonds
(finely chopped)
1 small piece of stem ginger (finely
chopped)
1 tablespoon golden syrup

3 tablespoons cold water

For the Amaretti cream:
10 Amaretti biscuits
250g/9oz fromage frais
1 tablespoon icing sugar (sifted)
1 tablespoon amaretto liqueur

- Preheat the oven to 180°C/350°F/Gas mark 4.
- Core the apples and score horizontally around their middles with the point of a sharp knife. Cut the figs lengthways, almost through into quarters, leaving them intact at the base.
- Mix the marzipan, almonds, ginger and syrup until smooth and roll into 8 balls.
- Place them in the centre of each fruit.
- Place the apples in a baking dish with the cold water and bake for 30 minutes.
- Add the figs to the tray and bake for another 10 to 15 minutes or until both types of fruit are tender.
- For the Amaretti cream, roughly crush the Amaretti biscuits and mix with the remaining ingredients. To serve, put 1 apple and 1 fig on each plate and top with a little of the cream. Serve hot, with the remaining cream separate.

Apple Charlotte

SERVES 4–6

INGREDIENTS:

900g/2lb cooking apples
100g/4oz caster sugar
150g/5oz butter
3 tablespoons water

Juice of 1 lemon
3 tablespoons sieved apricot jam
8 slices of white bread

- Preheat the oven to 180°C/350°F/Gas mark 4.
- Peel, core and slice the apples and put them in a pan with the caster sugar and 25g/1oz of the butter. Add the water, cover the pan and stew gently over a low heat

→

←

for 10 minutes. Then remove the lid, stir and turn up the heat, continuing to cook until you have a thick purée. Stir in the lemon juice and apricot jam and reserve.

- Melt the remaining butter and cut the crusts off the slices of white bread. Cut the bread into fingers, brush with the butter and use them to line a 20cm/8in mould or soufflé dish. Pour in the purée and cover the top with more butter-soaked bread.
- Bake on a baking sheet in the oven for 35 minutes, when the top will be crisp and golden brown. Remove and leave to cool for 10 minutes before sliding a palette knife round the edge and turning out on to a serving dish.
- Cut into wedges and serve with cream or ice-cream.

Rhubarb crumble

SERVES 4–6

INGREDIENTS:

900g/2lb rhubarb
150g/5oz sugar
100g/4oz butter

75g/3oz plain flour
75g/3oz demerara sugar
10 Amaretti biscuits (crushed)

- Preheat the oven to 200°C/400°F/Gas mark 6.
- Trim the rhubarb, cut into short lengths and put in a pan with the sugar. Stir over a low heat until the sugar has dissolved, then cover and simmer for 8 to 10 minutes, or until the rhubarb is soft. Spoon into a deep 1.5 litres/2½pt ovenproof dish.
- Rub the butter into the flour until the mixture resembles fine breadcrumbs, then stir in the demerara sugar and biscuits.
- Sprinkle the crumble over the stewed rhubarb and bake for 15 minutes, or until the topping is golden brown. Serve with cream or ice-cream.

Banana dosa

SERVES 4

INGREDIENTS:

4 ripe bananas (peeled and mashed)
200g/7oz rice flour
100g/4oz plain flour
2 tablespoons white sugar
2 tablespoons oil

½ teaspoon crushed cardamom seeds
Pinch of salt
100ml/3½fl oz water
Oil for greasing

- In a large bowl, place the bananas, rice flour, plain flour, sugar, oil, cardamom and salt. Make a well in the centre and pour in the water. Blend with a wooden spoon to give a thick batter, adding a little more water or flour if required.
- Heat a frying pan over a medium heat. Rub the surface with some oil using a brush or kitchen paper.
- Pour a large spoonful of the batter into the pan and spread it out lightly.
- Cook for 5 minutes or until golden brown underneath, then turn over and cook for a further 3 minutes.
- Serve hot, with ice-cream.

Crêpes Suzette

SERVES 4–8

INGREDIENTS:

100g/4oz plain flour
Pinch of salt
1 egg
1 egg yolk
300ml/½pt skimmed milk
15g/½oz unsalted butter (melted) plus extra for frying

For the sauce:
2 large oranges
50g/2oz butter
100g/4oz brown sugar
1 tablespoon Grand Marnier
1 tablespoon brandy

- Sift the flour into a bowl and make a well in the centre. Add the egg and the extra yolk into the well. Stir with a wooden spoon to incorporate the flour from around the edges. When the mixture thickens, gradually pour on the milk, beating well after each addition, until a smooth batter is formed. Stir in the butter, transfer to a measuring jug, cover and chill.
- Heat a 20cm/8in shallow frying pan, add a little butter and heat until sizzling.
- Pour in a little of the batter, tilting the pan back and forth to cover the base thinly. Cook the crêpes over a medium heat for 1 to 2 minutes until lightly browned underneath, then flip over with a spatula and cook for 1 minute.
- Repeat this process until you have eight crêpes. Pile them up on a plate as they are ready. Pare the zest from one of the oranges and reserve a teaspoon for decoration. Squeeze the juice from both oranges.
- To make the sauce, melt the butter in a large frying pan and add the sugar, orange zest and juice. Heat gently until the sugar is dissolved and the mixture is bubbling.
- Fold each crêpe in quarters. Add to the pan one at a time, coat in the sauce and fold in half again. Push to the side of the pan to make room for the others. Pour on the Grand Marnier and brandy and cook gently for 2 to 3 minutes, until the sauce has slightly caramelized.
- Serve, sprinkled with the reserved orange zest.

Sauces, dressings & stocks

While you can usually buy ready-made sauces, dressings and stocks, if you have the time to make them yourself, it is preferable to use fresh ingredients where possible. This is especially true for salad dressings, which are quick and easy to make. In the case of stocks, while it is generally more convenient to use stock cubes as it cuts down on cooking time, a rich homemade stock with fresh ingredients undoubtedly has an edge over a shop-bought one.

White/Béchamel sauce

MAKES 450ml/³/₄pt

INGREDIENTS

450ml/³/₄pt milk
1 bay leaf
10 whole black peppercorns
1 slice onion (1cm/¹/₂in thick)

50g/2oz butter
25g/1oz plain flour
Salt and pepper

- Place the milk in a saucepan and add the bay leaf, peppercorns and onion. Cook over a low heat for approximately 5 minutes, letting it come slowly to simmering point. Remove the saucepan from the heat and strain the milk into a jug, discarding the flavourings.
- Melt the butter gently in a separate pan. As soon as the butter melts, add the flour and, over a medium heat, stir quite vigorously to make a smooth paste.
- Add the milk a little at a time, stirring vigorously between each addition. When about half the milk is in, switch to a whisk and start adding more milk at a time, whisking briskly, until all the milk has been added.
- Over a low heat, let the sauce simmer gently for 5 minutes, whisking occasionally. Season with salt and pepper.

Barbecue sauce

MAKES 600ml/1pt

INGREDIENTS

2 tablespoons vegetable oil
1 onion (finely chopped)
3 garlic cloves (minced)
225ml/8fl oz tomato ketchup or tomato sauce

350ml/12fl oz cider vinegar
50ml/2fl oz Worcestershire sauce
75g/3oz sugar
1 teaspoon chilli powder
¹/₂ teaspoon cayenne pepper

- Heat the oil in a saucepan over a moderate heat and add the onion and garlic.
- Cook gently, stirring, for about 5 minutes. Add the ketchup, vinegar, Worcestershire sauce, sugar, chilli powder and cayenne.
- Reduce the heat and simmer, partially covered, for about 20 minutes, until the sauce has thickened slightly.

Tomato sauce

MAKES 600ml/1pt

INGREDIENTS

300ml/¹/₂pt white vinegar
1 teaspoon mixed spice
1.4kg/3lb ripe tomatoes (sliced)

25g/1oz salt
100g/4oz sugar

- Place the vinegar and the mixed spice in a saucepan, bring to the boil and remove from the heat. Cover and leave to infuse for 3 to 4 hours.
- Place the tomatoes in a heavy-based saucepan and simmer until pulpy.
- Rub the pulp through a sieve into a bowl.
- Clean the saucepan and add the strained pulp to it. Add the salt and cook gently until mixture begins to thicken
- Add the sugar and infused vinegar, stirring until fully dissolved.
- Continue simmering, stirring occasionally, until the mixture thickens to the consistency of whipped cream.

Creamed tomato sauce

MAKES 300ml/¹/₂pt

INGREDIENTS

6 medium ripe tomatoes
175ml/6fl oz water
125ml/4fl oz double cream

50ml/2fl oz plain yogurt
Salt and pepper

- Place the tomatoes in a bowl of just-boiled water for 30 seconds and skin. Then chop them finely.
- Place the tomatoes in a saucepan and add the water. Cover and simmer until the sauce is thick and creamy.
- Add the cream and yogurt.
- Season to taste with salt and pepper.

Mayonnaise

MAKES 300ml/¹/₂pt

INGREDIENTS

2 large egg yolks
1 teaspoon dry English mustard
powder
Pinch of salt

Ground black pepper
300ml/¹/₂pt groundnut oil or extra-
virgin olive oil
1 teaspoon white wine vinegar

- Put the egg yolks into a 900ml/1¹/₂ pt basin with a narrow base. Add the mustard powder. Season with the salt and pepper and mix well.
- Using an electric whisk, add the oil one drop at a time, whisking each drop in thoroughly before adding the next. When the mixture begins to thicken you can begin to add slightly more oil at a time.
- When about half the oil is in, add the vinegar. Pour in the rest of the oil in a steady trickle, whisking all the time.

Garlic mayonnaise

MAKES 300ml/¹/₂pt

INGREDIENTS

4 garlic cloves (minced)
2 large egg yolks
Pinch of salt

250ml/9fl oz olive oil
Juice of 1 small lemon
¹/₂ tablespoon boiling water

- Put the garlic, egg yolks and salt into a 900ml/1¹/₂pt basin with a narrow base. Mix well with a metal spoon.
- Using an electric whisk, add the oil one drop at a time, whisking each drop in thoroughly before adding the next.
- When about half the oil is in, start to add in drops of the lemon juice.
- When the mixture begins to thicken you can begin to add slightly more oil at a time. The mixture should become thick and well combined.
- Stir in the boiling water to prevent the mayonnaise from separating.

French vinaigrette

MAKES 150ml/¼pt

INGREDIENTS:

2 tablespoons red or white
wine vinegar
125ml/4fl oz light olive oil
1 teaspoon Dijon mustard

1 garlic clove
Salt and pepper to taste
Pinch of sugar

- Combine all the ingredients in a screw-top jar. Secure the lid and shake vigorously. Leave to infuse for 2 hours.
- Remove the garlic clove, then leave overnight before using.

Lemon vinaigrette

MAKES 150ml/¼pt

INGREDIENTS:

1 teaspoon Dijon mustard
3 tablespoons fresh lemon juice

125ml/4fl oz extra-virgin olive oil
Salt and pepper

- Whisk the mustard and lemon juice together.
- Whisking constantly, slowly drizzle in the olive oil.
- Season with salt and pepper

Other variations

Note that other ingredients can be added to the French vinaigrette:
- Finely chopped fresh herbs such as parsley, basil, marjoram and mint.
- Capers, finely sliced gherkins or diced shallots.
- 1½ tablespoons roasting juices (with oil drained) may be added if the dressing is intended for a meat salad.

Chicken stock

MAKES 1.8 litres/3pt

INGREDIENTS:

1kg raw chicken carcass
3 litres/5pt water
100g/4oz carrot (coarsely chopped)
100g/4oz celery (coarsely chopped)

200g/7oz onion (coarsely chopped)
3 garlic cloves
1 teaspoon salt
1 bouquet garni

- Put the chicken carcass in a large stockpot and cover with the water. Add the remaining ingredients and bring to the boil over a high heat.
- Skim off any cloudy scum that has risen to the surface and, once the scum stops forming, reduce the heat to medium and simmer, uncovered, for 2 hours. If you wish to reduce the chicken stock, stir over a high heat until it has reduced to the required amount.
- Strain the stock through a fine-mesh sieve and leave to cool. Refrigerate for 8 hours or overnight, then remove any fat from the surface.

Vegetable stock

MAKES 500ml/18fl oz

INGREDIENTS:

1 tablespoon olive oil
2 leeks (roughly chopped)
2 carrots (chopped)
1 celery stick (chopped)
1 small russet potato (chopped)
2 garlic cloves (halved)
1.2 litres/2pt water

50g/2oz dried red lentils
1 bay leaf
½ teaspoon peppercorns
½ tablespoon soy sauce
1 pinch dried thyme
6 sprigs parsley

- Place the oil in a large casserole dish over a medium heat. Sauté the leeks, carrots, celery, potato and garlic until slightly browned. Add the water and the remaining ingredients.
- Bring to the boil, then reduce the heat and simmer uncovered for 1 hour.
- Strain the stock.

Beef stock

MAKES 1.8 litres/3pt

INGREDIENTS:

2.7kg/6lb beef bones
1 large onion (sliced)
3 large carrots (chopped)
2 celery sticks (chopped)
1 large tomato
100g/4oz parsnip (chopped)
100g/4oz potatoes (cubed)

8 whole black peppercorns
4 sprigs fresh parsley
1 bay leaf
1 tablespoon salt
2 teaspoons dried thyme
2 garlic cloves
3 litres/5pt water

- Preheat the oven to 230°C/450°F/Gas mark 8.
- Place the beef bones, onion, and carrots in a large shallow roasting pan. Roast, uncovered, for 30 minutes or until the bones are browned, turning occasionally.
- Drain off any fat. Place the browned bones, onion and carrots in a large soup pot. Pour 150ml/¼pt water into the roasting pan and rinse. Pour this liquid into the soup pot. Add the celery, tomato, parsnip, potato, peppercorns, parsley, bay leaf, salt, thyme and garlic. Add 2.8 litres/4³/₄pt water.
- Bring the mixture to the boil. Reduce the heat. Cover and simmer for 5 hours.
- Strain the stock. Discard the meat, vegetables and seasonings.

Fish stock

MAKES 1.8 litres/3pt

INGREDIENTS:

2.3kg/5lb fish trimmings
5 onions (quartered)
5 celery sticks, including leaves
(chopped)
5 sprigs of parsley

5 bay leaves
1 teaspoon dried thyme
Salt and freshly ground black pepper
750ml/1¼pt dry white wine
3 litres/5pt water

- Place all the ingredients in a large saucepan set over a high heat. Bring to boiling point and lower the heat.
- Simmer for about 40 minutes, without a lid, then strain.

Conversion tables
&
Index

Weights

Imperial	Approx. metric equivalent	Imperial	Approx. metric equivalent
$1/2$oz	15g	$1\,1/4$lb	600g
1oz	25g	$1\,1/2$lb	700g
$1\,1/2$oz	40g	$1\,3/4$lb	850g
2oz	50g	2lb	900g
$2\,1/2$oz	60g	$2\,1/2$lb	1.1kg
3oz	75g	3lb	1.4kg
4oz	100g	$3\,1/2$lb	1.6kg
5oz	150g	4lb	1.8kg
6oz	175g	$4\,1/2$lb	2kg
7oz	200g	5lb	2.3kg
8oz	225g	$5\,1/2$lb	2.5kg
9oz	250g	6lb	2.7kg
10oz	275g	$6\,1/2$lb	3kg
11oz	300g	7lb	3.2kg
12oz	350g	$7\,1/2$lb	3.4kg
13oz	375g	8lb	3.6kg
14oz	400g	$8\,1/2$lb	3.9kg
15oz	425g	9lb	4.1kg
16oz (1lb)	450g	$9\,1/2$lb	4.3kg
1lb 2oz	500g	10lb	4.5kg

The Imperial pound (lb), which is 16 ounces (oz), equals approximately 450 grams (g).

Oven temperatures

°C	°F	Gas mark	Temperature
130	250	$1/2$	Very cool
140	275	1	Very cool
150	300	2	Cool
160–170	325	3	Warm
180	350	4	Moderate
190	375	5	Fairly hot
200	400	6	Fairly hot
210–220	425	7	Hot
230	450	8	Very hot
240	475	9	Very hot

Fluid measures

Imperial	Approx. metric equivalent	Imperial	Approx. metric equivalent
1fl oz	25ml	9fl oz	250ml
2fl oz	50ml	10fl oz ($1/2$pt)	300ml
3fl oz	75ml	12fl oz	350ml
$3^1/_2$fl oz	100ml	15fl oz ($3/_4$pt)	450ml
4fl oz	125ml	18 fl oz	500ml
5fl oz ($1/_4$pt)	150ml	20fl oz (1pt)	600ml
6fl oz	175ml	30fl oz ($1^1/_2$pt)	900ml
7fl oz	200ml	35 fl oz (2pt)	1.2 litres
8fl oz	225ml	40 fl oz ($2^1/_2$pt)	1.5 litres

The Imperial pint (pt), which is 20 fluid ounces (fl oz), measures approximately 600 millilitres (ml).

Spoon measures

All the measurements given in the recipes are for levelled spoonfuls (British Imperial Standard)
1 teaspoon = 5ml
1 tablespoon = 15ml

The tablespoon measurements below are equivalent to approximately 1oz (25g) of the following ingredients:

Breadcrumbs (dried)	3	Flour, unsifted	3
Breadcrumbs (fresh)	7	Rice (uncooked)	2
Butter/margarine/lard	2	Sugar (granulated, caster)	2
Cheese, grated (Cheddar)	3	Sugar (icing)	3
Cheese, grated (Parmesan)	4	Honey/syrup	1
Cocoa powder	4	Yeast (dried)	2
Cornflour/custard powder	$2^1/_2$		